JEALOUSY

JEALOUSY
Developmental, Cultural, and Clinical Realms

Edited by
Mary Kay O'Neil and Salman Akhtar

Routledge
Taylor & Francis Group

LONDON AND NEW YORK

First published 2018
by Routledge
2 Park Square, Milton Park, Abingdon, Oxon OX14 4RN

and by Routledge
711 Third Avenue, New York, NY 10017

Routledge is an imprint of the Taylor & Francis Group, an informa business

British Library Cataloguing-in-Publication Data
A catalogue record for this book is available from the British Library

Library of Congress Cataloging-in-Publication Data
A catalog record has been requested for this book

ISBN: 978-1-78220-644-6 (pbk)

Typeset in Palatino LT Std
by Medlar Publishing Solutions Pvt Ltd, India

To

Frederick Lowy

and

Muge Alkan

who are not prone to jealousy

CONTENTS

ACKNOWLEDGMENTS

We are deeply grateful to the distinguished colleagues who contributed to this volume. We appreciate their effort, their sacrifice of time, and their patience with our requirements, reminders, and requests for revisions. We are also thankful to Jan Wright for her skillful help in preparing the manuscript of this book. Oliver Rathbone and Kate Pearce of Karnac Books gave unerring support of this project and shepherded it through various phases of publication. To both of them, our sincere thanks.

Mary Kay O'Neil and Salman Akhtar

ABOUT THE EDITORS AND CONTRIBUTORS

Salman Akhtar, MD, is professor of psychiatry at Jefferson Medical College and a training and supervising analyst at the Psychoanalytic Center of Philadelphia. He has served on the editorial boards of the *International Journal of Psychoanalysis*, the *Journal of the American Psychoanalytic Association*, and the *Psychoanalytic Quarterly*. His more than 300 publications include eighty-six books, of which the following eighteen are solo-authored: *Broken Structures* (1992), *Quest for Answers* (1995), *Inner Torment* (1999), *Immigration and Identity* (1999), *New Clinical Realms* (2003), *Objects of Our Desire* (2005), *Regarding Others* (2007), *Turning Points in Dynamic Psychotherapy* (2009), *The Damaged Core* (2009), *Comprehensive Dictionary of Psychoanalysis* (2009), *Immigration and Acculturation* (2011), *Matters of Life and Death* (2011), *The Book of Emotions* (2012), *Psychoanalytic Listening* (2013), *Good Stuff* (2013), *Sources of Suffering* (2014), *No Holds Barred* (2016), and *A Web of Sorrow* (2017). Dr. Akhtar has delivered many prestigious invited lectures including a plenary address at the 2nd International Congress of the International Society for the Study of Personality Disorders in Oslo, Norway (1991), an invited plenary paper at the 2nd International Margaret S. Mahler Symposium in Cologne, Germany (1993), an invited plenary paper at the Rencontre Franco-Americaine de Psychanalyse meeting in Paris, France (1994), a keynote address at the 43rd IPA Congress in Rio de Janeiro, Brazil (2005), the plenary address at the 150th Freud Birthday Celebration sponsored by the Dutch Psychoanalytic Society and the Embassy of Austria in Leiden, Holland (2006), the inaugural address at the first IPA-Asia Congress in Beijing, China (2010), and the plenary address at the National Meetings of the American Psychoanalytic Association (2017). Dr. Akhtar is the recipient of numerous awards including the American Psychoanalytic Association's Edith Sabshin Award (2000), Columbia University's Robert Liebert Award for Distinguished Contributions to Applied Psychoanalysis (2004), the American Psychiatric Association's Kun Po Soo Award (2004) and Irma Bland Award for being the Outstanding Teacher of Psychiatric Residents in the country (2005). He received the highly prestigious Sigourney Award (2012) for distinguished contributions to psychoanalysis. In 2013 he gave the commencement address at graduation ceremonies of the Smith College School of Social Work in Northampton, MA. Dr. Akhtar's books have been translated in many languages, including German, Italian, Korean, Portuguese, Romanian, Serbian, Spanish, and Turkish. A true Renaissance man, Dr. Akhtar has served as the film review editor for the *International Journal of Psychoanalysis*, and is currently serving as the book review editor for the *International Journal of Applied Psychoanalytic Studies*. He has published nine collections of poetry and serves as a scholar-in-residence at the Inter-Act Theatre Company in Philadelphia.

Maxine K. Anderson, MD, trained in psychoanalysis in Seattle and London, England. She is a founding member of the Northwestern Psychoanalytic Society and Institute and a training and supervising analyst at several psychoanalytic institutes in North America and Canada. She is also a full member of the British Psychoanalytic Society and a fellow of the International Psychoanalytical Association. The richness of North American and British psychoanalytic traditions focused her thinking and writing interests on the forces for and against knowing, the ongoing tension between symbolic and a-symbolic functioning, and on the nature of reality. Dr. Anderson has published articles in the *JAPA*, the *Canadian Journal of Psychoanalysis*, and the *Journal of Analytical Psychology* on topics related to the internal forces which threaten whole-minded thought. Her most recent work, *The Wisdom of Lived Experience* (Karnac, 2016) reviews the intuitions and wisdom which arise from the ongoing dialogue between lived experience and cognitively based thought.

Joël Des Rosiers, MD, is a psychiatrist, psychoanalyst, poet, and essayist. A direct descendant of Nicolas Malet, the French revolutionary colonist and signatory of the Act of Independence, he was born in Les Cayes, Haiti. He moved to Canada as a child when his family was forced into exile. Des Rosiers later moved to Strasbourg, France, for his studies and joined the Situationist movement in the early 1970s. Throughout these years, he provided clandestine accommodation for dozens of refugees and *"sans-papiers"* in Alsace. While a medical student, Des Rosiers followed, during many years, the seminar on psychoanalysis led by Prof. Lucien Israël, a member of the Freudian School of Paris, who was analyzed by Didier Anzieu and Jacques Lacan. A writer and a thinker who has travelled widely, Des Rosiers has published twelve collections of poetry and two collections of essays, including *Metropolis Opera*, *Tribu*, finalist for the Governor General's Award, *Savanes*, winner of the Prix d'excellence de Laval, *Théories caraïbes*, winner of the Prix de la Société des écrivains canadiens, and *Vetiver*, laureate of the the Governor General Prize in translation. His last collection of poetry, *Chaux*, was awarded the Fetkann Prize in Paris. Des Rosiers received for his complete works the most prestigious literary prize awarded by the Quebec Government, the Athanase-David Prize, in 2011. For his last collection of essays, *Metaspora. Essai sur les patries intimes*, he received the MLA (Modern Language in America) Prize for Independent Scholars in 2014. As a member of the faculty at the Canadian Psychoanalytic Society, he leads the seminar "Literature and Psychoanalysis" and focusing on the challenges literature offers to psychoanalysis as a global theory of psychic production and meaning. Joël Des Rosiers practices psychoanalysis with a particular interest in psychosis, perversion, and cultural issues of migration. He is also a member of the IPA and the Canadian Psychoanalytic Society. He recently wrote the foreword of the first translation in French of *The Mark of Oppression*, by Abram Kardiner, the author of *My Analysis with Freud*.

Aleksandar Dimitrijevic, PhD, is interim professor of psychoanalysis and clinical psychology at the International Psychoanalytic University, Berlin, Germany. He received a PhD in clinical psychology from the University of Belgrade, where he taught for many years. He is a member of the Belgrade Psychoanalytical Society (IPA), and faculty at Serbian Association of Psychoanalytic Psychotherapists (EFPP), while he is practicing at Stillpoint Spaces Berlin. He is the author of many conceptual and empirical papers about attachment theory and research, psychoanalytic education, and psychoanalysis and the arts, as well as the editor or coeditor of ten books or special journal issues, the most recent of which is "Ferenczi's influence on contemporary psychoanalytic traditions" (with Gabriele Cassullo and Jay Frankel).

Susan Kavaler-Adler, PhD, ABPP, NPsyA, DLitt, is a psychologist and psychoanalyst in private practice, working with individuals and groups. She is the founder of the Object Relations Institute for Psychotherapy and Psychoanalysis in New York City, where she has served as executive director, training analyst, senior supervisor, and faculty member. She is also a prolific author who has published five books and over sixty articles, and has eleven awards for her writing. Her books are: *The Compulsion to Create: Women Writers and Their Demon Lovers* (Routledge, 1993; Other Press, 2000); *The Creative Mystique: From Red Shoes Frenzy to Love and Creativity* (Routledge, 1996); *Mourning, Spirituality and Psychic Change: A New Object Relations View of Psychoanalysis* (Routledge, 2003, winner of the National Gradiva Award from NAAP); *The Anatomy of Regret: From Death Instinct to Reparation and Symbolization in Vivid Case Studies* (Karnac, 2013); and *Klein-Winnicott Dialectic: New Transformative Metapsychology and Interactive Clinical Theory* (Karnac, 2014). Dr. Kavaler-Adler integrates psychoanalytic work on creativity, spiritual self-evolution, and erotic transference with mourning as a developmental process, and addresses the addictions to bad/traumatic eroticized objects that forestall mourning.

Christine Kieffer, PhD, is a psychoanalyst and clinical psychologist who serves on the faculties of the Chicago Institute for Psychoanalysis as well as Rush University Medical School, Chicago. Dr. Kieffer is the author of numerous papers and three coedited books: *Breast Cancer: A Psychological Treatment Manual* (1994), *Psychoanalysis and Women* (2004), and *Into the Void: Psychoanalytic Perspectives on Gender* (2005). She has edited special issues of *Psychoanalytic Inquiry* on Fathers and Daughters (2008), Psychoanalysis and Cyberspace (2012), and Psychoanalytic Perspectives on Bullying (2013). She serves on the editorial boards of the *Journal of the American Psychoanalytic Association, Psychoanalytic Inquiry*, the *International Journal of Self Psychology, and PSYCHcritiques*. Dr. Kieffer has recently published a monograph, *Mutuality, Recognition and the Self* (Karnac, 2014), that elaborates upon her integration of relational and intersubjective perspectives on psychoanalytic theory and treatment. Dr. Kieffer is the recipient of the 2013 Ticho prize given by the American Psychoanalytic Association. She has a dual specialization in child/adolescent as well as adult psychoanalysis and psychotherapy, and also provides group psychotherapy and couples counseling. She is currently serving as the chair of the Program Committee of the American Psychoanalytic Association and maintains a private practice of psychotherapy and psychoanalysis in Chicago and Winnetka, Illinois.

Judi B. Kobrick, PhD, is a Clinical Psychologist and Psychoanalyst who maintains a private practice in psychoanalysis and psychotherapy in Toronto, Canada. She is a founding member and president of the Toronto Institute for Contemporary Psychoanalysis, where she also serves as a faculty member and a training and supervising psychoanalyst. She is the past president of the Toronto Psychoanalytic Society and Institute and remains on its teaching faculty as well as being engaged in supervision. She was a longstanding member of the National Council of the Canadian Psychoanalytic Society. She has also participated as a member of the Committee on Women and Psychoanalysis and presently is a member of the Committee on Analytic Practice and Scientific Activities of the International Psychoanalytic Association. As an active member of the International Association for Relational Psychoanalysis and Psychotherapy she has written and presented internationally, clinical papers on eating disorders, gender, trauma and dissociation, marginality and creativity. She is currently participating on the Dean's Advisory Board for the Dr. Eric Jackman Institute of Child Study Laboratory School at the University of Toronto.

Jack Novick, PhD, is a child, adolescent, and adult psychoanalyst. Trained at New York University (PhD in clinical psychology), the Anna Freud Centre (child and adolescent psychoanalyst), and the British Psychoanalytic Society (adult, child, and adolescent analyst), he is a training and supervising analyst of the International Psychoanalytical Association, and serves on psychoanalytic institute faculties around the United States. Formerly chief psychologist, Youth Services, University of Michigan Department of Psychiatry, he is currently in private practice in Ann Arbor, Michigan. He served as a clinical associate professor at the University of Michigan Medical School, and was a founder and chair of research at Allen Creek Preschool, where he has also been

ABOUT THE EDITORS AND CONTRIBUTORS

a family consultant. Jack Novick is widely published in professional journals, and has coauthored five books. In 2013 and 2015, he was elected as a North American representative to the board of the International Psychoanalytical Association, and he is president-elect of the Association for Child Psychoanalysis.

Kerry Kelly Novick, AB, BA, is a child, adolescent, and adult psychoanalyst. She did her child training with Anna Freud in London in the 1960s, and her adult training at the Contemporary Freudian Society of New York. Formerly a lecturer in psychoanalysis at the University of Michigan Medical School, she is a child and adult training and supervising analyst of the IPA and on the faculties of numerous psychoanalytic institutes around the United States. A founder of Allen Creek Preschool, she is past president of the Association for Child Psychoanalysis, a councilor-at-large for the American Psychoanalytic Association, and chair of the IPA Committee on Child and Adolescent Psychoanalysis. Author of many papers, she has also coauthored five books.

Mary Kay O'Neil, PhD, is a supervising and training psychoanalyst who has recently moved from Montreal back to Toronto, where she is in private practice. She is the past director of the Canadian Institute of Psychoanalysis (Quebec, English) and a past North American representative on the board of the International Psychoanalytical Association. In addition, she has served on a number of IPA committees, including ethics committees at local, national, and international levels, and on the editorial board of the *International Journal of Psychoanalysis*. Dr. O'Neil received a PhD from the University of Toronto, where she was an assistant professor in the Department of Psychiatry. She completed her psychoanalytic training at the Toronto Institute of Psychoanalysis and is a registered psychologist in both Quebec and Ontario. The author of *The Unsung Psychoanalyst: The Quiet Influence of Ruth Easser*, she coauthored/edited six other books and has contributed numerous professional journal articles as well as chapters and book reviews. The subjects of her presentations, publications and research include depression and young adult development, emotional needs of sole support mothers, post termination analytic contact, psychoanalytic ethics and the analyst as art collector. Her research activities have been funded by foundations in Toronto and Montreal.

Brian M. Robertson, MD, is a training and supervising analyst of the Canadian Institute of Psychoanalysis, an associate professor in the Department of Psychiatry, McGill University, and in practice in Montreal. He is a former editor of the *Canadian Journal of Psychoanalysis*, a past director of the Canadian Psychoanalytic Institute (Quebec English), and a past president of the Canadian Psychoanalytic Society. He has presented and published in the areas of long analyses, psychoanalytic research, siblings and the internal world, and teaching and supervising psychoanalysis. In 1992, he was awarded the Miguel Pardos prize for his paper on the supervisory process, and in 2002, he received the Canadian Psychoanalytic Society's Citation of Merit.

Dhwani Shah, MD, is a clinical associate faculty member in the Department of Psychiatry at the University of Pennsylvania School of Medicine and an attending staff psychiatrist at Princeton University's Counseling and Psychological Services. He did his residency in psychiatry at the University of Pennsylvania School of Medicine, where he also served as chief resident. Later, he completed a fellowship in treatment of resistant mood disorders at the same institution, and then trained at the Psychoanalytic Center of Philadelphia. He is the recipient of several awards, including the University of Pennsylvania's PENN Pearls Teaching Award for Excellence in Clinical Medical Education, the University of Pennsylvania Residency Education's Psychodynamic Psychotherapy Award, and the Laughlin Merit Award for professional achievement. He has published papers on diverse topics, including neuroscience, mood disorders, and psychotherapy. Dr. Shah maintains a private practice of psychiatry, psychotherapy, and psychoanalysis in Princeton, NJ.

Richard Waugaman, MD, is a training and supervising analyst, emeritus, at the Washington Psychoanalytic Institute. He is clinical professor of psychiatry and faculty expert on Shakespeare for media contacts at Georgetown University. He has written more than 100 publications; fifty of them are on Shakespeare and on the psychology of pseudonymity. Since 2004, he has done archival research at the Folger Shakespeare Library. There he discovered one of the largest previously unknown literary sources for Shakespeare's works, in Edward de Vere's copy of Sternhold and Hopkins's *Whole Book of Psalms*. De Vere's annotations showed his unusual interest in some of these psalms, which are echoed repeatedly in Shakespeare's plays and poems. This discovery has unlocked new levels of meaning in Shakespeare's works, and has helped validate Freud's theory that Edward de Vere wrote the works of "Shakespeare."

Greg Zeichner, MLIS, is a cofounder and writer for the independent magazine, *The Journal of Interstitial Cinema*, which has covered rare films and pop culture since 2009. He received a bachelor's degree in film and television from NYU's Tisch School of the Arts and a master's in library and information science from Pratt University. He also studied scientific journal publication at University College London and is a member of Beta Phi Mu, the International Library and Information Studies Honor Society. He is currently an audiovisual librarian and archivist at the United Nations and did similar work previously at the Metropolitan Museum of Art, National Dance Institute, and Duart Film and Video. He has directed several short films and written several feature length screenplays. He grew up in the Washington, DC area and has lived in New York City for over twenty years.

INTRODUCTION

The subject of this book is jealousy. This emotion is closely related to envy but has been less thoroughly investigated in psychoanalytic literature. In popular parlance, the two designations are often used interchangeably. The fact is that envy and jealousy differ in many significant ways. Freud and Klein diverged in formulating their origins and consequences. For Freud, envy appeared on the psychic horizon during the phallic phase, whereas for Klein it arose during the early oral relationship with the mother. For Freud, envy was a matter of anatomy and quintessentially a female concern, whereas for Klein envy was a matter of nurturance and not at all gender-bound. For Freud, envy resulted in a competitive search for organ substitutes, whereas for Klein envy led to hateful greed. Overall, Klein wrote much more about envy than did Freud. In contrast, Freud paid greater attention to jealousy. Here too, his views were different from those of Klein. Freud traced the roots of jealousy to the repudiation of homosexual desire (a notion that is now considered obsolete) while Klein held that jealousy first raised its head with the arrival of a sibling. For both, however, envy was a dyadic and jealousy a triadic experience.

As psychoanalysis evolved further, more literature accumulated on envy and less on jealousy. A search of entries in the PEP-Web (the electronic compendium of over 118 years of psychoanalytic literature) readily confirms this impression. Envy appears in the titles of 169 papers, and jealousy in the titles of forty-two papers. Moreover, sixty-two papers on envy have appeared since the year 2000, while only eleven on jealousy have appeared during that same period. This lack of attention and theoretical updating prompted us to consider the phenomenon of jealousy more deeply.

Aiming to put together an up-to-date volume on this "anguish of triangulation," we invited twelve distinguished colleagues to shed fresh light on it from developmental, cultural, and clinical perspectives. They responded with enthusiasm and gave us the gift of their evocative and provocative thoughts with reference points ranging from the varied relationships within a family through race relations, literary imagination, and movies, to the highly nuanced and, at times, distressing ebb and flow of jealousy in the transference-countertransference matrix of clinical discourse. It is our hope that this rich tapestry of ideas would pave the way for enhancing empathy with those who suffer from the painful emotion of jealousy and to help free them from its cruel shackles.

PROLOGUE

CHAPTER ONE

The spectrum of jealousy: an introductory overview

Salman Akhtar

I would like to begin this chapter by quoting Marcianne Blevis's (2009) highly nuanced description of the individual afflicted by jealousy. Writing with disarming eloquence, she notes that:

> The jealous person is unable to trust anything. He doubts, suspects, or imagines extraordinary scenarios of deception, waiting for the other shoe to drop. Eventually, reality catches up with his theatre of illusions and his mistaken definition of love. He can't know or guess everything. It is obvious that his lover can never become totally transparent to him. Every human being needs her privacy, her secret garden. Yet for the jealous person, this state of affairs is intolerable. He needs total control over his subjects. (p. 3)

This portrait is remarkable not only for its literary quality but also for its bringing together a number of "meta-experiences" that go with jealousy. I will discuss such experiences soon. For now, it will suffice to say that jealousy is a painful experience that is frequently encountered in social, cultural, and clinical realms of life.

My contribution here is meant to highlight the nature of this phenomenon, trace its developmental origins, and explicate the therapeutic strategies for its amelioration in cases where it acquires a seriously distressing and morbid form. In order to accomplish these goals, I will first elucidate the phenomenological features of jealousy (and its absence), then conduct a comprehensive survey of psychoanalytic writings on the topic, and attempt to interweave pertinent insights from general psychology, psychiatry, and cultural anthropology. Following this, I will discuss the technical challenges in the psychoanalytic treatment of jealous individuals and conclude by making some synthesizing remarks and by pointing out areas that merit further attention.

Descriptive features

The etymology of the current English word "jealousy" is so well-traced by David Buss (2000) that paraphrasing him would simply not do. Hence, I quote him at length here.

> The word *jealousy* came into the English language through the French language. Comparable words in French are *jaloux* and *jalousie*, both of which derive from the Greek word *zelos*, which meant fervor, warmth, ardor, or intense desire. The French word *jalousie*, however, has a dual meaning. One meaning is similar to the English *jealous*, but *jalousie* also refers to a Venetian blind, the kind with numerous horizontal slats suspended one above the other. The Norwegian psychiatrist Nils Retterstol at the University of Oslo speculates that this meaning arose from a situation in which a husband suspicious of his wife could observe her undetected from behind the *jalousie*, presumably to catch her in the act of intercourse with another man. (p. 28, italics in the original)

The dictionary definition of jealousy includes phrases like "intolerance of rivalry or unfaithfulness ... hostility towards a rival or one believed to enjoy an advantage … [and] zealous vigilance" (Mish, 1993, p. 627). Three realms seem to be involved here: emotional, cognitive, and behavioral. Close contact with someone afflicted with jealousy lends support to such categorization. In *the realm of emotions*, jealousy involves mental pain and mistrust. The former results from the subjectively experienced rupture of a self-object relation that was taken for granted (Akhtar, 2000; Freud, 1926d; Weiss, 1934). The latter is a reaction to the trauma of betrayal (actual or imaginary) and guards against recurrence of mental pain. In *the realm of cognition*, many disturbances are evident. The jealous individual sees meaning where there is no meaning, exaggerates the importance of environmental cues, and shows difficulty in considering alternate explanations for what he or she has deduced. A jealous wife, for instance, chides her husband who welcomes a couple entering their house for dinner by telling the female guest that she is looking "very nice"; the wife finds this an evidence of her husband's wanting to have sex with that woman. A jealous husband turns red with rage when, after giving a paper, his academician wife thanks her mentor before talking to him; he concludes that she does not love him at all. The jealous person's cognition is characterized by rigidity, loss of figure-ground relationship, and "narrow-mindedness" (Brenman, 1985) which has "the function of squeezing out humanity and preventing human understanding from modifying cruelty" (p. 273). In *the behavioural realm*, disturbing actions involve constantly looking for "clues" and "proofs" of betrayal, checking the lover's (or spouse's) email and text messages, and confirming their whereabouts (by repeatedly calling or actually showing up). Spying in other forms, stalking, and hiring private detectives also form the gamut of a jealous individual's behavior. Fortunately, in most instances, jealousy does not lead to such behaviors; it remains a private, if deeply troubling, experience. At other times, matters get out of hand and then not only the behaviors listed above come into operation but rage, violence, and even murder may take place.

Putting together the affective, cognitive, and behavioral manifestations of jealousy, it can be safely concluded that hostile mistrust, hyper-vigilance, and destructiveness constitute the central triad here. Blevis's (2009) monograph on jealousy contains all this and more. She notes that pervasive mistrust and the wish for omnipotent control are not the only features of jealousy. Among its other elements are (i) inability to understand that love cannot be controlled; (ii) perceptual errors (whereby a misspoken sentence, the slightest delay in responding to a phone call, a momentary shift in the eye gaze is imbued with paranoia and triggers panic); (iii) a split attitude towards the imaginary rival, who is consciously hated and devalued put preconsciously (or unconsciously) admired and envied; (iv) a profound sense of having lost the love that one was receiving, (v) a traumatic destabilization of identity; (vi) the activation of deep insecurity about one's "lovability"; (vii) insistent claims for attention and love; (viii) the potential of perverse sadomasochistic excitement in the experience of being "ignored" and "excluded," and finally (ix) a peculiar, thought-numbing alienation from the object of one's desire.

Even with this rich and nuanced portrait at hand, some questions about the nature of jealousy remain unanswered. These include the following.

- *Can a certain amount of jealousy be deemed "normal"?* From St Augustine's declaration that "He that is not jealous, is not in love" (cited in Buss, 2000, p. 27) to Freud's (1922b) allowing that ordinary "competitive jealousy" might be "normal," there exists a notion that a modicum of jealousy is inevitable in intimate relationships. Indeed, there is some evidence (Buss, 2000) that both women and men tend to regard a partner's absence of jealousy as lack of love.
- *What distinguishes normal jealousy from abnormal jealousy?* The sort of jealousy referred to above as normal is mild, fleeting, and correctible by reality testing. At times, a certain playfulness also characterizes the experience. Morbid jealousy, in contrast, is disturbing, persistent, and immune to corrective evidence from reality. Unlike normal jealousy which has the potential of fueling competitiveness with the rival and enhancing eroticism within the couple, pathological jealousy saddles the individual with chronic worry and becomes a torment for the partner.[1]
- *Are there "cocreated" elements in the experience of jealousy?* The impact of jealousy on one's lover or spouse is evident via the latter's feeling wrongfully accused, constantly watched, and treated unempathically. Such distress on the partner's part (and his or her defensive maneuvers of concealing one's whereabouts or restricting one's contacts) is customarily seen as a consequence of the jealous individual's tyranny. However, a deeper question exists here. Could the person predisposed to jealousy have "deliberately" picked a lover/spouse who possesses an extra quantum of jealousy-inducing triggers? For

instance, an inwardly insecure man might marry a crowd-pleasing popular theatre actress, or a woman with shaky self-esteem might get involved with a recently divorced man with a four-year-old coquettish daughter in order to "facilitate" the subsequent development of jealousy. Such "actualization" (Akhtar, 2009a, p. 4) accords the jealous person's complaints a realistic quality. To a certain extent, then, the couple's suffering is cocreated insofar as both partners are unable to free themselves from their characterological traps and both continue to hurt each other.

- *Can jealousy be "induced" or is the jealous person predisposed to such suffering?* Iago's cunning and relentless efforts to make Othello believe that his wife, Desdemona, is having an affair with Cassio (Shakespeare, 1603), would have us believe that jealous feelings can be induced by others. This might be true to a certain extent. There might exist environmental triggers that unleash the "green-eyed monster"; these include a partner's glance at an attractive stranger passing by, his undue friendliness with a good-looking waitress in a restaurant, or even his expression of love for his children from a previous marriage. However, such "induction" and "triggering" is generally more effective in people who already have a predisposition to jealousy.

- *Are there variables in one's personal background that predispose one to intense jealousy?* This question brings us to the psychoanalytic explanations of the origins of jealousy. Before covering that literature, however, going over a jargon-free and matter-of-fact passage from Ayala Pines's (1998) book, *Romantic Jealousy*, might serve us well. Pines states that the predisposition to jealousy:

> … is influenced by our family background: a man whose mother was unfaithful to his father or whose parents had violent outbursts of jealousy is likely to have far greater predisposition to jealousy than a man whose father and mother felt secure in each other's love. It is influenced by our family constellation: a woman who was outshone by a prettier or brighter sister is likely to have a greater predisposition to jealousy than a woman who was the favorite child in the family. It is also influenced by childhood and adult attachment history: a person who had a secure attachment to his mother will be less likely to become jealous than an anxiously attached person, and a person who was betrayed by a

trusted mate is likely to develop a greater predisposition to jealousy in the future. (pp. 6–7)

This descriptive portrait of vulnerability to jealousy is a good stepping-stone for us to enter into the chamber of metapsychology.

Psychoanalytic perspectives

Freud's views

Freud (1911c) first formulated the mechanism underlying jealousy in his study of the Schreber case. He directed his comments to alcoholic delusions of jealousy and delusions of jealousy in women. In both scenarios, he traced the origin of jealousy to latent homosexuality. An alcoholic was disappointed in his love for women and turned to men for company. His "drinking buddies," however, soon became "the objects of a strong libidinal cathexis in his unconscious" (p. 64). This, in turn, was transformed into jealousy by the following associational chain: "It is not *I* who love the man—*she* loves him" (p. 64, italics in the original). As a result, the man begins to suspect the women in relation to all the men who he himself is tempted to along similar lines: "It is not *I* who love the women—*he* loves them" (p. 64, italics in the original). The jealous woman suspects her male partner of paying excessive attention to all the women that she herself wants to be sexually involved with. Her dynamic was thus the exact replica of the male alcoholic. However, Freud added that the jealous woman is also attracted to women owing to "the dispositional effect of her excessive narcissism" (p. 64). Eleven years later, Freud (1922b) returned to the topic of jealousy and declared that:

> Jealousy is one of those affective states, like grief, that may be described as normal. If anyone appears to be without it, the inference is justified that it has undergone severe repression and consequently plays all the greater part in his unconscious mental life. (p. 223)

Freud felt jealousy was composed of three layers: (a) competitive, (b) projected, and (c) delusional. *Competitive jealousy* could be regarded as "normal." After all, the thought of losing one's love object does cause narcissistic injury and a tendency towards self-blame. Freud added though that:

Although we may call it normal, this jealousy is by no means completely rational, that is, derived from the actual situation, proportionate to the circumstances, and under the complete control of the unconscious ego; for it is deep in the unconscious, it is a continuation of the earliest stirrings of the child's affective life, and it originates in the Oedipus or brother–sister complex of the first sexual period. (p. 223)

The jealousy of the second layer, *projected jealousy*, is the result of the projection of one's own unfaithfulness (or the impulses towards it) upon the partner. The dynamic is the same in men and women. Those who cheat suspect others of cheating. Freud made the interesting observation that a certain latitude given to each partner's temptation to flirt with others serves as a safety valve and diminishes the need for repressing such impulses; this reduces the possibility of developing jealousy. *Delusional jealousy*, the third among Freud's nosology, also emanates from projection. However, the love object in this instance is of the same sex as the subject.

Delusional jealousy is what is left of a homosexuality that has run its course, and it rightly takes its position among the classical forms of paranoia. As an attempt at defense against an unduly strong homosexual impulse, it may, in a man, be described in the formula: 'I do not love him, *she* loves him'. (p. 225, italics in the original)

Freud quickly added that in most psychotic cases one finds an admixture of all three types of jealousy: competitive, projective, and delusional.

Freud's pupils and early followers

Ferenczi (1909) echoed Freud and, in reporting upon a female patient who was presumably also seen by the master, attributed the origin of jealousy to repudiated homosexual desire: "She projected it on to her husband (whom she had previously loved) and accused him of infidelity" (pp. 65–66). In a later paper, Ferenczi (1912) recounted the woeful tale of his own housekeeper. Her husband, a chronic alcoholic, repeatedly accused her of marital infidelity and of flirting with their master's male patients. Ferenczi offered all sorts of details about this alcoholic man's fascination with him and concluded that "The conspicuous feature of homosexual transference to myself allows of the interpretation that his jealousy of me signified only the projection of his own erotic pleasure in the male sex" (p. 161).

Jones too (1929) agreed with Freud that jealousy resulted from the projection of warded-off homosexuality. However, he arrived at this conclusion by a somewhat different and circuitous route. He held that the jealous person was possessed by narcissistic dependency. Such dependency had resulted from severe oedipal guilt which led to fear of the father and a desire for homosexual submission. This, in turn, led to fear of women from which infidelity arose; the projection of infidelity caused one to experience jealousy.

In contrast to such loyalty to Freud's formulations, Klein (1927) traced the origin of jealousy to the child's reaction to the arrival of a sibling. Noting that relationship with brothers and sisters plays a fundamental role in character formation,[2] Klein stated that:

> Every analysis proves that all children suffer great jealousy of younger sisters and brothers as well as of older ones. Even the quite small child, which seemingly knows nothing about birth, has a very distinct *unconscious* knowledge of the fact that children grow in the mother's womb. A great hate is directed against this child in the mother's womb for reasons of jealousy, and—as typical of the phantasies of a child during the mother's expectancy of another one—we find desires to mutilate the mother's womb and to deface the child in it by biting and cutting it. (p. 173, italics in the original)

Klein added that similar sadistic impulses are often directed against older siblings because the child feels weaker in comparison to them, even if this might not be the case in reality. Another important aspect of Klein's theorization involved the complex relationship between envy and jealousy. She distinguished envy as a dyadic and jealousy as a triadic experience. However, the way the two emotions were related becomes a little muddled in her writings. At one place, she spoke of infantile envy of the maternal breast and declared that "To this primary envy, jealousy is added when the Oedipus situation arises" (1952, p. 79). At another place, she reported that:

> There is a direct link between the envy experienced towards the mother's breast and the development of jealousy. Jealousy is based

on the suspicion of and rivalry with the father, who is accused of having taken away the mother's breast and the mother. This rivalry marks the early stages of the direct and inverted Oedipus complex, which normally arises concurrently with the depressive position in the second quarter of the first year. (1957, p. 196)

At a third place, however, she states that the oedipal "envy, rivalry and jealousy—at this stage still powerfully stirred by oral-sadistic impulses—are now experienced towards two people who are both hated and loved" (1952, p. 80). This leaves the impression that oedipal jealousy was a revival, even if a powerful one, of oral sadism (directed at mother and siblings). Thus who was the child's original rival—a sibling or the father—remained unclear in Klein's writing. In all fairness to her though, it should be acknowledged that the inseparability of the two (after all, it is the father who impregnates the mother and causes siblings to be born) and her locating the oedipal development in the second year of life makes the separation of envy and jealousy rather murky. What does remain clear about Klein's formulation is that projection of homosexuality plays little role and oral sadism (even though accentuated by the oedipal configuration) a big role in the genesis of jealousy.

Brunswick (1929), working with a female psychotic patient suffering from jealousy, found a compromise between the Freudian and the Kleinian positions. She agreed that homosexuality underlay jealousy but felt that such erotic inclination arose not from the Oedipus complex but from an earlier preoedipal level. Riviere (1932) gave this formulation a further twist. She felt that the desire to steal something from the mother or to rob her of her possessions was, in its projected form, the basis of jealousy. Riviere acknowledged that such robbing fantasies can undergo "genitalization" (i.e., acquire an adult sexual connotation) but are in fact infantile and oral in origin. She stated that in the jealous person

> ... the "loss of love" or "search for love" in question refers ultimately to something deeper than a genital relation to the desired parent. The quality of the attachments in such people, moreover, is often that to a part-object, thus facilitating the change of real objects and explaining the relative indifference shown to their objective personality. The "search" or "loss" in such cases can be traced back to *oral envy*, and to the deprivation of the breast or father's penis

(as an oral object)—the object with which the parents in coitus are at that level felt to be gratifying each other. I would mention here the very prevalent confusion between the *words* "envy" and "jealousy" which finds a quite precise derivation in this oral primal scene experience in which the two feelings would be indistinguishable. This and only this experience furnishes a rational basis for the acute and desperate sense of lack and loss, of dire need, of emptiness and desolation felt by the jealous one of a triangle and reversed by the unfaithful. (pp. 420–421)

Fenichel (1945) too discerned early oral fixation at the base of jealousy. Oral sadistic wishes directed toward the mother were projected on the dyadic partner of adult life who, as a result, appeared treacherous and cunning. Working independently in Calcutta and seemingly unaware of Riviere's and Fenichel's contributions, Chatterji (1948) presented detailed clinical material to support his conclusion that "Pathological jealousy is not one of genital oedipal level but is of purely oral origin" (p. 21). Barag (1949), reporting from Israel on a male case, however, went back to the early Freudian formulation and did not evoke oral fixation in the genesis of jealousy.

Later analysts

Siedenberg (1952a, 1952b) noted that a particular kind of wish-fulfilment takes place in jealousy regardless of whether it is of day-to-day type or of clinical severity. A modicum of feigned jealousy and gently teasing "accusations" of flirtatiousness add spice to the romantic life of a well-functioning couple. The husband who teases his wife about her fondness of their gardener enjoys unconscious pleasure of oedipal victory (with the gardener standing for the son and he himself for the father) while in reality committing no transgression. The same goes for the wife who jokes about her husband's "love" for his young research assistant. In both instances, a certain lightheartedness is retained and the experience of jealousy is self-dosed and enjoyable.[3] When such playfulness is lost, jealousy turns deeply distressing. However, even in such instances, one can discern a wish-fulfilment to take place. By bitterly accusing the partner of unfaithfulness, the individual betrays the desire that the parent who was the object of childhood erotic desire indeed be sexually loose—so that one's illicit desires can be gratified on a clandestine basis.

Such covert wish-fulfilment in jealousy is responsible for the fact that the jealous individual thwarts all reassurance and, contrary to all expectation, seeks "confirmation" of his or her suspicions.

Schmidberg (1953) emphasized the intense early need for the love object, oral sadism, and desire for omnipotent control. She thus remained loyally within the drive theory model and that too as it pertained to the oral phase. In contrast, Ortega (1959) approached the problem of jealousy from a Sullivanian (i.e., interpersonal) perspective. He posited that jealous individuals are deeply insecure about their worthiness to others. As a result, their rivals need not be demonstrably superior; they are *felt* to be superior because one considers oneself worth nothing. Moreover, competing with them constitutes an effort to seem more adequate than the jealous person actually feels.

Writing a decade later, Pao (1969) questioned the inevitability of the link between repressed homosexuality and jealousy. He traced the origin of jealousy to disturbed object relations of early childhood. Pao stated:

> Because three persons act as the "stars" of the jealousy drama, it may be intimated that jealousy must be experienced at a time when the developing and maturing child acquires the ability to clearly distinguish persons around him. At such times, he must have already been able to distinguish self from others, to establish a certain degree of object constancy, and to formulate a rudimentary set of self-representations and object-representations. The intrusion on the dyadic relation between the mother and the child by a third person, such as the father, sibling, or others, is inevitable. Therefore, every child knows jealousy feelings as soon as his ego equipment permits him to conceptualize them. But, to formulate the self-representations and the object-representations in order to stage or re-stage the jealousy drama requires something special. (pp. 633–634)

This "special" thing was an actual event (e.g., birth of a sibling, separation from the mother) that created insecurity about attachment and belonging. The ensuing grief then got exacerbated by the feelings of exclusion during the oedipal phase. Pao went on to declare that jealousy is a complex mental state that involves all three components of the psychic structure: id (manifested by oral sadism), ego (manifested by projection of impulses to be unfaithful and by narcissistic self-holding), and superego (manifested by punishing criticism of the partner and also of the self). Pao's observation regarding the role of early trauma was "confirmed" by Spielman (1971) and Wisdom (1976); the latter described the jealous reactions of a twelve-month-old boy to the birth of a brother in striking details.[4]

Neubauer (1982) added a new twist to the phenomenology of jealousy by distinguishing it not only from envy but also from the infrequently invoked concept of rivalry. According to him:

> *Rivalry*, the striving for the exclusive access to the source (of needed supplies), implies an assertive, aggressive struggle against the rival … Rivalry is an act, based upon the wish not to lose the object to the rival. Thus, in rivalry, the contact with the object is maintained. *Envy* is based either on the awareness of superior attributes of others or an idealization of these attributes. The libidinal component of this admiration is linked to resentment, self-devaluation, and sadness. *Jealousy* is the resentment of the love the third person receives or expects. It comes into operation when additional developmental factors are added to the rivalry, when gender identity is established, that is, when the phallic-oedipal organization has developed and when the triadic relationship has oedipal characteristics. (pp. 123–124, italics added)

Neubauer went on to state that rivalry can be mastered through competition or coexistence and jealousy by repossession of the object's love. Envy, however, poses greater difficulty since it involves aggression directed at the very object that is admired and loved. Neubauer's contribution was followed by two other significant papers on jealousy during the 1980s even though neither of them referred to his ideas. Coen (1987) offered a highly nuanced and multiply determined portrait of jealousy. In this view, jealousy is both a substitute for and a defense against full and deep intimacy with another person. It is a masturbatory equivalent which involves perverse scenarios of sexual relatedness.

> The cast of characters includes at least four roles: male and female sexual protagonists, an observer, and an audience witnessing the interaction between the three. The need for concrete evidence relates to denial, mistrust, and guilt, especially about feared

destructiveness, as well as masochistic and narcissistic enhance-
ment. The object choice in pathological jealousy involves a fantasied
protector, and is basically homosexual, narcissistic. These defend
against the dangers of passive needs of another person different
from oneself, as well as of aggressive destruction. (p. 107)

Pierloot (1988) extended the jealous individual's tormented object relations to the realm of "impersonal objects." Noting that impersonal
objects (e.g., fetishes, transitional objects) often stand for part-objects
(in both a figurative and a literal sense), he elucidated the symbolic significance of Othello's handkerchief and Lady Windermere's fan (from
the eponymous play by Oscar Wilde, 1893). Thus the pain of jealousy
suffused not only one's relationship with human beings but also with
the inanimate objects that linked one with those human beings.[5]

More recent contributors

One monograph (Mollon, 2002), an edited volume (Wurmser & Jarass,
2008), an interesting paper (Lewin, 2011), and Blevis's (2009) slim but
impressive book constitute the more recent contributions on jealousy
that merit our attention. Mollon's (2002) monograph, titled *Shame and
Jealousy*, attempted to bring together the work of Melanie Klein and
Heinz Kohut. It proposed that a disruption of early parental empathy
leads to an evaluation of the self as lacking or inferior in some way.
This, in turn, causes a vulnerability to shame and jealousy. The contributors to Wurmser and Jarass's (2008a) edited volume also stressed
the role of shame in the genesis of jealousy. Their essential thesis was
that jealousy arises from the inevitable experience in human relations
of being "the excluded third" (in the primal scene, most clearly, but also
while witnessing mother's attention to a sibling). They also noted the
"advance" from jealousy to murderous vengefulness. Wurmser and
Jarass (2007), in their own contribution to the book, maintained that "The
sequence of *shame* → *envy and jealousy* → *revenge* → *feared retribution by
even more archaic forms of humiliation* turns into a characteristic vicious
cycle of repeated traumatisation" (pp. 173–174, italics in the original).
    Lewin (2011) proposed the novel concept of "parallel identification"
which worked as a shield against the painful experience of jealousy.
Such identification was a sort of manic defense and functioned in the
following way:

> The identifying subject merges with his object of desire through compulsive imitation. This merger holds the subject in a developmental cocoon of non-being that negates his perception of any rivals for the object's love. Parallel identification inhibits conscious jealousy, subsequently blocking the subject's capacity to evolve through empathy and fantasy. (p. 551)

Individuals using such a defense had arrived at the precipice of jealousy and withdrew from it by creating an impenetrable shield of self-sufficiency. There is a "make-pretend merger" (p. 568) with the love object underneath this shield which is held in place by uncrossable boundaries against two-person relatedness.

This brings our survey of psychoanalytic literature on jealousy full circle back to Blevis's (2009) book which I mentioned at the very outset of this discourse and to which I will refer again in the treatment section of this chapter.

Critique, synthesis, and further ideas

While holding some water (especially vis-a-vis the projection of one's own unfaithful impulses), Freud's vase of hypotheses had many holes. *First*, it is heavily tilted in favour of the vicissitudes of libido and takes little account of the role of aggression. *Second*, it places emphasis on the oedipal determinants of jealousy and overlooks that jealousy could arise from preoedipal conflicts as well. *Third*, it bypasses the contribution made by actual traumatic events during childhood (details below) to the vulnerability to jealousy. *Fourth*, it assumes homosexuality to be invariably ego-dystonic and in need of repression and projection. *Fifth*, it fails to account for jealousy in overtly homosexual men and women. *Sixth*, its separation of "alcoholic" and "female" categories is logically untenable. And *finally*, it shows a phallocentric bias in postulating narcissism as a basis for jealous insecurity in women and not in men.

Such weaknesses in Freud's conceptualization coupled with the overall shift in psychoanalysis from drive theory to object relations approach led to the emergence of alternate explanations regarding jealousy. At first these explanations accommodated Freud's emphasis upon latent homosexuality, even though they often did so in labored ways. Later on, this particular etiological dimension was totally dropped. Oral sadism, early disappointment in caretaking figures, and traumatic

THE SPECTRUM OF JEALOUSY 17

turning away of a major love object became the major causative explanations for jealousy. Complex fantasies, ego restrictions, and compromised
superego functioning were added to the psychoanalytic description of
jealousy as well.

Klein's distinction of envy as being dyadic and jealousy as being
triadic was largely upheld by subsequent contributors. However, some
further thought is needed about this demarcation. After all, there is
a reason to covet an attribute (e.g., better looks, greater intelligence)
that someone else possesses and that reason often turns out to be the
belief that if one has that attribute then one would be more admired and
loved by others (a third party). Envy thus contains a covert scenario of
jealousy. Conversely, hatred for a rival receiving (in reality or imagination) a loved one's attention implicitly acknowledges admiration for the
rival. Jealousy thus contains a covert scenario of envy. The two emotions, it seems, are always intermingled and can only be separated in
their extreme forms. Their frequent interchangeability in colloquial discourse thus seems far from linguistic sloppiness; it actually contains a
bit of wisdom. Mention of such colloquial wisdom brings us to consider
the sociocultural aspects of jealousy.

Sociocultural aspects

The experience of jealousy is ubiquitous. With rare exceptions (e.g., the
Banaro of New Guinea reported upon by the great anthropologist,
Margaret Mead, 1931), all cultures show evidence of its existence.
What differs from one culture to another is the act/event that triggers
jealousy. Sexual liaison with someone other than the spouse, regarded
to be the most powerful "justification" for developing acute jealousy,
is not universally found to be so. In polygamous and polyandrous
societies and among "swingers," sexual involvement with more than
one partner is accepted as a norm (Gilmartin, 1986). Jealousy among
the members of these groups is stirred up by emotional infidelity and
social gossip. Moreover, cultures that uphold monogamous marriage as
an ideal are more prone to stir up jealousy in general. Cultures that sup-
press women on a conscious basis (while idealizing and fearing them
unconsciously) are more prone to cause male romantic jealousy in particular (Pines, 1998).

The link between idealization and jealousy becomes more evident
when we discover that jealousy shares a feature with nostalgia. Both

experiences have a bitter-sweet quality. The bitterness in them has to do with the loss of an idealized self-object state. The sweetness has to do with the memory of (in the case of jealousy) and the hope of reunion with (in the case of nostalgia) that idealized object. To be sure, nostalgia has more sweetness and jealousy more bitterness but both emotions contain the bittersweet flavor.

The bitterness of jealousy, if truly unbearable, can break hearts, rupture bonds, and lead to destructive acts. When manageable, the same bitterness can become fuel for sublimation. Vying to obtain similar, if not greater, acclaim than others accord to a rival can become a force for personality growth (Edward, 2011). Under fortunate circumstances, such jealous competitiveness can yield productive results. This is as true for athletics as it is for science. The Harvard-based geneticist, Richard Lewontin (1968), declares that science is a competitive and aggressive enterprise and "a contest of man against man that provides knowledge as a side product" (p. 2). Within hard sciences, the well-known rivalries between Robert Koch and Louis Pasteur, Thomas Edison and Nicola Tesla, and Humphry Davy and Michael Faraday have contributed much to theoretical advances and new discoveries. Within literature and art, the jealous competitiveness between Arthur Rimbaud and Paul Verlaine, William Wordsworth and Samuel Taylor Coleridge, and Ernest Hemingway and F. Scott Fitzgerald have also propelled artistic creativity. And, within our own field of psychoanalysis, the tensions between Freud and Ferenczi, Klein and Winnicott, and Kohut and Kernberg have enhanced theory and technique.

The relationship between jealousy and creativity is not exhausted here. Great works of literature have been devoted to this emotion. Almost all the great love epics of the world include reference to jealousy and its disastrous outcome. Shakespeare's *Othello* (1603) might be the best known of a focused literary work on jealousy but it is hardly the only one. Tolstoy's (1889) *The Kreutzer Sonata*, Hardy's (1891) *Tess of the D'Urbervilles*, and the much hated and much loved experimental novel, *Jealousy*, by Alain Robbe-Grillet (1957) recently made a list of ten top novels about jealousy prepared by the Man Booker Award winning British novelist, Howard Jacobson (cited in *The Guardian*, November 4, 2009). Fiction is not the only literary genre fascinated by jealousy, however. Poetry too bows its head at the poisonous altar of the emotion. Major and minor poets in all languages have penned songs, sonnets, and ballads about jealousy. One poem that stands out for its brevity, its psychological-mindedness, and its keen awareness of the sadomasochistic agenda of jealousy is William Strode's (1598–1645) "On Jealousy".

> There is a thing that nothing is,
> A foolish wanton, sober wise;
> It hath noe wings, noe eyes, noe eares,
> And yet it flies, it sees, it heares;
> It lives by losse, it feeds on smart,
> It joyes in woe, it liveth not;
> Yet evermore this hungry elfe
> Doth feed on nothing but itselfe. (1620, p. 51)

Strode's poem underscores the experience of loss, defensive vigilance, and masochism in jealousy. In contrast, Rupert Brooke's (1887–1915) poem, "Jealousy," emphasizes the envy of the rival and the sadistic impulses towards both the rival and the betraying beloved.

> When I see you, who were so wise and cool,
> Gazing with silly sickness on that fool
> You've given your love to, your adoring hands
> Touch his so intimately that each understands,
> I know, most hidden things; and when I know
> Your holiest dreams yield to the stupid bow
> Of his red lips, and that the empty grace
> Of those strong legs and arms, that rosy face,
> Has beaten your heart to such a flame of love,
> That you have given him every touch and move,
> Wrinkle and secret of you, all your life,
> —Oh! then I know I'm waiting, lover-wife,
> For the great time when love is at a close,
> And all its fruit's to watch the thickening nose
> And sweaty neck and dulling face and eye,
> That are yours, and you, most surely, till you die!
> Day after day you'll sit with him and note
> The greasier tie, the dingy wrinkling coat;
> As prettiness turn to pomp, and strength to fat,
> And love, love, love to habit!
> And after that,
> When all that's fine in man is at an end,
> And you, that loved young life and clean, must tend

A foul sick fumbling dribbling body and old,
When his rare lips hang flabby and can't hold
Slobber, and you're enduring that worst thing,
Senility's queasy furtive move-making,
And searching those dear eyes for human meaning,
Propping the bald and helpless head, and cleaning
A scrap that life's flung by, and love's forgotten, —
Then you'll be tired; and passion dead and rotten;
And he'll be dirty, dirty!
O lithe and free
And lightfoot, that the poor heart cries to see,
That's how I'll see your man and you! —

But you
—Oh, when THAT time comes, you'll be dirty too! (1908, p. 45)

Jealousy also undergirds the central theme of many significant plays and movies, including Peter Shaffer's (1979) *Amadeus*—a stunning theatrical piece dealing with an admixture of envy and jealousy. Films such as *Laura* (1944), *Mildred Pierce* (1945), *Niagara* (1953), *East of Eden* (1955), *An Affair to Remember* (1957), *Suddenly Last Summer* (1959), *The Beguiled* (1971), and *Fatal Attraction* (1987) are some outstanding movies about jealousy.[6] Though not directly about this emotion, the Mike Nichols's evergreen *The Graduate* (1967) and Stanley Kubrick's *Eyes Wide Shut* (1999) also tackle the theme of romantic jealousy in powerful and evocative ways.

Such sublimated outcomes pertaining to jealousy must not make one overlook that at its core, the affect is corrosive of both the self and its relations to loved others. A nationwide survey of marital counsellors revealed that jealousy is a problem in one third of all couples seeking couples therapy (White & Devine, 1991). Jealousy can also lead to aggressive acts, violence, and murder. Spousal murder is often precipitated by intense feelings of jealousy (Chimbos, 1978; Mullen, 1996). Such dark outcomes of jealousy bring us back to clinical concerns and therapeutic management of jealous individuals.

Therapeutic considerations

A good beginning point here is constituted by Blevis's (2009) therapeutic approach to such patients.[7] Her way of working with them is anchored in the conviction that the one afflicted with jealousy is fighting a battle that is not contemporary but from his or her past. Bringing forth the muzzled voices and frozen sentiments related to the time when someone deeply important (e.g., mother, father) turned away from the child remains profoundly important. Blevis demonstrates a truly impressive skill in discovering such "buried treasures" of pain and linking them up with their contemporary interpersonal versions. The pathways she traverses to reach the past are varied and include a subtle enactment on the patient's part (p. 15), a telling dream (p. 27), seemingly inexplicable intrusions into the patient's free association (p. 39), and so on.

While reconstruction remains the mainstay of Blevis's approach, she is forever prepared to make transference interpretations, thus vivifying the past as it is lived out in the "here and now" of the clinical relationship. Moreover, she is keenly aware of the regressive pull exerted by the masochistic pleasure of jealousy and, in that realm, is willing to go beyond interpretation and reconstruction to strict limit-setting. Note the following comment of hers:

> I had to put our work online when Frank, almost to the point of rage, announced that he wanted to destroy all our recent hard-won insights and return to the jealousy he so enjoyed. If he wanted to follow that path, it would have to be without me. (p. 43)

Such limit-setting and "spoiling" of the sadomasochistic pleasures inherent in jealousy requires a brave tough-mindedness to accompany the characteristic soft-heartedness of the analyst. The analyst might have to go out on a limb and the patient might have to bear considerable suffering in such moments. Blevis acknowledges that "To unearth the past takes courage because it requires questioning situations that would be more comfortable to leave unexamined" (p. 16).

At times, the patient comes to this point and cannot bear the material that is getting "de-repressed" and/or becoming evident as a result of taking a new look at his formative years. The jealous woman, who built the "personal myth" (Kris, 1956) that her jealousy originated with her teenage discovery of a lurid extramarital affair of her father, and who now finds out that she had been painfully "dropped" much earlier by her mother (when her younger sister was born), cannot tolerate the latter discovery; it destabilizes her too much and makes her feel too angry with her mother whom she needs for all sorts of other reasons.

The jealous husband, filled with rage at his vivacious (taken by him to be seductive) wife, who "accidentally" hears the family gossip that his younger sister might be the product of a secret liaison his mother had when he was five or six years old, is loathe the recognize the shadow of such a past upon his current marital transactions. Arriving at such junctures, some jealous patients drop out of treatment.

However, a one-person psychology explanation of this sort can also be self-serving on the analyst's part. Shifting the responsibility of the impasse or disruption to the patient can evade the analyst's contributions to the difficulty. Therapeutic inexperience, technical rigidity, empathic failure of a sustained variety, and specific countertransference blocks to careful listening can all contribute to failed treatments. To be sure, working with intensely jealous patients is not easy. The analyst has to be simultaneously involved in many tasks, some of which seem contradictory. For instance, the analyst must empathize with the pain of the patient (at the suspicion that her boyfriend is interested in another woman) without lending his imprimatur on the validity of her perceptions leading to that pain. Conversely, the analyst must resist the temptation to "educate" the patient about social norms. Statements such as "It is within proper etiquette to compliment a woman guest about her looks," or "Glancing over at a waitress does not mean your husband is inclined to be unfaithful to you," do not help. They only make the patient feel misunderstood. Even more risky is to include the words "jealousy" or "jealous" in one's interpretations. Such labels, tempting though they might be, are to be strenuously avoided. This is because the patient whose analyst refers to him or her as "jealous" or calls his or her feeling "a pang of jealousy" experiences such utterances as pathologizing and invalidating. Yet another difficulty arises from the pressure that the patient puts upon the therapist to "agree" that the partner's behavior was indeed improper. The "screen" functions of this demand also need to be interpreted. In other words, the patient's need for the analyst to "confirm" that a partner has been inattentive masks the necessity for the validation of an earlier betrayal by a parent.

As treatment unfolds, the analyst gradually realizes that the patient is making a contradictory demand upon him: to confirm the "badness" of the offending party and thus validate that the patient *is* being betrayed but at the same time to reassure that the patient is lovable and is being loved. From this eroticized threesome battle (the aggrieved patient, the desirable side of the partner, and the betraying side of the partner), the analyst can find his way to the underlying oedipal triangulation, at first, and then to a preoedipal split in the mother–child relationship. The analyst might then learn that both these configurations had found "credibility" in external fixating events of the patient's childhood (e.g., father's affair during his daughter's teenage years; mother's giving birth to a sibling when the patient was barely fourteen months old). A firm commitment to the "principle of multiple function" (Waelder, 1936) anchors the analyst's work ego under such circumstances. It also allows him to discern that in parallel to the externalized crises, subtle transferential re-creations of early traumatic scenarios are also taking place. These need to be interpreted as well and in fact, addressing them might render the analyst's interventions much greater credibility than merely extra-transference interpretation and/or reconstruction would afford.

An important prerequisite to conduct such work is a deep and ongoing contact with one's countertransference. The sadomasochistic tableau of jealousy is induced via projective identification into the analyst but this almost never takes a coarse or explicit form. A man jealous of his wife's attention to her brother might attempt to induce similar jealousy in the analyst; he might brag about the large sums of money he is donating to his cardiologist and make the analyst fee excluded and inferior. Attention to disguised derivations of such sorts is very helpful in formulating interpretations of transference of jealousy. All in all, a well-attuned oscillation between transference and current reality, between perception and affect, between reconstruction and interpretation, and between validation and deconstruction is what is needed in order to be helpful to jealous individuals.

Concluding remarks

In this chapter, I have delineated the emotional, cognitive, and behavioral components of jealousy. I have distinguished "normal" from pathological jealousy and, by surveying the extensive psychoanalytic literature on the topic, have traced the origins of the vulnerability to the latter. After a brief foray into the sociocultural realm, I have returned to the clinical realm and elucidated the pitfalls and challenges in treating individuals with intense jealousy. Now, as I arrive at the conclusion of this contribution, I note that three areas still need attention. These include: (i) evolutionary foundations of jealousy, (ii) gender differences in the experience of jealousy, and (iii) the complete absence of jealousy in some individuals. Brief comments upon each of these follow.

From the evolutionary perspective, jealousy is an adaptive or problem-solving device whose aim is to help us cope with a host of reproductive threats. Jealousy pushes us to ward off rivals with nonverbal threats, verbal injunctions, and aggressive behaviors. It communicates commitment to the partner and precludes his or her straying by heightened vigilance. To be sure, this motivational substrate of jealousy is not conscious. It is based upon "emotional wisdom passed down to us over millions of years by our successful forbearers" (Buss, 2000, p. 6).

The second matter that has remained unaddressed is the gender difference in the experience of jealousy. Evolutionary psychologists, psychoanalysts, and empirical researchers of human behavior concur that men and women experience jealousy differently and react to it in separate ways. This does not mean that members of either gender experience more or less jealousy than the other.[8] In fact, there is ample empirical research to demonstrate that men and women report virtually identical levels of jealousy (Buunk & Hupka, 1987; White & Mullen, 1989). They differ, however, in what they feel most jealous about and how they express their bitterness at the real or imagined exclusion. Both men and women are hurt by infidelity of their partners but men are far more distressed by their women's sexual infidelity and women by their men's emotional infidelity (Shackelford, Buss, & Bennett, 2002). Another difference has been observed by DeSteno and Salovey (1996). These researchers note that when a woman knows that her man is attracted to a particular feature in another woman and the woman drawing his attention has that feature, she feels jealous. Men, in contrast, feel jealous of men who excel in areas important to their own self-definition. In other words, women's jealousy is more object-related, men's more narcissistic. Finally, there is the issue of jealousy leading to violence. Here too, one finds differences in the two genders, with men being more likely to be driven by jealousy to commit violent acts and murder (Buss, 2000; Paul & Galloway, 1994; Pines, 1983, 1998).

The third and last area needing comment is the absence of jealousy in certain individuals. Freud (1922b), as noted earlier in this discourse, was skeptical in this context and regarded absence of jealousy as merely a conscious experience underneath which lurked the unconscious, repressed emotion. At the other extreme is the argument that if one has experienced a secure attachment in childhood, possesses robust self-esteem, trusts the partner, and carries no impulses to be unfaithful oneself, then one would be immune to jealousy. A realistic compromise between such skeptical and credulous viewpoints on the absence of jealousy is to regard the vulnerability to mild jealousy as ubiquitous and to regard excessive jealousy as pathological. In other words, those who claim to be never jealous likely have the morbid intensities of the affect in mind while making their pronouncements. But if nothing at all, including actual sexual infidelity of their partner, distresses them, then one has to question such "pathological tolerance" (Pinta, 1979) and the deficiency of healthy entitlement that leads to it. To paraphrase Nietzsche (1905), who said "A small revenge is humaner than no revenge at all" (p. 71), we can end this discourse by declaring that a bit of fleeting and correctible jealousy is more congenial to mental health than a complete absence of the emotion. If a dollop of playful eroticism gets added to such mild jealousy, matters are even better.

PART I

DEVELOPMENTAL REALM

CHAPTER TWO

Jealousy among mothers

Maxine K. Anderson

Jealousy may be underrepresented in our psychoanalytic under-standing, often being confused with envy, likely because jealousy and envy are entwined in our experience. Simply put, envy refers to the desire to have what someone else has; jealousy is this (envy) as well as wanting the other person not to have it" (Spielman, 1971, p. 60). In envy, one covets what another person possesses and feels less in not possessing that object. The relationship involved in envy is the dyad. In jealousy, the configuration is the triad and the coveted object is usu-ally another's love or attention. One is jealous when a third person seems to have intruded and taken or possessed that affection. In jealousy, there is usually envy of the now-lost affection plus the bitterness toward the intruder who appears to be responsible for that loss, the one who seems to have stolen the coveted love. Many authors emphasize that jealousy harbors more intense feeling, bitterness, and hatred, as well as the long-ing and loss.

In the psychoanalytic literature, different authors give different emphases to envy and jealousy, depending largely upon their theoretical orientation. Thus, Kleinian authors (Klein, 1975; Riviere, 1932; Spillius, 1993), who focus on the earliest object relationships, stress the importance of envy that may emerge in the earliest stages of the differentiation of the ego functions. During this time, otherness only threatens to deprive or to persecute, and the loss of control of the supplies one needs feels catastrophic. These vulnerable states may trigger a pain such that spoil-ing the now un-possessed good is felt to be preferable to letting it exist beyond the grasp of the envier. Envy also isolates the envier who barely notices the existence of others; the focus of envy operates on primarily narcissistic considerations. That is, the focus is on one's own need and satisfaction without concern for others (Spielman, 1971).

While jealousy involves more developed levels of relatedness to objects in its recognition of triangularity in relationships, it is important to consider that jealousy is rooted in the earlier experiences of envy. For this discussion of jealousy between mothers, an appreciation of the entwinement of envy and jealousy will be assumed. In both circum-stances, narcissistic pain accompanies the sense of loss; it may be mild or if more intense, it may be experienced and expressed as mortifying humiliation. A varying degree of anger or aggression may also accom-pany envy or jealousy, and it is likely that the degree of aggression will parallel the depth of the narcissistic pain.

Developmental considerations

Earliest development begins with emergence or awakening within the dyad of the mothering presence. While the newborn has innate expectations for self and other (Mancia, 1981; Panksepp & Bevin, 2012; Trevarthen, 1996), it is generally thought that the newborn experiences a merged dyad for the first several weeks or even months of life. Indeed, Winnicott (1975) suggests that during this time, there is "no such thing as a baby" (p. 99), separate from his enveloping maternal environment. The gradual dissolution of this merger, which occurs as the infant gains a sense of a separate self is of course important developmentally. Envy is likely to be triggered when the infant feels deprived of that previous soothing merger and yet aware of its continued existence. This would be a kind of "warmth but not for me" state of mind. The previously soothed self feels bereft and in pain as it senses that the warmth has been lost and yet still exists. Loss of contact with, and also loss of control of that so-needed warmth are both basic to envy. In good enough developmental circumstances, the child gains a sense of continuity in his being less dependent on maternal supplies for his very existence, and thus less prone to envy. But in families with several children, the mingling of envy and jealousy may be prominent among the older children who have to navigate the experience of a new baby taking the supplies previously offered to them. This may be done smoothly if the mother appreciates the older children's growing emerging selves, but traces of the previous pains may persist.

In the good enough developmental situation, as the child gains the sense of her continuity-of-being, the capacity to share and to appreciate the existence of others generally grows. Jealousy may then be thought of as coming on line as it occurs when the ego is more developed, especially in terms of the awareness of separateness: the ego has developed beyond the need to possess and to maintain the exclusive relation with the prized other, but it still strives to maintain the illusion of having a special if not central place with that so-valued other. The envy of the new baby may have been significantly metabolized by the mother's intuitive recognition of her need to appreciate her growing child's capacities. Maintaining him in a place of warmth and love is often vital in fostering the emergence from the entrapping envy. But navigating envy of the lost supplies still leaves the triadic feelings of loss of privilege to others, as signified by the intensity of oedipal strivings. How and whether the child manages this phase-appropriate jealousy is likely shaped by her innate resilience to painful affect, but also to the empathic offerings from the parental figures.

While the goal of envy is to eradicate the sense of having been diminished by losing control of existing supplies, the goal in jealousy is to regain the wished-for relationship. This may bring hope in terms of restitution as a goal in jealousy. An important consideration in both envy and jealousy is shame. Lansky (2005) and Schore (1991) suggest that shame, the sense of diminishment or being compared negatively in one's own as well as others' eyes, is a primary cause of the psychic pain which underlies both envy and jealousy.

Contributions of affective neuroscience

Psychoanalysts may be enriched by the contributions of contemporary affective neuroscience, which informs us that there are innate affects—the legacy of evolution—which color our emerging experience (Panksepp & Bevin, 2012). Research reveals that all vertebrates investigated have deeply embedded ancient mid-brain structures that give rise to various affects. The arousals which mammals including man experience when quiescent well-being is disturbed are tinged with rather specific responses, such as fear or rage, sexual urgency, or separation distress. These specific affects trigger in stereotypic ways the action needed to quell the disturbance: Fear propels the animal to flee, rage to attack, threats to attachment expressed as distress calls speak clearly and urgently to the mother who is impelled to respond. These innate affects propel one toward tension-relieving action. The threats to attachment trigger impulses in adult females toward nurturing and tender care, aspects of what we consider to be part of maternal instincts. And a specific pro-social neural circuitry that Panksepp calls CARE seems to have developed by way of evolution in response to the length of vulnerability of the infant and his frequent need for attentive, comforting care. The hormone, oxytocin, facilitates this caring, nurturing bonding behavior in all mammals tested. Oxytocin also modifies the more aggressive affects in both males and females. We might consider it a civilizing biochemical, important in the development of attentive care and transformation of pain and distress. Indeed, neuroscientists suggest that oxytocin and the caring circuit are the bases of the development of empathy and compassion.

All of this is brought forward to underscore the degree of complexity and the significant impact of many underlying emotions having to do with care in this discussion involving jealousy between mothers. It is important to realize that the emotions which comprise envy and jealousy, which include loss, separation, fear, and rage, are not superficial, but innate and urgent, often triggering deep pain.

Mothering pairs

Two of the most obvious pairings of mothers are those between mother and daughter, and between mother-in-law and daughter-in-law. The relationship between a mother and her daughter, of course, impacts the quality of the mothering involving the two women when the daughter has a baby of her own. The way she was mothered will be implicit in the daughter's ministrations to her own baby. While she may not be able to consciously remember how she was mothered, we know via the functions of implicit memory that she will naturally tend to her baby as she felt tended to when she was a baby, although contemporary learning from friends and others will also lend impact.

Mary was the older of two daughters, a long-welcomed baby to a happily married couple. Her mother did not work outside the home during Mary's early years, and Mary grew up within an atmosphere of attentive care and maternal time devoted in an unpressured way toward her and her four-year-old younger sister's care. As she came to consider motherhood herself, Mary intuitively seemed to replicate the spaciousness and attentiveness for her babies that she had experienced from her own mother. This included her thoughtful choices about career that allowed the flexibility needed for full-time patient attention to her children in their early years. Also, it seemed that she was able to avoid the pressures that her peers often experienced amid competing choices about career and family. Mary's sense of security about her mothering was based in part upon her having felt well-held in mind by her caretaking persons during her early years. While Mary's mother, feeling internally well-grounded, was subject to the normative jealousies which arise when daughters marry and begin their own families, her internal security allowed her to appreciate the new freedoms and perspectives available to grandparenthood. She offered counsel to her daughters only upon their request. The normative effects of loss and jealousy can be mitigated when spacious thought, attentiveness, and self-respect offer underlying sturdiness to the personality.

Mary's friend, Nancy, grew up under different circumstances: She was the product of an unplanned pregnancy for a couple in their late teens. Each came from family situations governed more by impulsive behavior and abrupt rules than by thought-based values. As an unplanned child, Nancy felt herself to be an irritant or even a burden to her often overwhelmed mother. In contrast to Mary's inner sense of ease and safety amid attentive care, Nancy's inner experience was more shaped by impatience, doubt, and abrupt "happenings." Not guided as much by thought and restraint and often functioning on a concrete level, she felt more at risk in a hostile world. When she began to date in adolescence, Nancy encountered her own unthought-about pregnancies with surprise and, at times, a sense of entrapment. Her children, unplanned themselves, and thus lacking the atmosphere of attentive regard, often felt the world to be unpredictable, and even a bit dangerous. The normative jealousies, attendant with loss and change, for Nancy and her own mother might well have been exacerbated due to the underlying insecurities, which shaped their insecure sense of self. As the examples suggest, if the grandmother can graciously step aside and allow her own daughter (Mary) to explore and discover this new mothering role, offering lessons as needed, she may not feel painfully jealous about not being the primary caretaker. But very often the need for control (Nancy and her mother), and/or the pain of relinquishment of the primary caretaking role makes this difficult for a new grandmother. Similarly if the new mother has trouble trusting her own experience, automatically privileging the mothering role of her mother, she may develop resentment and even jealousy. She may feel shunted aside by the apparently greater influence and power of the older mothering person. A young mother's mistrust of her own experience might be played out when she tries to overcompensate for what she felt were deprivations from her own mother. In many ways, the echoes of the mothering pair live on.

A potentially more complex relationship is that between the young mother and her mother-in-law, because this pairing almost invariably includes each woman's relationship with the same man (the young woman's husband as the mother-in-law's son). This mothering pair is actually comprised of a triad. Whether a good enough relationship of mutual regard among all members of the triad is possible depends on the nature of the relationship between each two members of the triad.

A mother's loss of her son to another woman seems to inflict pain and loss, no matter how secure and sturdy she may feel. Naomi came from an economically privileged family, which conveyed the message that Naomi and her siblings could expect little hardship in their lives, due to the insulation offered by their economic privilege. This assumption of emotional ease then led to jolting surprise and pain when the jealousies attendant to loss and exclusion could not be bypassed. This circumstance occurred especially as Naomi's son, Norman, met and married Alexa, a woman who did not seem to meet the expectations of his mother. Whether any woman could have met Naomi's "standards" may be a reasonable question. Her sense of entitlement likely augmented the normative pains of loss and jealousy. Norman had trouble declaring much independence from Naomi's powerful questioning of the marital match. Naomi implicitly

JEALOUSY AMONG MOTHERS   35

anticipated priority to mother Norman's and Alexa's children according
to her own "standards." Her unquestioned sense of offering her grandchildren all manner of economic gifts in spite of the wishes of Alexa especially made for ongoing tension between the mother and mother-in-law.
Norman often found it easier to disappear into his work in order to avoid
this tempest, which seemed at times impossible to quell.

Norman's workmate, Nathan, came from an apparently less privileged family background where hard work was necessary to overcome
economic adversity. But good physical health, sturdy temperaments,
and that measure of luck which we all need at times offered his family
the template of optimism that sincere work amid respect for self and
others could lay the basis for emotional well-being needed for a successful life. Nathan and his sister grew up within this atmosphere, working
as necessary to pay for schooling and preparation for their adult lives.
In his twenties, Nathan met and married Susan, a classmate. Nathan's
mother, Laura, was pleased to welcome Susan into the family, while
also aware that the family relationships would never be the same. Her
son's happiness, respect for Susan in her own right, and her wish for
grandchildren made this a happy change. Laura's basic sense of well-
being allowed her to accept the inevitable losses but also made way
for new possibilities as she grew into an available but not overweening
grandparent. Each adult in the triad, Nathan, Susan, and Laura was
able to respect the changes without rancor or jarring pain, and in so
doing to welcome the new opportunities which opened up for each in
the evolving family.

Complexity abounds in this generational consideration because the
relationship between both grandmothers is important to consider. All
of these relationships and the senses of inclusion/exclusion, security/
insecurity, and the multiple transference manifestations between the
generations influence the relative strength and variety of jealousies
experienced. Because these relationships are deeply involved with
entwined emotions and fantasies, as are all familial configurations,
the focus here is on less complex mothering pairings to illustrate some
aspects of jealousy.

A closer look at mothers' jealousy

As noted earlier, women exposed to children generally develop caretaking urges. Women involved in caretaking the same children—be

they stepmothers, housekeepers, nannies, teachers, therapists—may develop jealousies which may not be overtly recognized but which will certainly be felt and likely acted upon in overt and covert ways.

1) The first vignette involves the mother who employs a nanny or housekeeper for her own children. Especially if there are young children involved the caretaking emotions aroused are bound to include jealousy, perhaps on both sides: Anna is a married professional woman who for professional reasons needs a nanny to care for her growing children, a girl of three years and a baby about eight months of age. Beatrice, an unmarried competent girl in her twenties has been employed by Anna because of a personal fit between the two women. If the underlying inborn affects of caregiving are stimulated by the mere presence of infants it is possible that Beatrice could have these caregiving affects stimulated in her, especially if she plays an important role in the caretaking of young children. The degree of jealousy in each woman will of course depend on the evolving relationship between them, how much of the nurturing role Anna plays, and how much she leaves to Beatrice. Anna's own need for nurture may tip the jealousy balance even to a proprietary degree in Beatrice. Likewise, Beatrice's goals for herself, whether this role as caregiver is primary in her life, will also be vital. While both women remain healthy and balanced in their relationship the jealousy each may have for the other will likely be manageable.

In the second vignette Albert and Carole, both professionals, got married in their early thirties. By their tenth anniversary, they have three children, ages nine, seven, and five years. In order to support their active working lifestyle and manage the growing household they have employed Donna, a single mother with a young child of her own, as a live-in housekeeper and nanny. Donna's duties include—besides the daytime care of the children and the routine care of the house—cooking evening meals for the children and often for the parents as well. Her live-in duties comprise a full-time job; she feels devoted to the family and the household. Her employers appreciate her work and contribution to the family and pay her well.

Carole, who has been deeply involved with her profession, has left much of the everyday care of the children to Donna. In the twelfth year of marriage, Carole is diagnosed with cancer and dies within several months of the diagnosis, despite the best medical care available. Albert and the three children are devastated, as is Donna, who responds by doubling her efforts for the children's and indeed Albert's care.

The children, now eleven, nine, and seven years of age, look to her care and solace, which is of some comfort as they grapple with the loss of their mother. Albert is also grateful for Donna's presence and care of the household as he mourns Carole's loss. Under these circumstances, a woman in Donna's position may become a motherly and indeed a wifely figure in the household. All may be trying to reconstitute the family and to keep the devastating loss for the father and children at bay. In another outcome, jealousy could more likely reach painful proportions. The whole family copes in this manner for about four years after which time Albert remarries, to a long-time colleague and friend, Evelyn. She becomes the titular stepmother for the children now fifteen, thirteen, and eleven years of age. Donna finds it difficult to make way for Evelyn. While not an especially dominant personality, Donna feels she has been unfairly set aside with Evelyn's arrival. Evelyn, emotionally astute, quickly sees how significant Donna has been to the family. Evelyn, in fact, is a bit daunted by Donna's seemingly towering presence in the household as she plays such a pivotal role in both the mothering and the housekeeping. Admittedly, the children are in their teens, less needy emotionally but they do look to Donna out of affection and familiarity. They are also hesitant as well to accept a new stepmother, an outsider. While they are pleased for their father in his new relationship, they feel the disturbance of change and wonder about their feelings for this new woman in their lives. Obviously a complex set of emotions for each member of the household ensues.

Since the focus here is on the jealousy between mothers and the feelings between Donna and Evelyn, each woman's individual dynamics will influence how she responds to the other woman. If Donna's sense of entitlement and resentment over the seeming intrusion of Evelyn becomes dominant her jealousy, in terms of her feeling excluded from her previous central position in the family, will be a factor. If Evelyn feels reticent or daunted by Donna's centrality, she may give way, and agree to be the demeaned one in the relationship. She may actually not feel as much jealousy as Donna, in that she does not feel dispossessed of her previous position; instead she may feel a bit envious of Donna's previous centrality while also grateful for her stabilizing strength in the family. While adjustments in the new family configuration will be important to navigate, if Evelyn has a sturdy sense of herself in the face of feeling daunted by Donna she will be able to remain centered and likely manage the various emotions in her relationship with

Donna. If, however, Evelyn feels too demeaned in relations to Donna she might become more reactive, or regressed. Albert may be able to offer sustenance if he has access to his emotions and can understand the complexity between the two women. Obviously there are a lot of emotional variables involved. Donna, feeling displaced from her previous role, may continue to experience painful jealousy. Her sturdy self could prevail, or she could react with rancor, or demean Evelyn—there are lots of ways her jealousy could be played out. If the two women can talk about their mutual situation, that might bring empathic thought into the situation and could offer relief. However, in a domestic situation in which there is a power differential (employer and employee), it might be unusual for the dyad to have access to such emotional sharing.

The women's relationship with the children of Albert and Carole of course could trigger both envy and jealousy. If Donna has a strong, enduring motherly role with the children, it is likely that Evelyn would feel a mixture of admiration, jealousy, and envy: admiring but jealous of the nurture Donna had provided and still offers, and likely envious in terms of feeling that Donna has something which Evelyn would wish to have as well with the children. Again, the levels of maturity accessible to Donna and Evelyn would be pivotal as to what can be mediated by thought and what would need to be enacted directly or by projective identification.

The therapist's jealousy

A third vignette comes from my early practice: a mother brought her four-year-old son for therapy, worried about his increasingly tempestuous behavior. In my initial meeting with the mother prior to seeing the little boy, I was impressed with how obviously pregnant she was, and how seemingly oblivious she was about the likely impact of her pregnancy on her four year old. I could see that the mother was feeling overwhelmed with her second pregnancy as it was not a planned event. During this exploratory interview, it seemed that she could barely recognize her own feelings, and indeed could not recognize that her son might be disturbed by the looming change in the family that an added baby would bring. While she could not to seek emotional help for herself, she readily allowed that her son might be able to use my help in sorting out his difficulties. Perhaps, this might be as close to help for her own emotions as she could allow herself at that time. I offered a twice a week schedule with her son, and also an hour every two weeks support for her and as an appropriate update about her son's emotional situation.

The four-year-old boy was very responsive in play therapy, making use of the availability of a place for his feelings to be labeled and understood. He was readily able to put words to his "worries" about his mother's changing shape but also to his concern that things would change in other ways, including his dawning awareness of the new baby that would displace his position of being his mother's only child. His curiosity about the world beyond his family was also budding and found expression in his vibrant play.

In a way that I did not realize at the time, he became a special child to me with his bright imagination and his insightful play. He became much less "worried," and significantly more buoyant, and actually cautiously welcoming of the new baby as his curiosity was freed up and his concern lessened about his wish that the baby would not be born. When the new baby was about four months old, about six months into the therapy, the mother in one of her meetings with me said rather abruptly that she wished to stop her son's treatment. Her words were etched in my memory: "I need him to have a few neurotic symptoms; I am not recognizing him as my own child anymore." I was startled by this unexpected response, albeit because I thought her son's work was going so well! And indeed, I felt in retrospect, that was the problem: he was growing in ways that I could appreciate, but which seemed foreign to the mother. I had tried to keep her informed of his growing ease with his feelings, but she felt that she was losing touch with her child, that someone else's influence was holding sway. I believe, looking back, that my enthusiasm for my little patient's insight and the easing of his fears led me to overlook the mother's growing concern, her jealousy I think, about the role I was playing in her son's life. And I must admit I have wondered whether my enthusiasm for his growth included a bit of jealousy on my part, my own subtle wish to be the favored mother in his mind. That role might have been represented in the boy's dream on the last day of our work. On that final day, he told me a dream: *He was on a beach holding a beautiful blue marble, and all of a sudden it got lost in the sand, and somehow he knew that he would not be able to find it until he was sixteen years old* (end of dream).

He seemed to know that the dream had to do with something valued becoming lost. We both thought of the marble being lost in the sand as representing the ending of our work; he smiled shyly as we spoke about that, and we both admired how the dream could speak about emotions in such a meaningful way. We both felt sadness as well during this the final session of his therapy. I did not have follow-up with the boy, as the family relocated to a distant city within a few months.

I have thought of that dream from many angles over the years, admiring its insight and hopeful prophecy as well as its representing a meaningful way to understand emotions which, the dream suggests, will be lost from sight until this little boy reached adolescence. Current thoughts also bring the scope of jealousy into view as represented in the dream.

In terms of jealousy arising in the mother, I can envision the blue marble of the therapeutic work as an expression of the little boy's attraction to the way we had worked, and the kind of attentive mothering that the therapy had been able to facilitate. Psychotherapy does offer that kind of attentive care, which we often speak of as maternal reverie. But the dream may also suggest that this attentive care and understanding had to be lost from sight, due to his mother's discomfort with the impact of the therapy, that is, the freeing up of his emotions. He would, the dream suggests, have to wait until he could begin to explore outside the family ("when he is sixteen years old") before he could find that space for thought again. But in another way the blue marble could be a representation of a parallel situation in the little boy's mind: his and my blue marble space, leaving out his mother, could have been a defense or "payback" for her internal blue marble (new baby) creating a relationship which would exclude him. This formulation may be appreciated in retrospect but there was no way to speak to it at the time, the dream having been presented on the last day of our work.

In reflection, I have wondered whether I may have entered into an enactment in being more attentive to the boy than was prudent for the therapy, for I too was a bit mesmerized by his capacity for insight and the liberation of his curiosity. Indeed, I as well may have felt some jealous rivalry regarding this young patient, wanting to be his favorite mother. In my focus on his therapy, I may not have paid sufficient attention to the impact it would have on my little patient's mother. It is likely that at some level she feared that she was losing him to a rival, to my mothering ways. And possibly any jealous or rivalrous part of me would not have been as alert to how endangering the mother's unaddressed jealousy would be for the therapy, let alone for the boy's relationship with her. From another angle, the mother may have experienced envy of the attentive work her son was receiving while she was having to bear the burdens of growing responsibility in caring for her second baby. Even though she had elected not to see someone for her own needs, I came to feel in retrospect that if I could have paid more careful attention to her vulnerabilities, the likely envy and more prominent jealousy could have been contained on both our parts and her son's work might have been allowed to continue.

I will never know, of course, whether more prudence on my part would have protected the therapeutic work, but I became more aware of parental (and my own) envy and jealousy as an issue in subsequent psychotherapeutic work with children.

Discussion

These vignettes from life and the consulting room demonstrate the range of emotions involving innate affects, which arise in the complex entwinements of the two and three person dynamics of envy and jealousy. Appreciating the enormous complexity of emotion between mothers and daughters, and mothers-in-law and daughters-in-law, a focus on less complex interactions seemed reasonable in terms of tracing strands of envy and jealousy among mothering pairs. The second vignette, involving housekeeper Donna and stepmother Evelyn, illustrates various aspects of envy and jealousy on both women's parts and how the maturities and immaturities of each personality might shape the outcome.

The vignette from my therapeutic work with the little boy illustrates how envy and jealousy can erode trust (that of the patient's mother) and become a blind spot (in the therapist) that can significantly impact the work.

The dream in this last vignette also suggests how intimate work (the blue marble) can trigger jealousy in the one felt to be excluded from that intimacy (the mother) or who so wishes that intimacy could be between her and her son. As therapists, we may well be cautioned about the intensity of jealous feelings in the emotional heat of the therapeutic encounter involving various family members who may feel left out of the intimacy of the therapeutic dyad.

Dreams may well express and predict affects of loss and jealousy even among our consciously less sophisticated selves. On the eve of her daughter's wedding, a mother confided to her other as-yet unmarried daughter that she had a disturbing dream: *She dreamed that her right arm had been cut off.* The astutely listening daughter suggested soothingly that while her mother was glad for her other daughter's upcoming marriage, she also anticipated feeling significant loss. With this comment, the mother seemed to realize the vivid metaphor of the dream (of losing her right arm) and felt comforted by her daughter's spontaneous interpretation of her anticipated loss, and the perhaps more hidden jealousy at losing her marrying daughter to another.

Caretaking functions, then, involve complex emotions which cannot be avoided and are likely not always predicted. While they may be difficult to navigate smoothly, we might be heartened by the awareness that we each have an ongoing bodily dialogue between our cerebral hemispheres that embeds aspects of a caregiving dyad. Right hemispheric functions foster the sense of *inner* space which forms the basis for the depth and comfort which comes from feeling "held in mind," while the left brain offers the binding function of conceptual thought which transforms waves of sweeping emotion into mental objects or thoughts by way of representation and language (Kaplan-Solms & Solms, 2000; Solms, 2013).

The right brain in its more ancient, receptive, intuitively based functions receives and integrates bodily states of being as well, while the left brain facilitates the more detailed, cognitively based efforts of getting to know and to master oneself and one's environment. Differentiation by the left, and integration by the right—a dyad which works well most of the time and which may serve as a model for most of our more conscious caregiving functions.

But even the left and right brains in their varying functions seem to have different attitudes toward one another as well as toward the world: the right in its wide-ranging receptivity is oriented to external and internal space. Wired to receive all input simultaneously rather than to parse and discriminate, its attitude is one of nonjudgmental openness and patience. The left brain, in contrast, in its language facilitation and its tendency to categorize and differentiate towards mastery, does compare and contrast, so it does seem to be judgmental and indeed contemptuous of anything less structured, minimizing the softer-voiced, patient presence of the right. Since language seems front and center in our own experience we, in turn, tend to be influenced by this cognitively based attitude and to downplay the value of the quiet, intuitive potential that characterizes the right brain. It may seem ironic, therefore, to consider that the deepest wisdom seems to reside in this more ancient right hemisphere. That is, not in the differentiating products of cognition, but in the intuitive functions of integration that the right brain offers.

The open receptiveness of the ancient right hemisphere does not pay special attention to the products of cognition. While the left privileges thought with its necessary boundaries, the right hemisphere focuses mostly on sensory based lived experience. This means that the right relies on the unconscious registrations of our bodily selves, which over time and integration give rise to our intuition. And intuition that reaches beyond the boundaries of thought may be considered to hold open space for as yet undreamed-of expressions of reality. The more ancient hemisphere then may also offer the deepest sources of wisdom, because intuition may reach more widely and deeply than can bounded thought. But it is difficult to fully trust our intuition given the allure of the intellectual brain's promises of clarity and certainty.

Our conscious, mothering selves, then, might take a lesson from the dialogue between the inner caretaking functions of the right and left hemispheres, and if possible learn especially from the quiet lessons of the receptive, nonjudgmental, right brain: that a widely receiving, open view may offer a realistic perspective about and refuge from the painful affects that arise amid difference and judgment. Open receptivity (right) that embraces painful affects (left) such as jealousy and envy, which otherwise beleaguer us all.

CHAPTER THREE

Sibling jealousy

Brian M. Robertson

Sibling relationships have been marked by jealousy since the dawn of our species. Biblical authors documented its existence in Genesis with two legendary accounts of jealousy between siblings. The first concerned that of Cain, the firstborn son of Adam and Eve after their expulsion from Eden, and his next-born brother, Abel. The theme of sibling relations returned later in Genesis with the story of Joseph and his brothers.

In the first account, both brothers made sacrificial offerings to the Lord. Both offerings were drawn from their work in the fields and we assume were sincerely presented to the Lord. However, the Lord had respect for Abel's sacrifice, but for Cain's he had none. Cain was enraged at the rejection of his offering, "... and his countenance fell." The Lord rebuked Cain for his anger against the Lord and Abel. To add to Cain's humiliation, the Lord lectured him sternly, saying, "Why are you angry, and why has your countenance fallen? If you do well, will you not be accepted?" The Lord then followed these words with those that many parents have echoed through the millennia, "If you do not do well, sin is couching at the door; its desire is for you, but you must master it." Nevertheless, despite these commands, the outcome was the first of many sibling murders, as, "Cain rose up against his brother Abel and killed him" (Genesis: chapter 4).

The story of Joseph and his brothers is more complex. It begins with a situation of sibling rivalry, including intense jealously, and its immediate aftermath. Jacob, Joseph's father, had taken Joseph as his favorite, "because he was a son of his old age." He gave his favorite a coat of many colors. When his brothers realized that their father loved Joseph more than them, "they hated him and could not speak peaceably to him." Their hatred was enhanced when Joseph recounted a dream in which his brothers, symbolized by sheaves in the field, bowed down in obeisance to Joseph's standing sheaf. Joseph then told a second dream to his father and brothers. The theme of this dream was similar to the first: the sun, the moon, and eleven stars, representing his parents and his brothers, bowed down before him.

Later, Joseph was sent by his father to tend his family's flock with his brothers. His jealous brothers' initial intention was to murder him but there was ambivalence in the group and one brother, Reuben, persuaded them to follow an alternative plan. Rather than murder Joseph, he suggested that they throw Joseph into a waterless desert pit. Privately, Reuben had decided to rescue Joseph from the pit and return him to his father unharmed. The brothers stripped Joseph of his prized coat and cast him into desert pit. At that point, they sat down to eat. While eating the brothers sighted a passing trading caravan and hatched another plan that spared them from shedding their brother's blood. They sold Joseph as a slave to the traders. To conceal their behavior, they killed a goat and dipped Joseph's coat in the blood. Their intention was to claim that they had found the coat but knew nothing of Joseph's fate. They then took the bloody coat and showed it to Jacob. The old man, recognizing the coat, was deceived. He realized that the torn coat bore bloody witness to Joseph's death, most probably killed by some wild beast. His father's grief was overwhelming: "Jacob rent his clothes, put sackcloth upon his loins, and mourned for his son for many days" (Genesis: chapter 37).

Many centuries have passed since these biblical accounts, but sibling rivalry and its accompanying jealousy remains as a potent force in human affairs. More recent case reports and anecdotes will serve to underline the timelessness of the biblical accounts of sibling jealousy. In an early publication, Winnicott (1931) documented sibling conflicts that typically beset the lives of two and three year olds. He described "a crisis of separation": separation from the mother and replacement in her affections by a new sibling. He reported the case of Joan, aged two years and five months, who was an only child until her brother was born when she was thirteen months old.

> Joan had been in perfect health until this event. She then became very jealous, she lost her appetite and consequently got thin ... She has remained like this, is very irritable and her mother cannot leave her without producing in her an anxiety attack ... She pinches and even bites the baby and will not allow him things to play with. She will not allow anyone to speak about the baby, but frowns and ultimately intervenes. (pp. 3–4)

Winnicott notes that, "The parents are exceptionally nice people, and the child is a perfectly healthy and loveable child" (p. 3). Commenting on this case, J. Mitchell (2013b) considers that Joan has "a trauma of separation." This sibling trauma has two dimensions: the loss of the mother, and the appearance of a new baby who replaces the toddler. Jealousy is the dominant affect, spawning, in this age group, the accompanying emotions of anger, rage, fear, sadness, and depression. As with Joan, toddlers may resort to violent action against the intruder.

A less violent anecdote involves Jimmy, a four-year-old boy, his recently born sister Rachel, and their parents. Being an enlightened couple, they had sought their pediatrician's advice as to how to ease Jimmy's distress, fully expected once his new baby sister arrived home. The pediatrician suggested that the parents buy their son a large toy to coincide with the arrival of his sister. Following this reassuring advice, the parents proceeded to buy Jimmy a large truck, trucks being his favorite toys at this time. Rachel duly arrived and all seemed well for a time. Jimmy, prepared months in advance by both mother and father, appeared at first to have accepted his sister's appearance. At times, he was even affectionate with the baby. However, one evening, about a month after Rachel's birth, the parents were sitting together watching an early evening news broadcast. Mother was breastfeeding Rachel. Her brother, who had been playing elsewhere in the house, entered the room and stood staring intently at the nativity scene unfolding before him. There was something in Jimmy's attitude that commanded his parents' attention. Fixing his parents with an angry stare, Jimmy pointed to his large, recently acquired truck that stood close to the television set, hitherto unnoticed, and said loudly, "Nothing's been the same around here since that truck came into the house!" He then turned abruptly and stamped out of the room.

J. Mitchell (2013b) comments that such recent observations of sibling rivalry and jealousy have their amusing side, associated with childhood wishes and fantasies. This defends us from recognizing their violent underpinnings and their linkage with biblical accounts of sibling jealousy and violence. If the killing of babies was not prohibited, the toddlers could be Cain in adulthood, or the deeds could be those of Joseph's brothers.

These varied accounts of sibling jealousy and its aftermath are widely separated in historical time and in the authors' intentions. However, they contain a number of common elements that I will use to define jealousy in general, with particular reference to sibling jealousy.

Definition

Jealousy is defined as the state of "feeling or showing a resentful suspicion that one's partner is attracted to or involved with someone else"; it is intimately involved with the state of being "fiercely protective of one's rights or possessions" (*Oxford Dictionary of English*, 2003). Jealousy, as defined psychologically, expands on this definition. Clanton and Smith (1998) describe jealously as "The negative feeling that accompanies the fear that one will lose the affection, the support, and the services of another person" (p. 5). Citing Bohm (1967), they add that the person whose affection or support may be lost has a real or imaginary experience with a third person. Both of these definitions emphasize the two main elements of jealousy: the threat of losing a partner's love and the ominous presence of a third person. The jealous situation continues to be referred to as the "eternal triangle," usually referring to the jealous individual, the mate, and the rival. Jealousy can also arise in situations that are clearly not sexual in the generally accepted sense. If siblings are involved, then the "partner" of these definitions is replaced by a parental figure and the two other individuals involved in the triangle by rivalrous siblings. Jealousy is a complex state of mind that may contain a variety of emotions. Individuals may experience pain, distress, self-blame, anxiety, sadness, anger, agitation, fear, and betrayal (Mullen, 1990).

Freud (1922b) placed jealousy on a spectrum ranging from the "competitive or normal," through projected, to delusional jealousy. Of normal jealousy he commented,

> It is easy to see that essentially it is compounded of grief, the pain caused by the thought of losing the loved object, and of the narcissistic wound, in so far as it is distinguishable from the other wound; further, of feelings of enmity against the successful rival, and of a greater or lesser amount of self-criticism which tries to hold the subject's own ego accountable for the loss. (p. 223)

He continued that though labeled as normal, this jealousy is "by no means completely rational," and derived from the actual triangular situation, rather "… it is rooted deep in the unconscious, it is a continuation of the earliest stirrings of the child's affective life, and it originates in the Oedipus or brother and sister complex of the first sexual period" (p. 223).

Freud makes a pertinent observation when he suggests that adult jealousy originates in particular childhood developmental stages. In this contribution, we are concerned with sibling jealousy which brings us to the "brother and sister complex." Neubauer (1983), in a paper discussing the importance of the sibling experience, provides a definition of jealousy that specifically relates to siblings. He states, "Jealousy is the competition with a sibling or parent for the love of the person with whom they share" (p. 327). Neubauer also succinctly defines two allied affects that are closely linked with sibling interactions: rivalry and envy. Rivalry he defines as "the competition among siblings for the exclusive or preferred care from the person they share" (p. 326). Envy differs from jealousy in that it encompasses the "wish for the possession of attributes that a parent of sibling has, such as penis, strength, breast" (p. 326). In these definitions, sibling jealousy and rivalry are defined in the context of triadic relationships while sibling envy is linked to dyadic relationships. Some of the more recent psychoanalytic approaches to sibling relationships deal with sibling jealousy and its potential effects on many facets of individual development.

Psychoanalytic approaches to sibling jealousy

As noted above, Freud wrote a good deal about the importance of sibling relationships, including the significance and complexity of his own, without, however, advancing a detailed metapsychological approach that would complement his formulations of parent-child relationships. His many references to siblings and their relationships have been recently documented (Sherwin-White, 2007). Concerning sibling rivalry and jealousy, Freud was explicit about the effects on his own life. In a letter to Fliess, Freud (1897) wrote:

> ... I greeted my one year younger brother (who died after a few months) with adverse wishes and genuine childhood jealousy; and that his death left the germ of (self) reproaches in me. I have also long known the companion of my misdeeds between the ages of one and two years; it is my nephew, a year older than myself, who is living in Manchester and who visited us in Vienna when I was 14 years old. The two of us seem occasionally to have behaved cruelly to my niece, who was a year younger. This nephew and this younger brother have determined, then, what is neurotic, but also what is intense, in all my friendships. (p. 268)

The multiple aspects of sibling relations that affect psychological development have been a neglected aspect of psychoanalytic investigation until recently; instead, the parent-child relationship has preoccupied psychoanalysts in their theoretical and clinical writing. Child analysts and child psychoanalytic therapists have been exceptions to this trend (Houzel, 2001; Kieffer, 2008; Rustin, 2007).

Juliet Mitchell, in a series of publications (Britton, Cohen, & Mitchell, 2009; Mitchell, 2003, 2013a, 2013b), explores the specific effects of siblings on the development of an individual. She also formulates a theoretical basis of this specificity. She is critical of the bias towards what she refers to as the vertical axis in psychic life, parent-child relations, in psychoanalytic writings, both clinical and theoretical. This she contrasts with the horizontal axis sibling relations, including sibling bonds and unconscious complexes linked to these bonds. She states the core of her theory as follows:

> The sibling par excellence is someone who threatens the subject's uniqueness. The ecstasy of loving one who is like oneself is

experienced at the same time as the trauma of being annihilated by
one who stands in one's place. (2003, p. 10)

The danger for the sibling is annihilation of the self by the intruder who
threatens to take the individual's place. The response to this trauma is
intense and often violent. This is in contrast to the threat of castration
in the Oedipus complex. Ambivalence being the condition of human
intimate relations, the sibling's impulse to murder is coupled with love.
Mitchell suggests that this love is initially narcissistic, linked as it is to
love of the self. As development proceeds under favorable conditions,
this love is transmuted into the love for another, like the self but different. Sibling ambivalence teeters between murder and sexual wishes.
Actual sibling incest is rare but sexual exploration and play between
siblings is probably very common.

With a nod to Lacan, Mitchell states that the "Law of the Mother"
prevails over siblings. It is the mother who is the prime mover in taming sibling rivalry and jealousy, forbidding outright murder and incest.
The mother maintains the vertical differential between herself and her
children and the horizontal differentiation between siblings. Under her
law, all siblings are accorded a place of their own from which they cannot be displaced, that is, annihilated. She also initiates and promotes
sibling relationships. Siblings then become "one of a number," or a
"seriality" and evolve into a band of brothers or a sisterhood.

In parallel with Juliet Mitchell, René Kaës (2009) published *Le complex fraternal* in which he explores in detail the intrapsychic presence of
the sibling complex. Well known for his work in group analysis, Kaës
attributes his understanding of the sibling complex to his prior inves-
tigations of group dynamics and group analysis. He joins Mitchell in
understanding the sibling complex as a universal component of the
psyche, transcending the individual. As such, the complex has a formative role, along with the seminal Oedipus complex in the development
of an individual's psychic structure. Kaës defines a complex as an organized grouping of ideas and memories of great affective significance
derived from childhood relationships that are partly or totally unconscious. The sibling complex serves to structure all levels of the psyche:
emotions, attitudes, and adaptive behavior. Further, the sibling complex
is a triangular intrapsychic structure of both narcissistic and object love,
hate, and aggression, directed by the subject at another, recognized as
"brother" or "sister." The triangle is completed by those elements that
link and oppose the subject and the other in conflicts specific to the

complex. In parallel with Mitchell, Kaës understands that this complex results in the various forms of love and hate, directed toward the
sibling—*le semblable contemporain*, the intruder—*l'autre*, who becomes
the same, familiar and different. Experiences with siblings are thus distinct from those lived with parents. There are various forms of the sibling complex and its accompanying fantasies: the intruder and the rival;
the imaginary twin; bisexual fantasies; the narcissistic double; sibling
incestuous fantasies.

Kaës understands the sibling complex intersubjectively, stating that
understanding of the unconscious should not be based solely on considerations of individual psychic structure. An intersubjective understanding of psychic structure is necessary from both clinical and
metapsychological viewpoints. He writes of unconscious processes
between two or more subjects, involving shared defenses, co-repression
and co-denial, unconscious alliances between subjects, and shared
mechanisms of return of the repressed, leading to acting out in the interpersonal relationship of the siblings and their substitutes.

Kaës (2009) shares with Mitchell, and with Coles and Vivona, the concept of the sibling complex as the horizontal axis of the psyche whereas
the Oedipus complex forms the vertical axis. According to Kaës, "These
two axes cross one another, struggle against each other, stir one another
up, sometimes fall back on one another, but neither can exist in its full
form without the other" (p. 7).

Coles, in a series of publications (2003, 2014) takes a somewhat different vantage point than Mitchell. While acknowledging Mitchell's contributions, she states that Mitchell's:

> ... deeply held Freudian beliefs lead her to an essentialist position,
> in which siblings are again reduced to hated rivals. I agree that the
> birth of a sibling can herald a catastrophic and murderous reaction,
> but it does not follow that the intrinsic nature of sibling relation-
> ship is predicated on displacement ... in my work with some of
> my patients, they express loving feelings towards their siblings/
> peers, and these feelings play a significant part in the structure of
> the psyche. (2003, p. 92)

Coles stresses that human love is by definition ambivalent, always a
variable mixture of love and hate. She also emphasizes that the position of the sibling in the relationship plays an important role in the

formation of the individual's psyche. Coles also argues that sibling love contributes positively to psychosexual development; it may also sponsor object choice in adulthood. Of relevance to the case vignette discussed later in this chapter, Coles notes that in some of her cases, an extremely severe superego was linked to sibling abuse and cruelty. She notes that, "Sibling cruelty seems to eat into the psyche with a ferocity that is commensurate with the actual experience and gives a different twist to the harsh superego" (p. 94). She also observes that an excessively strong sibling relationship, marked by intense ambivalence, is often accompanied by parental inattention or neglect. Here, she touches upon both Mitchell's and Kaës's idea of the dynamic interaction of the vertical and horizontal dimensions of psychic life.

Vivona (2007, 2010) also discusses the effects of sibling identification on subsequent development. She points out that children may use differentiation as well as identification to enhance their distinctiveness from fellow siblings as a means of managing sibling jealousies, conflicts, and ambivalences. Vivona accepts Mitchell's contributions, including the importance of a horizontal dimension of psychic life in the determination of an individual's identity. She states that the particular intrapsychic challenge of this dimension is to: "… find one's unique place in a world of similar others … The lateral challenge is fraught with conflict and ambivalence; its resolution imbues psychic structure" (2007, p. 1192).

According to Vivona, differentiation is an intrapsychic adaptation to such rivalries and part of identity formation. Differentiation as an intrapsychic process comes about through four mechanisms: (i) *comparison* of self with others; (ii) *recognition* of the actual or potential qualities of self and others; (iii) *projection* onto siblings qualities concordant with those perceived in siblings; and (iv) *amplification* in oneself of discordant or opposite qualities. Differentiation allows siblings to stake out a unique but limited territory wherein, albeit ambivalently, rivals can be kept out and aggression somewhat tamed. It also carries a cost as a compromise formation in the sibling dimension. There is a danger for siblings in that one may have the identity of the "good one" while another is designated as the "bad one"; thus identity and desire may become restricted over the course of development.

In the following section, a clinical vignette drawn from an analysis in which sibling relationships and their intrapsychic components formed a significant portion of the analytic work is presented.

Clinical vignette: the effect of sibling jealousy

Celia, a classical musician, recently separated, came for a consultation with the following complaints. She had developed persistent feeling of sadness, guilt, and fatigue after separation from her husband. In addition, she had a long-standing sense of inadequacy in her work as a classical musician, despite noteworthy career achievements and success. She was also concerned about a new relationship with a fellow musician with whom she had shared a number of concert stages. These meetings had resulted in an affair during her marriage. This relationship with its intense emotions and passionate sexuality had precipitated the end of her marriage; it was the breaking point in a troubled relationship.

During the initial consultation, Celia told me a childhood memory which became a "selected fact" for us over the course of her analysis. When she was six years old, Celia had come down to a family breakfast to hear her brothers, Joe—three years older, and James—six years older, holding a learned mathematical discussion about square roots with their mother. She recalled thinking, as she listened to the family talk, that she would never in her life possess the expertise with square roots that her brothers claimed to possess. This avowal at age six echoed through subsequent years, surviving her stellar education at leading universities. It also survived despite the fact that her university achievements surpassed those of her two siblings. Prior to obtaining her doctorate in music, she had attained an honors degree in mathematics.

Celia was born into comfortable circumstances. Her father, who had died some years before she entered analysis, was a writer with a considerable reputation and some financial success. Although basically sound, the family atmosphere was not without conflict and strain. The presence of Celia's maternal grandmother, with her domineering and self-righteous ways, created tension between her parents. Celia was close to her father and when, later in life, he developed an anxiety disorder, she was a comforting and reassuring presence. Her relationship with her mother was more troubled. As a quiet, observant, and sensitive child, overshadowed by her dominating brothers, she felt distant from her mother, who, for a period of time, referred jokingly to her daughter as "Miss Mouse." Initially very hesitant to criticize her mother, it slowly emerged that Celia had experienced her mother as remote, even disinterested, for much of her childhood and adolescence. She also was convinced that her mother favored her brothers.

Prominent in her analysis was the relationship that developed with her older brother, James, throughout Celia's childhood and beyond. As she grew out of infancy, this brother became a threatening and bullying presence in her young life. Over the course of the analysis, details of this sibling abuse slowly emerged. At the time of Celia's birth, James had become problematic for her parents as well. Neither seemed to have been capable of dealing with his demanding nature and aggressive outbursts. At no time could Celia recall either of her parents defending her against James, or being aware of his abusive behavior towards her.

A number of themes emerged in the analytic material that pointed to the importance of siblings and sibling substitutes in Celia's internal world, and their effects on her past and current life. This horizontal dimension of intrapsychic life was ever-present in the clinical material. In the early years of her analysis, much time was spent in dealing with her feelings about the separation from her husband. Over time, it became clear that a major element in this unhappy object choice was linked to Celia's unresolved issues with her brothers, in particular with those involved with the bullying James. The middle years of her analysis were marked by the emotional fluctuations of her developing relationship with her colleague, and former lover, Charles. He also represented a brother figure, although markedly different from her eldest brother. In these years, we worked through repetitions of internalized sibling object relations, as they manifested in her relationship with Charles, and in the transference.

In the final phase of the analysis, Celia and Charles became engaged. After further hesitations and some emotional turmoil for both, they married. Both remained somewhat guilty about the effects of their relationship on their former spouses, and on their young adult children. Although Celia was happy in her new marriage, she remained plagued by difficulties. Problems with her professional life continued if not worsened in this phase of her analysis. The familiar litany of personal inadequacy, hopelessness, and despair, coupled with ruthless self-criticism, was frequent—at work and at home with Charles. Typically, before concert performances, Celia suffered considerable anxiety. She imagined she would play poorly and be criticized mercilessly for her failures; public humiliation in front of her colleagues would follow. Reality consistently contradicted these imaginary scenarios; her musical abilities have been well received by fellow musicians, her audiences, and by critics.

She was also plagued by jealousy of Charles's capacity to work consistently as a prominent musician without apparent conflict or despair. Celia added to her woes by persistent thoughts that her feelings and her failings would have deleterious effects on her relationship with Charles, leading to the breakup of their marriage. Her moods did affect him to the point where, baffled by what he perceived as her gloom-filled distortions about her professional abilities, he would become impatient with her, thereby worsening her despair.

It was at this point in the analysis that further details of her treatment at the hands of her oldest brother began to emerge. These details came into sharp focus following Celia's association of a marital argument, and the sharp words that followed, with a particularly violent episode of bullying by her brother during her childhood. She was constantly on guard against James's aggression, ready to raise her arms against his attacks. As Celia said, "I was always on guard, hyper-vigilant in James's vicinity." She became the "Ms. Mouse" of her mother's teasing comment. She dreaded being on "show" in any way, as she put it, or drawing attention to herself. Any such action on her part in James's presence could be greeted by a blow, by sarcastic insults, or both. Frequently, he would grab her by the throat, saying threateningly, "Want to make something of it?" She particularly recalled the unexpected shocks she endured as a result of his attacks. For example, there were many times that she was struck very hard by various objects he hurled at her with full force and without warning.

As Celia's analysis entered its final stages, it became more apparent that her continuing problems involving her professional and personal life were linked to her habitually constrained behavior in the analysis. Her consistent use of the ironic mode in her analytic discourse at times irritated me although I did not take this issue up with Celia at the time. Later, it became clear that my irritation was linked to aspects of her hidden aggression involving the sibling abuse that she had suffered at the hands of her brother.

It was also a manifestation of her own sibling rivalry and jealous competitiveness with me as a brother figure in the transference. In a dream that involved a fellow musician whom Celia spontaneously identified as a brother figure, the brother/colleague sat at his desk looking at her "as if he had more important things to do." I then interpreted my own position as such a figure. Celia responded sharply, saying, "Well, look at this office here. There's no fretting here. No things not handled. It's like mission control, papers arranged, always ink in the pens, the computer never crashes, no lost music scores or agendas."

Her difficulties in her new marriage became the focus in the final phases of the analysis. That these problems were linked to her unresolved sibling conflicts became increasingly apparent. Charles was depicted in sessions as having no inner struggles or external problems in his own work as a musician, in stark contrast to her own work-related despair. Her portrait of his carefree life did not fit with her accounts of his anxieties when stressed at home or at work. When their paths crossed at musical gatherings, Celia complained that he surrounded himself at such meeting with "admiring females" while at the same time ignoring her presence.

In one later session Celia began by saying that she was "at the bottom of the pile." She had a busy day of rehearsals during which she had played a number of solo pieces. Characteristically, she had begun to feel that her colleagues were disapproving of her, finding her playing inadequate, and thinking that she was disorganized. She arrived home overwhelmed, tremulous, and exhausted. She then told her husband, who had attended one of rehearsals, that she was a failure in the eyes of her colleagues. Exasperated, Charles replied that she was "crazy," as he had thought of her at the rehearsal as beautiful, brilliant, and musically gifted. He also told her that she appeared to love her negative feelings more than him, which upset her greatly. I was able to point out that her various descriptions of her husband's behavior at home and elsewhere were almost entirely negative. Furthermore, these accounts were at variance with what she had told me over the years about the loving, passionate side of their relationship. In the next session, Celia admitted with some hesitation that she continued to find Charles "excruciatingly attractive" and that the "physical side of things between us is as powerful as ever." This presaged a lengthy period of working through in her analysis of turbulent emotions and painful conflicts in her marriage, linked at least in part to powerful, unresolved sibling jealousies and rivalries.

My analysis of Celia consolidated my own thoughts about the importance of the sibling complex in psychosexual development. Coincident with her analysis, I also had other patients in treatment whose current conflicts were linked with their own sibling complexes. My patients' accounts of their sibling jealousies and rivalries, with their intense, ambivalent emotions, so often disruptive of family life, were the interpersonal indicators of underlying intrapsychic conflicts linked to sibling object relationships. My own clinical experience suggests that sibling rivalry is a common occurrence. Parents who are asked how often are jealousies, rivalries, and sibling fights part of daily family life will answer with resigned or exasperated statements such as "Constantly!" or "When do they not fight!".

Each sibling complex is different, taking its own form, from the basic template. This makes the sibling complex akin to the Oedipus complex in that the basic elements are present in individual forms, shaped by the family dynamics, parental attitudes, and cultural forces. In Celia's case, she faced real difficulties in her struggle to find a place for herself as the newest member of the sibling group, and of the family as a whole. It appears that her older brother exhibited an intense jealousy towards Celia from an early age, a jealousy that lingered into adult life. His particular sibling jealousy contained a complex mix of emotions as Mullen and others have noted (Buss, 2000; Mullen, 1990; Mullen & Martin, 1994). Her very presence in the family seemed to have caused James by turns, pain, distress, humiliation, anger, rage, all linked under his overriding jealousy. His jealousy of Celia provoked bullying attacks on her that lasted through much of her young life. She was for James the one who threatened his uniqueness and who traumatized him by in some way taking over his place in the family. Celia then was assigned the role of the dangerous intruder and rival who wants, in James's words, "to make something of it," to take her own place in the family. As J. Mitchell has noted, we are inclined to greet stories of sibling jealousy and rivalry with amusement, and associate them with childhood wishes and fantasies. Celia's story tells us otherwise. The biblical intensity of James's hateful and abusive behavior towards his sister is a lesson in the much under-reported and studied topic of sibling abuse, as damaging in many cases as adult abuse of children. During her analysis, James still remained a menacing figure for Celia. A family reunion had brought the family together. James had an altercation with Celia's adolescent son during the day. That night, Celia had a nightmare in which Saddam Hussein was loose and dangerous on the family property.

In her adult relationships with sibling substitutes, Celia still struggled with the shadowy figure of her jealous and abusive sibling. These sibling conflicts and ambivalences strongly influenced both her object choices and her professional life. Her first marriage was contracted with a colleague considered an outstanding musician. This man professed his devotion to Celia but was consistently sarcastic and patronizing in his attitudes towards her, in both their private and shared professional lives. With Charles, many of the same issues surfaced in their relationship but were eventually worked through to a considerable extent in her analysis. Her long-defended rage against competitive and dominating sibling figures surfaced in substitute forms both in her analysis and in her private and professional life. Her persistent defensive use of the negative in her second marriage, coupled with her traumatically induced defensive use of guilt, allowed her to remain trapped in the painful situation of her childhood experiences. In the transference, her anger and competitiveness with me as a transference figure were manifested initially by my mounting irritation at the ironic distance she tended to take from her own narrative and the analytic process.

Concluding remarks

Sibling jealousy, and its inevitable accompaniment, sibling rivalry, is one of the earliest developmental challenges that face all children. Furthermore, as I have attempted to illustrate with my clinical vignette, it is a highly conflictual and emotionally intense series of events that continue to influence key areas of an individual's interpersonal and intrapsychic life. How sibling jealousy is dealt with by an individual will long affect such crucial matters as future object choices, the nature of friendships through the life cycle, and the ability to live as a productive member of human groups. Several authors have noted that jealousy is accompanied by a variety of emotions that in turn may trigger a wide variety of actions from the individuals involved. These emotional patterns are equally true of sibling jealousy. These emotional patterns have been noted in the biblical accounts of sibling relationships (e.g., the story of

Joseph and his brothers). It is also important to be aware that sibling jealousies and rivalries are the surface manifestations, dramatic as they may be, of underlying unconscious processes. If the conflicts and motivations of the oedipal phase of development are the foundations and heralds of adult desire, then the underpinnings of sibling jealousies are the struggle to encompass the fact, often traumatic, of another like oneself, but different. This struggle is one of the essential elements in the composition of the individual subject who must come to terms with someone who is an equal but separate subject—the sibling.

CHAPTER FOUR

Jealousy, envy, and friendship in adolescent girls

Christine Kieffer

In this contribution, I will develop some ideas about the role of friendship in female development, tracing the influence of jealousy and envy as both facilitating and destructive dimensions along the path to adulthood. I will examine the developmental literature in adolescence, with a particular focus upon girls and women, but with some brief clinical examples drawn from both females and males, including transference material. However, female development will remain the principal focus, with particular emphasis upon the development of the sense of self as subject and the development of intersubjectivity and mutual recognition. In lieu of an extended clinical vignette, I will use Elena Ferrante's *The Neapolitan Novels* (2014b), a set of books that traces the development of two girls—later, women—throughout their lives. I will highlight the ameliorative aspects of friendship vis-à-vis jealousy and its overall impact upon development in the direction of maturity. It is also hoped that a focus upon this remarkable set of books, a *Bildungsroman* set in the slums of Naples, will shed some light both upon the construction of female identity amid patriarchy, and the emergence of strivings towards a more nuanced and independent identity. Allow me, though, to begin with some short clinical vignettes.

Three brief vignettes

Clinical vignette: 1

Less than a minute or so before my patient, Ms. Y, arrived for her session, the doorbell to my office rang, signalling the arrival of twenty-four long-stemmed roses for my anniversary, an unexpected present from my husband. I quickly stashed the gift inside a hallway closet that was empty due to an early September heat wave and returned to the consultation room.[1]

When Ms. Y arrived, however, she greeted me with a perplexed and slightly resentful look: "Do you *know* that there is a bowl of roses in your *closet*?!" She then lay down and I asked for further associations. She was in a troubled marriage, and felt thwarted in what had seemed to have become a stultifying life as a house-wife and mother. Her associations had focused upon what she had presumed to have been a gift from a secret lover, who had enclosed a card containing a *billet doux* with an invitation to our next tryst. That is, a much more exciting life than was hers. (Or mine.)

Some information about Ms. Y's development background might be useful at this time. In her adolescence, she had found herself in competition with a one-year older sister who had been greatly admired both for her beauty and her popularity. Alas, Y's sister had also been one of those "mean girls" so often voted the most popular, and Ms. Y was often treated dismissively and sometimes with derision, if she herself had obtained some recognition. Ms. Y had been an excellent student, but this set of abilities had been undervalued in her family (at least for the girls). Her mother, who had been a celebrated beauty in her youth, certainly had emphasized the importance of good looks and popularity over intellectual achievement, and Ms. Y had despaired of competing with them. When Ms. Y began steadily dating a boy she had become enamored of, her sister had swooped down and "stolen" this boy. The loss of her first love—particularly to the sister who "had it all"—had been particularly devastating to Ms. Y, and she had become more distrustful as well as more generally devaluing of herself as she grew to adulthood. These themes naturally had come into the transference, and the discovery of the flowers had done much to intensify Ms. Y's transference (both sibling and maternal) during the period in which the flowers had been discovered.

Clinical vignette: 2

An adolescent, Ms. Z, who had often spoken with anger about her mother for having been neglectful of her throughout her life, had begun to spontaneously and heatedly express anger in another vein entirely (at least, seemingly) from the issues that had brought her in: her mother now seemed to her to have it ALL: a better figure, a better career than Z thought she would ever have, a great sexual relationship with her husband (Z's father) after all these years, and a relationship that my patient felt completely left out of.

These new feelings emerged with the unexpected intensity of a thunder clap heralding the beginning of a summer storm. After two years of analysis during which she had stressed a sense of neglect by her mother—by whom she had felt abandoned for a glamorous and demanding career, returning home to dinner alone with her husband after Z had been put to bed—my patient had become focused intensively upon jealousy of her mother which earlier had been muted by her plaintive sense of neglect, that was gradually replaced by mockery for her mother's lack of maternal talents. Z at first had emphasized that she had always felt a greater attachment to her housekeeper/nanny who had been with the family for many years. Z had denied what was obviously my own decision to work, thinking of me implicitly as a kind of nanny—the most recent kind, hired to take care of Z as an older adolescent.

After focusing initially upon the preoedipal dimensions of the eating disorder and lack of popularity that had been presenting problems for Z, along with her earlier memories of a felt abandonment by her mother, an oedipal dimension had emerged, with jealousy coming into the foreground as envy faded.

As these conflicts were worked through, Z's anorexic tendencies ended, along with the bullying she experienced in a previous school, and were replaced by a young woman who earned excellent grades as she began to focus upon one day becoming a surgeon; an easygoing popularity developed, and a steady relationship with a schoolmate began. Also, she had become quite a beauty herself. (Interestingly, she and her boyfriend were nicknamed "the old married couple" by their classmates.) So it seemed that there was room for her and for her mother—both—after all.

Clinical vignette: 3

A patient recalled a cherished memory of her childhood in which she put on a pair of her mother's stiletto heels: "They were black suede and I wobbled on them as I stood before the large round mirror of a vanity table, admiring myself in them. I then selected Mama's favorite lipstick—a deep and luscious red—and carefully applied it. It felt wonderful!" When asked for further associations, she added that she had been six years old, and the time of the memory was shortly after she had moved to a new apartment with her mother and sister, after the parents separated. However, neither parent had uttered the words "separation" or "divorce," and my patient had been bewildered as to why her father had not simply come home in the evening. "He told me, 'It's too far away from where I work,' although I quickly pointed out to him that there was an elevated train just a block away from our new apartment. I was further puzzled because Papa seemed to take such a strong interest in the apartment itself—in its parquet floors and balcony—and visited us often so it seemed as though he was living there with us, although he was not. Eventually, his visits tapered, and we began to see him only at our grandparents' house. My formerly vivacious mother seemed to just fade away, sleeping all day, just getting up to make us meals, but not always, and staying in her bathrobe, without bothering to get dressed at all. And she always had been a fashion-plate. That year, I tried to stay out playing on the street for as long as I could before coming home to a darkened house. Strangely, she did not admonish me to return—to not stay out too late—as she always had done before. Sometimes I had the feeling that she almost had forgotten me."

As we analyzed my patient Carol's recollections, we were struck by the symbols of feminine power and sexuality utilized as talismans designed to bring back a wandering father and to restore a previously lively household, albeit one in which the parents sometimes fought bitterly. Little girls often like to dress themselves up in Mama's glamorous clothing, anticipating their future adult roles and in competition with her. Little boys do the same, as do those with nontraditional gender/sexual orientation. This scene is an iconic one.

Carol felt herself caught between a desire to revive a seriously depleted mother ("dead mother," Green, 1980) and a wish to replace her, alongside a now ambivalent striving to identify with a woman whom she no longer could idealize. She also was aware of a sense of guilt: Had her own wishes to replace her mother been so toxic? The scene of Carol before the mirror opened up to us a view of some deeply held but long buried conflicts that enabled us to understand her distress in a fresh way, and became a touch-stone throughout the analysis.

We gradually uncovered the legacy of this experience in Carol's romantic life: She had felt unconscious guilt concerning earlier envy and jealousy of her mother, atoning through a masochistic relation to men in her romantic life. This was the issue that brought her to analysis: repeatedly being attracted to unavailable men, and culminating in rejection by them. At the same time, Carol felt contempt for her mother in "just lying down and sleeping her life away," while she experienced herself as wanting to triumph, which she did but only in her work life. The divorce had occurred at an unfortunate time for Carol in terms of her developmental trajec-tory, but her mother's capitulation to self-pity and depression had exacerbated its impact. Carol needed a mother whom she could idealize, against whom she could compete, and around whom she could work through her Oedipus complex. Her childhood fantasy of having destroyed her mother with the strength of her wishes had led to an unconscious need to defeat herself in her adult love life.

Jealousy, envy and adolescence: a farewell to childhood

"I can't fill her shoes" ... "he has big shoes to fill" ... "the man had big footprints" ... these phrases are symbolic of describing a relationship with someone admired by one who is anticipating a succession and per-haps a triumphant exceeding of expectations one day. Children envy their parents, dare to compete with them—sometimes for prizes not entirely understood—and eventually come to stand alongside them. They stand wobbling in the high heels, and if all goes well, the parents are able to recognize in themselves echoes of their own long-ago striv-ings. The identification is mutual.

As children move towards an oedipal phase of development, envy is increasingly mixed with jealousy as they sense the parents have a special though perhaps mysterious relation to one another, that they gradually realize does not include them. And as siblings come along—particularly the first successor—there is yet another collision with a new experience of jealousy, sometimes sparking a temporary regression as they vie to regain their baby-place once more. It is a consolation to realize they can do so much more than the baby, and eventually accept that their parents' need for them to "be a big boy" has its own rewards. But what is the relationship between envy and jealousy?

In his much celebrated *Comprehensive Dictionary of Psychoanalysis*, Salman Akhtar (2009) explains the difference between envy and jealousy in the following way: he notes that Melanie Klein's (1957) theorization of envy involves part-object relationships and takes place within a *dyadic* relationship. That is, envy is an emotion directed at the love object itself, in which, in addition to seeking gratification, the child also wishes to be the source of such omnipotent goodness. This may lead to a greediness that includes a desire to "exhaust the object entirely, not only in order to possess all of its goodness but also to deplete the object purposefully so that it no longer contains anything enviable" (Segal, 1974, p. 41). In contrast, as Akhtar (2009) noted, "... jealousy aims at the possession of the love object and removal of a rival" (p. 96). He further argues that jealousy pertains to the following dimensions of relations with others: jealousy has its origin in both the Oedipus complex and in the sibling experience: "an admixture of love for the desired person and hate for the rival; and is an emotion distinct from envy" (p. 96).

Peter Neubauer (1983) has further differentiated between rivalry and jealousy in family relationships in the following way: He describes rivalry as originating in the experience of siblings as rivals for the exclu-sive or preferred care by a parent. Envy, for Neubauer, refers to the wish of the possession of attributes that a parent or sibling has, such as penis, strength, or breasts. In contrast, he defines jealousy as the competition with the sibling or parent for the love of the person whom they share.

Adolescence provides the person with an opportunity to rework conflicts around envy and jealousy into adult ideals, aspirations, and relationships. This is what Louise Kaplan (1995) referred to as a "farewell to childhood," with a second opportunity in adolescence to work through earlier, unresolved conflicts. Envy may become a positive emotion in which the hero worship of adolescence may lead to the inspiration to develop one's own capacities. Thus, fantasy can lead to actual achievements. The envied characteristics and capabilities of the older mentor may be envied but may become a guide to aspiration. There is also a positive aspect to sibling relationships: the older sibling, closer in age than a parent, may represent a more realistic role model, and present a more attainable goal. Thus, envy can beckon towards a whole object relationship, and children can learn to accept that one cannot have everything.

Jealousy of a hated rival who has proven more successful in obtaining access to a desired love object may similarly be transformed as the adolescence matures. The adolescent may decide to emulate the rival and become more like him or her, and may learn, as he moves into a larger world, that there are other possibilities—in love and in work. An immersion in the broader world outside the family and school may help to bring about this insight, along with catch-up development giving one's own desired attributes. Short boys may grow up, pimples disappear, breasts finally emerge, intellectual gifts grow more valued than muscles by the peer group now eager to get into college. The narcissistic mortification of not having kept up with pubertal changes among one's early adolescent peers eventually recedes. And finally, the role of friendship may have an ameliorative effect upon the conflicts and deprivation of one's own household. While undoubtedly the rivalries, envies, and jealousies of families may be experienced just as acutely among friends, there are also more opportunities to find age cohorts in the community who may share common interests and who may provide support as well as competition.

The Neapolitan novels of Elena Ferrante

Elena Ferrante's quartet of books, *The Neapolitan Novels*, which include: *My Brilliant Friend* (2012), *The Story of a New Name* (2013), *Those Who Go and Those Who Stay* (2014a), and *The Story of the Lost Child* (2015) focus upon the enduring friendship between two girls growing up in a Neapolitan slum, following their lives from the blossoming of their friendship at the age of six into old age. Now translated into English from the original Italian[2] by Ann Goldstein, this set of novels is a *Bildungsroman* that focuses in particular on the life of Elena from whose perspective the book is narrated, but also upon her lifelong, passionate friendship with her friend, Lila. We are given an extended glimpse into the lives of girls and women, particularly within the vicissitudes of a tempestuous relationship between two gifted girls from the Mezzogiorno—one who escapes and one who remains immersed—and their effect upon one another throughout their lives. In addition to illuminating the lifelong impact of their friendship upon development, Ferrante also demonstrates how even "those who go" never quite escape the imprint of early childhood experiences, with the *stradone* (the population that failed or refused to escape) endlessly beckoning the pathway home. Throughout the set of books, there is an enduring theme of jealousy in which Nino, a boy from the "neighborhood," grows into both a heartthrob and a serious scholar immersed in the student unrests that rocked Italy during the 1960s and 1970s—a figure who appears (and disappears) unexpectedly throughout the book. Lila, despite (or perhaps because of) knowing Nino is her friend's first love, steals him away for a secret affair. Later, Nino appears in a crowd of listeners at Elena's first book launch in Florence, to defend her when an attendee stands up and attacks the quality of her writing. In the last book of the series, Elena and Nino finally embark on an affair in Naples, have a daughter together, but Nino, now a staid member of Congress, has resumed more traditional mores, and refuses to leave his wife and family for Elena, although divorce was still illegal in Italy at the time. Nino serves as a sort of Italian trickster character—the man who juggles two families, one with the wife and one with the paramour, and is never entirely with or without either one. Elena remains suspicious of Lila's influence on him, aware that Lila seems a bit too ready to hint at signs of Nino's contented married life, revealing this information in a way that suggests mixed motives: malice combined with a desire to confront her friend with the truth. By this time, Lila has had her own late-in-life baby (both friends had married earlier and had children), who is stolen from her while they walk on a crowded street in the neighborhood.

The current of strife that pervades the two girls' bond is not confined only to men, however. While Elena's family permits her, with some reluctance, to attend high school and go to college, Lila, an equally talented scholar, is prevented from doing so by a family which feels that her powerful personality and rebelliousness must be tamed. Indeed, neither family could truly fathom the idea of an educated woman, and certainly not one who had come from their own family. It was unthinkable, and merely the whim of an adolescent girl. Lila is, instead, made to join the family shoemaking business, and soon marries the local neighborhood success (and Mafioso), settling into a life firmly rooted in this unlettered and stifling world, a world in which women are unquestionably second class, and with very limited options. Elena, despite her academic success, remains secretly envious of her brilliant friend's intellectual and imaginative gifts and, in retaliation for Lila's love affair with Nino, has thrown her friend's childhood writing, *The Blue Fairy*, into the Arno while she is studying in Pisa. What if Lila is the "real" writer, she asks herself, as if there can be only one.

The friendship of Elena and Lila is forged around an experience centering upon another man: Don Achille, the elderly Mafioso who rules the neighborhood, feared by all. As they are working out the construction of their friendship, their bond begins with a dare in which Lila encourages Elena to throw her prized and only doll into the cellar of the Don's house, after tossing her own prized doll there as well. The cellar seems like a dungeon from which no one may return, doll or girl. This act of relinquishment cements the friendship and foreshadows the later loss of Lila's child. Somehow, after great hesitation and trembling, they gain entrance into the cellar but find no dolls there. Lila concludes that Don Achille must have taken the dolls away in his big, black briefcase, which they have seen him carry as he leaves the house. Lila insists upon an immediate confrontation despite her friend's terrified protests. When Achille opens the door, Lila boldly confronts this ogre. The Don is amazed both by her demand and the little girl's fearlessness, and decides to give them money to buy new dolls. He pauses, as he turns to go back inside: "Remember that I gave you this gift." This is a reminder that, in the future, something will be asked of them, and seems like a vague foreshadowing of the loss of Lila's little girl, her most precious possession of her old age.

This scene with the Don has a magical, fairy-tale quality to it: he seems just like an ogre (*orca*, in Italian), and it becomes emblematic of a kind of relation that the girls have with men. In the narrow culture of the *stradone*, men are either monsters who must be placated and sometimes confronted, or they are unreliable heartbreakers. But in any case, all are no good. It is only women who may be truly counted upon, and even then, not entirely. Elena and Lila come to rely upon one another throughout the novels, separated only temporarily by jealousies. Their jealous rivalry over Nino seems, in some respects, more like a device to avoid a psychological merger and maintain their individuation than is a striving for attainment of a desirable object.

Interestingly, Elena's former husband, Pietro, proves to be a far better man: a man who can recognize and honor his wife's vocational goals and demonstrate a devotion to his two daughters' care. Elena, however, escapes from her husband finding him boring, after Nino comes looking for her. She seeks the enlivening embrace of the bad boy, and spurns the man who could truly be there for her. As Joseph Luzzi (2013) has suggested, the cultural and economic divide in Italy, labeled the *Southern Question*, pervades this set of books, and Pietro and Nino are emblematic of both sides of the divide. As Luzzi has noted, the books are not only set in Naples, but "they *are* Naples, as they teem with the city's dialect, violence and world view" (p. 12). I would add that Lila is the personification of Naples *herself*, with her unquenchable will for survival and for power that exists alongside an unquestioning acceptance of the rules of the neighborhood all the same.

Somehow Lila believes that the world outside the neighborhood is for Elena, even as she envies her friend's greater opportunities. For her part, Elena ultimately cannot escape the neighbourhood—the very street where she was born, and eventually finds her way back for good. However, she continues to write and travel to promote the books. But in the end, Elena's erudition has not allowed her to escape entirely from a regional mindset. And yet, despite her envy of Elena's increasing erudition and continued prospects, Lila had earlier volunteered to pay for her friend's continued schooling when she finds out that Elena's parents have been reluctant to give her even a paltry sum for tuition. But in the inflexible system of Italian schooling, Lila was unable to change her mind, return to complete lower school and then go to college; that decision had been made for her at the age of ten and she is trapped. Nevertheless, Lila is able to put her native intelligence to use in developing a computer company in her neighborhood. So both friends remain within the confines of the *stradone*.

It is in adolescence that the impact of Elena's and Lila's bond seems to be most profoundly formative, although the days of grammar school in which the two are clearly bonded by their unusual intellectual and imaginative gifts are certainly important. In adolescence, Lila enters into marriage with a neighborhood bigwig—the son of a Mafioso who owns a large grocery store—after being chosen by him. It seems almost like an arranged marriage, one from the past century in which Lila simply capitulates. Nevertheless, a woman of Lila's fierce will never wholly accepts such an arrangement, and she eventually breaks free of this stultifying relationship. As Elena watches this unfold, it becomes another among many object lessons that propel her forward into her studies at excellent colleges in northern Italy.

Later, recalling the book, *The Blue Fairy*, that Lila wrote as a child and that Elena jealously threw into the Arno while in Pisa, Elena reflects that "Only she and I could write like that," aware that one of their bonds is a shared love of language and of books. "I, I and Lila, we two with that capacity that together—only together—we had to seize the mass of colors, sounds, things and people, and express it and give it power." Elena is aware that the career that she presently enjoys—her success as writer and scholar—was inspired and shaped by both her friendship with Lila as well as her rivalry. The intensity of their feelings about one another, which sometimes encompasses taking pleasure in the other's misfortunes (Elena said that she sometimes wished her friend dead), seems to fuel their ambitions. Lila, having emerged from that first adolescent marriage, uses her braininess to found a prosperous computer company with the aid of a more simpatico partner/lover, Enzo, who was albeit from the same neighborhood. Lila's and Elena's friendship survives a level of conflict that might well torpedo a marriage or even fracture a family. They serve as both muse to one another and as tormentor.

What does Elena Ferrante teach us about friendship, jealousy, adolescence, and identity?

The second individuation of adolescence, a term coined by Peter Blos (1967), describes a process of emotional disengagement from the internalized object relations with one's parents in adolescence. While psychological separateness during childhood depends upon a secure internalization of the parental homeostatic functions, acquisition of such separateness during adolescence requires a reverse process. This, coupled with the characteristic drive upsurge of this period, results in a certain degree of ego instability. Progressive and regressive trends alternate, at times, with disturbing rapidity. Regressive trends encompass a move backward toward earlier modes of expression. On the other hand, progressive modes, both defensive and autonomous, can lead to new self-configurations. There is usually a marked and insistent disengagement from earlier parental norms that have been internalized in the form of superego dictates, alongside an increased reliance upon the values of the peer group. Blos emphasized the utility of role experimentation and trial identification that can lead to a broadening of ego autonomy and an enhanced sense of inner solidity and constancy.

While Blos (1968) spoke with some distaste of the dramatic experimentation of the adolescents that he treated during the 1960s and 1970s, most of the role experimentation in adolescence is relatively mild, and despite dramatic shifts in ego state, most emerge from the adolescent period with a stable identity and ego ideals. The issue of identity is one that is not directly highlighted in the work of Ferrante, but much of the early and later life of the two heroines of her Neapolitan novels seem to unfold in both rebellion against and capitulation to life along the *stradone* and the limited roles allotted to Italian girls of their day. A friend who grew up in Brooklyn, reared by immigrants from Sicily, told me that she felt that she had actually grown up in the fourteenth century. She was stressing that life in the Mezzogiorno had not really changed since the Middle Ages, with most of its inhabitants living century after century, toiling on subsistence farms, with gender roles rigidly adhered to, and policed, with vigor. While I am told that things have gradually changed, particularly with the discovery of minerals and the development of southern Italy as a dumping ground for chemical companies (so, perhaps changed for the worse), in the timeframe of Ferrante's female heroines, my friend's lament also could be said of Elena and Lila: growing up in an environment not so different from the Middle Ages, particularly with respect to female identity and male-female relationships. Lila and Elena are depicted throughout the books, but most empathically in adolescence and young adulthood, as striving to define themselves as individuals in an environment which is rigidly stratified for both men and women, but with particularly few choices for young women of intelligence and ambition.

In Napoli of the 1950s–1960s, most women in the lower classes dropped out of school in the fifth grade, went to work in factories, or if they were luckier, in stores or other trades, until they married, usually in their late teens. Children—many children—soon followed, accompanied by increasing obligations to tend to the aging parents of both their families and those of their husbands. To be fair, the choices of their men were similarly limited, although many eventually (or sooner) had women on the side—the wealthier of those among them creating second, shadow families whom they supported but not as husbands. Divorce was illegal in this very Catholic country. Marital infidelity was out of the question for women in the country where female purity was prized (think of all those Madonna and child paintings in the museums) and it was considered tacitly permissible, as a crime of passion, to murder an unfaithful wife.[3]

I write this in order to locate the lives of these two girls within a sociocultural context that makes their intellectual accomplishments all the more astonishing. However, Elena is "the one who goes," while Lila is "the one who stays." Elena is able to carve out more choices for herself although, as Ferrante depicts, the mark of those traditional mores have nevertheless had their centrifugal pull on her despite her sophistication. While we may read these novels, taking for granted that a girl from the slums of Naples may become a professor and writer, it truly is an astonishing feat, particularly during that time frame. It is Lila's fate that is far more typical.

In the absence of traditional ego-ideals and sources of identification available to middle-class American adolescents, all that these Neapolitan girls have are themselves, and they provide sources of emotional regulation, and later mutual recognition as their paths diverge over time. They recognize one another's gifts and each, in her own way, affirms and supports the other's strivings for development as author of her own life. Inevitably, emotions of jealousy and envy arise, and yet these young women are able to transcend these emotions, fuelling their ambitions.

Ferrante is known in Italy as a feminist who is focused upon the particular conflicts between the notion of woman as object and the emerging sense of identity of woman as subject with her own desires, needs, and whims. Woman as subject is steadily contrasted with the dictates of a rigid and patriarchal Italy, the norms of which persist into the current age, but which were particularly dominant during the times in which her characters as well as she, herself, came of age. Ferrante was born in 1943, but has withheld her true identity from the press. "Elena Ferrante" is a pen name that she indicated was being used in order to avoid a focus upon her stories as autobiographical. In other words, she wanted to preserve her subjectivity as well as her privacy.[4]

The norms of the Mezzogiorno are frequently contrasted in her work with those of northern Italy: the dominance of emotion (however, florid and uncontained) over reason, a preoccupation with individual honor and vengeance as a means of restoring it over empathy and a rational settling of disputes, and the predominance of the family over the concerns of the state or *patria*. That is, a preoccupation with narcissistic injuries prevails and is often nursed. It seems that for the downtrodden southern Italian male, honor obtained through dominance over women and the immediate family is one of the few things that can be controlled, and maintenance of male honor appears to be always in fragile balance. In Ferrante's writings, these conflicts between north and south are sometimes articulated when Lenu (a diminutive of Elena) and Lila switch back and forth between a Neapolitan dialect (the rough and sometimes scatological language of her youth) and classical Italian learned in school.

Although the political struggles of the student rebellions of the 1960s and 1970s take center stage in the first two books of the series, feminism and women's rights are not discussed, but rather the plight of women is demonstrated through the lives of Ferrante's protagonists. Whereas the relations between men and women are portrayed in depth, Elena's struggle to write and maintain her career, particularly after leaving Pietro and the household help that was provided in their home, occupies a significant part of the protagonist's life. Her character talks bitterly of the ongoing conflict between motherhood and devotion to one's work, for example, daring to stray from the icon of the Madonna as symbol of selfless motherhood that is venerated in Italian churches and paintings throughout the country. Ferrante does not shrink from portraying Elena's daughters' critical reactions to their mother, particularly as they come into their own adolescence and become the authors of their own lives.

Some links between these novels and the preceding clinical vignettes

I would like to direct my attention to some of the links between Ferrante's novels and the brief clinical vignettes that I presented at the beginning of this chapter. Both the Neapolitan novels of Elena Ferrante and my case material highlight a compensatory reaction to deficits in the maternal-daughter bond. (However, it should be kept in mind that the role of friendship in development is also an important one in its own right.)

Elena's and Lila's mothers were subjugated to the machismo and poverty of Napoli. Both were portrayed as unable to recognize their daughter's considerable gifts, greeting them with alarm instead of delight. Instead, they sought to conscript their daughters into a lifetime of obeisance—to accept their place in a hierarchy dictated by the mores of the Mezzogiorno. I believe that their mothers' failures to mirror their daughters' considerable intellectual abilities and to provide them with sources of idealization may have propelled their two daughters into a more intense friendship—one with heightened twinship and alter ego experiences that served to partially fill in what had been missing in their relationships with their mothers. Of course, the need for twinship experience is essential for children, and perhaps particularly for adolescents, as they differentiate themselves (to an optimal degree) from their immersion in family life. But that is contingent upon a good enough relationship with parents—and for daughters, in particular, with their mothers. But what if the mother is not idealizable, and/or cannot recognize her daughter as an independent center of initiative? And what if an entire culture cannot permit this, as was true for the two friends in Ferrante's books? They then have to turn to themselves, in an intense friendship that then may mirror some of the struggles toward separation and individuation that occurs between mother and daughter.

Both Elena and Lila, while experiencing intense feelings of envy and jealousy, also supported one another with the kinds of unstinting ardor that usually is found in the most intimate of connections—parent-child, siblings, and close friends or lovers. Elena reminds us that she and Lila were intermittently intimate friends and intimate *enemies*. Elena noted that she had sometimes hoped for her friend's death and had dropped the original of *The Blue Fairy* (Lila's work) into the Arno. And Lila had made it her business to take Nino from Elena. These sorts of oscillations in their bond reminded me of the struggles that occur in the earliest of bonds as mother and child learn to permit separation and individuation. When such experiences are not offered in the family, the adolescent turns to her friends with particular ardor.

In each of the clinical vignettes that I presented so briefly at the beginning of the paper, each female patient—two women and one adolescent—revealed that her mother had not been available as either a figure of idealization or mirroring. And each patient had developed symptoms of chronic envy and jealousy that appeared in various degrees in the course of their analyses.

Ms. X had a mother who was most narcissistically invested in her other, older daughter, experiencing her as an alter ego. It had seemed to Ms. X as though there had only been enough love available for one daughter, and she had been left out from the beginning.

While Ms. Y had envied her mother, she split her maternal objects into either sexy but distant career women, or passive but adoring housekeepers. Y had entered an analysis with an image of her mother as having abandoned her for an important career, saving all of her love for her husband. It was only in the second year of analysis that she had come to realize that her earlier sense of abandonment had disguised awareness of her envy of a woman whom, it had seemed to Ms. Y, truly had it all, yet someone who would not share her secrets of success. The character, Lila, too, was aware that her mother and father continued to still harbor sexual passion toward one another despite their harsh lot in life, glimpsed through their exchanged glances in the kitchen by their keen-eyed daughter, although Ferrante does not suggest that this disturbed Lila.

Perhaps Carol's mother seemed closest in temperament to the defeated women portrayed by Elena Ferrante: abandoned by her husband, she retreated to her bed, ignoring her children. A woman without subjectivity, passion, or volition. Carol had vowed never to be anything like her mother, and had become best friends with another girl who felt similarly about her own mother.

At this point, you might be wondering: What about some of the ways in which these disappointments, thwarted strivings, and rebellions manifested themselves in the analytic encounter? What were the vicissitudes of these patients' relations to me, and what did it evoke in me as their analyst?

For Ms. Y, a girl in adolescence, I began to note that it seemed safer to think of me (at least unconsciously—Y was shy about making this connection at first) as but another in a line of housekeepers/caretakers (keeping things tidy instead of mucking about with her in the messiness of her feelings), rather than to consider that it might be likely that I, too, had a family whom I was leaving in coming to the office each day. And for my part, hearing Y criticize her mother so severely had evoked in me some not inconsiderable feelings of guilt. I found myself inwardly wanting to defend Y's mother at times—or, at least, to present alternate views. It was noteworthy that, at the end of the analysis, as the patient prepared to head for the West Coast to college, she was seriously considering medical school, and with a later specialization in surgery. (Not exactly a career that would keep her at home, and might well necessitate a housekeeper!) She had begun to reconcile the fantasied mother with the actual mother and she and her mother had developed a warmer relationship.

X and I were of the same age cohort and so it was perhaps natural that she found it easier to gravitate toward a sibling transference with me. But her mother and elder sister had seemed to have many characteristics in common. X's discovery of the roses stashed in the waiting room marked the beginning of a stage in which she felt more comfortable in exploring aspects of the negative transference. My initial reaction to X's accusatory question about the flowers had flooded me with shame: When the flowers had arrived, during a previous patient's hour, he had just been lamenting that he "just knew" that I must be living a better life than he. Not wanting to add further "fuel" to the transference, I quickly had tried to hide the flowers in a hall closet—thus burying the evidence. Instead, X had found what I had tried to conceal. (Despite the very warm early September day, she had brought a jacket she wished to hang up.) Whereas we all understand, after all, that marriage is not just a bed of roses (including Ms. X), while in an unfolding transference I had seemed to become to her an amalgam of her narcissistically preoccupied mother and her sister whose achievement had seemed impossible to reach. At the end of her analysis, Ms. X began law school and now is a successful partner, with grown children, still married. Perhaps there are enough bouquets for all of us, after all.

It is maybe not surprising that Carol had tended to cling to a highly idealized view of me throughout the analysis. Had Carol seen me as impotent, the analysis would not have gotten off the ground. It was only much later, during a long analysis, that Carol had felt secure enough to experience some disappointment in me: Did I seem tired today? Or distracted? I had, after all, missed the essential point of what she had just been telling me. *Again.* Could I really understand the aching emptiness in her stomach when she turned the key and entered a darkened room? Or the hastily thrown-together dinner presided over by a slumped over, sour-mouthed figure in stained pajamas? And how did I truly feel about *my* children? All these signs of ambivalence—distrust and resentment—gradually became knowable, and then speakable. And as they did, Carol slowly resumed dating and a quest for a partner once more. They now live together … reasonably content. Relinquishing the ideal allowed for the enduring possibility of good enough.

Concluding remarks

I would like to conclude with some observations about adolescence as a time of consolidation of the capacity for intersubjectivity along-side the development of relative independence of the self in relation to others. This is an area of particular struggle for adolescent girls, as demonstrated by the predominance of symptoms of eating disorders, excessive reliance upon the peer group, and the relegation of intellec-tual and career achievement in pursuit of popularity with males, as well as a more general affirmation from the surrounding community. It is a well-documented fact that, just as their male peers are benefitting from an increase in formal operations and other intellectual aptitudes afforded by the physiological, emotional, and mental changes in ado-lescence, their equally gifted female peers become less vocal in class and shy away from demonstrating what they know (Gilligan, 1983; Sadker & Sadker, 1994). Those adolescent girls who attend same-sex schools are significantly more able to avoid this achievement gap, how-ever. Ferrante's depiction of the ways in which Lenu and Lila support one another throughout their lives—particularly during their years of schooling and adolescence, but also beyond—is a demonstration of how this might be useful.

The cultivation of jealousy, particularly within a patriarchal culture such as the Mezzogiorno, can be particularly fraught for adolescent girls who are coming into their own as authors of their own lives. As Muriel Dimen (2003) has noted, it is difficult for women to exit the role of object, whether they are simply walking down the street or at the workplace. In *My Brilliant Friend*, Elena notes that the correct way to pass by a group of catcalling young men hanging out of their cars is to put one's head down meekly and silently walk past. This behavior wins respect albeit at the cost of subjectivity, not to mention an abject acceptance of objectification. However, one day, as Elena was walking with Lila, the following scene occurred. The Mafioso brothers—the Solaras—are ogling her. Lila was exempt from this treatment because she was still, at thirteen, to menstruate and develop; she was just a child in their eyes. Lila, not yet schooled in proper behavior for young women, and scornful of it in any case, responded to their treatment of her friend with a string of vicious insults in Neapolitan dialect, the content of which was all focused upon, perhaps unsurprisingly, a take-down of their manhood. This was a response that would only get one pulled into the car and whisked away, to be done to as one would a whore. And they responded by trying to pull Elena in with them. Lila, however, saved both herself and her friend, by pulling out her shoe-maker's knife (she had been apprenticed to her father's shoe shop after being denied continued schooling) and holding it menacingly to Marcello's throat. Ferrante stresses that Lila displays absolutely no hesitation and an utter commitment to following through. Marcello and his brother, Michele, were so astonished and frightened by this young girl's ferocity that they abandoned their project of rape. Who objectified whom, and whose subjectivity was preserved? Such is life on the *stra-done*. Read Ferrante's description of the gaze in which both Michele and Lila lock eyes, and one is reminded of Muriel Dimen's (2003) observa-tion that "the gaze" captures both subject and object, gazer and gazed upon. This incident marked the beginning of an ongoing relationship between Lila and Michele, part contest and part something else, includ-ing respect, that lasted their entire lives.

This dance of domination that expresses patriarchy serves to distract from an appreciation of self and other as subjects rather than objects, one which could lead to an opening up of an intersubjective matrix in which self and other may recognize one another as subject, that is, as those with independent centers of initiative. This is a mode of relating that Benjamin (1998, 2004) terms "mutual recognition." Relational patterns of chronic jealousy represent the mirror opposite of mutual recognition, as states of chronic impairment in narcissistic regulation. While the more basic template for this pattern of domination is undoubtedly laid down in the preoedipal and oedipal periods of development, it is during ado-lescence that the steps and overall tempo of the dance are refined and attain their unique characterological patterns. Elena and Lila, as ado-lescents, represent two forms of female (heterosexual) adolescent reac-tion to patriarchal dominance: submission or defiant refusal, either of which may interfere with the potential for freedom and intimacy which mutual recognition enables.[5]

An important contribution to the understanding of gender, particu-larly as it manifests itself in jealousy and throughout adolescence, has been made by Lynn Layton (1998, 2005), who has presented a model of gender identity as a negotiation between (and among) fluid and hetero-geneous gendered selves. Layton has stated that she views difficulties in maintaining a stable sense of self-esteem as reflecting difficulties in negotiating a sense of agency while maintaining connection. She then argues that a pressure to conform to and internalize a binary, circum-scribed gender identity results in a form of chronic narcissistic injury—an injury that restricts capacities to be both "agentic" and relational. This, in turn, results in gendered versions of narcissism and narcissistic expres-sion (like archetypal insanely jealous lovers). Gender, particularly in its extreme, caricatured forms, represents ways to express—in a perverted form—disowned aspects of agency or relational strivings. A classic example is the woman who marries the powerful man rather than striving to become powerful herself. The societal requirement to wedge oneself into a normative gender identity is thus a narcissistic blow. Of course, some authors, such as Irene Fast (1984), have argued that a tod-dler learns that one cannot "have it all." This is one of the earliest of les-sons. Judith Butler (2002), who coined the term "gender melancholy," has made a similar observation. Layton maintains that the narcissistic wounds that result from gender inequality subtly interfere with devel-opment on more general dimensions since every social interaction is potentially gendered. Certainly, the characters of Lila and Elena suf-fered their own struggles in coming to terms with the "gender binary," particularly in coping with adolescence, and the conflict embedded within women between loyalty to the self (often portrayed as loyalty to a career as an author) versus loyalty to the family (children as well as the men in their lives) has been a favored theme throughout Elena Ferrante's work.

In conclusion, it is the task of the adolescent to negotiate an adult identity in which the individual is able to separate and individuate from the family of origin, and to create new bonds in which he or she will come to recognize self in relation to other. The work of Elena Ferrante has illustrated some of the particular struggles that girls face, particu-larly in adolescence, on the road to womanhood.

CHAPTER FIVE

Absence of jealousy

Aleksandar Dimitrijevic

T here are several possible options to date the beginning of psychoanalysis. Not the least feasible among these is to focus on October 15, 1897: the day when Sigmund Freud, unknown yet highly ambitious, communicated his belief that he had discovered the key to what he believed to have been the secrets of the psyche. He wrote a letter to his Berlin-based friend, Wilhelm Fliess, and described the basic pattern of what would later be called "personality dynamics": a particular form of relationship boys form with their parents between the ages of three and five. He expressed his pride at deciphering *Oedipus Rex* (Sophocles, 429 BC), the tragedy that tortured nineteenth-century German culture (see Rudnytsky, 1992), interpreted in the same vein Shakespeare's (1603) *Hamlet*, which had become the major puzzle of European intellectuals roughly a century earlier (see, for instance, Shapiro, 2010), and provided an important piece of self-analysis: "I have found, in my case too, being in love with my mother and jealous of my father, and I now consider it a universal event in early childhood" (cited in Masson, 1985, p. 106).

This pattern will later be named the "Oedipus complex" and will be considered to represent the crucial point of classical psychoanalysis. Its basic features are a) children (not only boys) establish relationships with both parents simultaneously, instead of relationships with just one caregiver at a time, b) children need to learn that not everything is allowed, that some things, even if possible, are prohibited, and c) very intensive emotions of positive and of negative charging, that Freud named "being in love" and "jealousy."

If we agree, thus, to connect the beginning of psychoanalysis with the introduction of the idea of the Oedipus complex, that would imply that the awareness of the importance of jealousy was with us all this time. Add to this the fact that as many as 13 percent of all murders in the United States are family murders and many of those are caused by jealousy (R. S. Miller, 2014, p. 315). Based on these two facts, one would expect a huge number of psychoanalytic publications devoted to the topic of jealousy. However, Freud devoted it only a couple of pages in a short paper from 1922 and searching the PEP-Web shows only forty-one titles containing the words "jealous" or "jealousy," of which some are book reviews, several are devoted to its pathological forms, and several to distinguishing it from envy. What, then, is this powerful emotion that is believed to be centrally important, can become lethal, but is understudied nonetheless? And, is it possible to live without it?

What is jealousy?

Worthy though it may be, studying jealousy is not simple. Its omnipresence may easily be deceptive. It has been described in all art forms countless times and since the beginning of human civilization. Some think that jealousy is implicitly present in the tenth of the Ten Commandments in the Bible: "You shall not covet your neighbor's wife; and you shall not desire your neighbor's house, his field, his male servant, his female servant, his ox, his donkey, or anything that is your neighbor's" (Deuteronomy 5:21); there, it is undifferentiated from envy. Evolutionary psychologists (cited in R. S. Miller, 2014, pp. 320–326) see jealousy as a primordial emotion that was selected due to its evolutionary usefulness—parents being cautious, or suspicious, of their mates' possible infidelity have higher chances for the survival of their progeny.

This evolutionary viewpoint may also be unique in that it sees jealousy as a positive and beneficial emotion. In everyday life, in psychoanalysis and in the rest of psychology, jealousy is always a negative emotion, needless to say, poetically speaking even "the green-eyed monster" (*Othello*, 3.3.169). In the words of French philosopher Roland Barthes:

> As a jealous man, I suffer four times over: because I am jealous, because I blame myself for being so, because I fear that my jealousy will hurt the other, because I allow myself to be subjected to banality. (cited in Toohey, 2014, p. 7)

Direct psychological study of jealousy thus requires a lot of skill and patience. Our psychoanalytic clients or research subjects are most usually reluctant to admit being jealous, as this is an emotion many think of as embarrassing, revealing fragility or weakness.

To make matters worse, jealousy is not completely distinguished from other emotions or traits: In Latin, it is synonymous with envy, and in English with being demanding, possessive, covetous, begrudging, emulous, and invidious (ibid., p. 3). Its distinction from the other negative emotions may have been noticed by the Austrian dramatist and poet, Franz Grillparzer (1791–1872), who provided a telling description of jealousy in his poem titled "Suffering Is So Sweet for Those in Love," where he wrote that "Jealousy is a passion, which zealously searches for that which produces suffering" (1830, p. 389).[1] Grillparzer, in this way, tells us that the basic element of jealousy is some form of masochism, a zeal that may lead us to wish to be constantly connected to the very source of our suffering, while, in contrast, other negative emotions may fade away or we do our best to distance ourselves from them. In the scarce psychological literature about jealousy one can find an idea that it consists of three elements—hurt, anger, and fear (R. S. Miller, 2014, p. 315), while Freud saw grief and narcissistic wounding (1922b, p. 223) in it. Be that as it may, studying a compounded emotion must be particularly challenging.

For quite some time now, jealousy is being seen as triadic, in contrast to envy, which should be dyadic: "To be jealous, one must have a relationship to lose and a rival to whom to lose it" (R. S. Miller, 2014, p. 315). This is, as already mentioned, in accordance with the basic psychoanalytic approach, first elaborated in Freud's correspondence. We understand that an infant is able to initiate and modulate social interaction (Beebe, Cohen, & Lachmann, 2016), but only with one person at a certain moment. Thus, both parents or another caregiver can provide comfort and the basis for attachment security (Grossmann, Grossmann, & Waters, 2006), but for the infant they do not have substantially distinct roles. It is only in toddlerhood that kids start playing with parents in different ways and that fathers become very important on their own, and because of this it is said that in the course of development, mother is a given object while father is a discovered object (Akhtar, 2005b). Paternal behavior has long-term effects due to fathers' introduction of rough-and-tumble play, which fosters children's—and especially boys'—capacity for exploration.[2] The psychoanalytic developmental model labels ages three to five the "Oedipus stage" and expects that it is then that children start feeling clear preference for one of the parents. While in infancy they could only wish for something that belonged to someone else, now they can also be jealous of someone who might have a privileged relationship with the person they deeply care about. Freud would expect it to be the parent of the opposite sex, although in *The Interpretation of Dreams* (1900a), he wrote about younger siblings provoking basically the same reaction. Children of this age might start inquiring thus: "Mommy, will I be able to marry you after daddy dies?", or say: "I will dream of you when I fall asleep." And at any sign that the precious parent might show affection to someone else, the child may feel threatened to lose his or her love. It is for this reason that a child may tell a parent that he or she "does not live here," "does not belong with us," that "there is no place for you here," or even to "go out and sleep in the street and freeze." Analogous emotions may appear in the relationship with siblings, usually the younger ones, where the aggression may be more obvious in behavior. Consequently, competitiveness becomes very prominent and parents must be careful to handle it wisely. Freud thought that this feeling of jealousy was of central importance for further emotional development, because children would become afraid of revenge by the parent they were jealous of. He, thus, repeatedly stressed how important the resolution of the dynamics among these emotions was (1924d).

Heinz Kohut was the first to write about the fact that the oedipal stage does not have to produce the Oedipus complex (1982). Based on his clinical observations, Kohut claimed that if parents realized that their children were merely playing out, "exercising," the hitherto unknown forms of social interaction, and if parents reacted to this empathetically, then children would grow up without fixations in this developmental stage, nontraumatized and optimally frustrated. This should also make children grow into adults not prone to falling victim to intensive feelings of jealousy, or, in other words, not bearing inside them the zeal to constantly search for what may make them suffer.

This must be a comfortable option, if it is indeed possible. It certainly deserves more scrutiny, together with the less studied personality dynamics of those who cannot be jealous, not because they are very mature, but, quite the contrary, because they may suffer from the incapacity to be aware of their feelings of jealousy. In this text, I will discuss exactly these issues: Is the absence of jealousy possible? Why do we idealize a utopian world without jealousy? And, finally, is there a relationship that, per definition, if you will, cannot contain jealousy?

Pathological absence of jealousy

Fragility

Culture and arts, psychoanalytic patients, and people in general—more or less everything has changed between Freud's times and ours. Social relationships become more numerous and superficial, emotional expression less restricted and controlled, sexual liberties widely propagated, families smaller with fewer and fewer children, marriages shorter and less important, and so on. This started becoming obvious to some psychoanalysts in the 1960s and 1970s. To put it briefly, they discovered that the classical, Freudian approach could not help some of their patients. These persons were looking for something different and experienced analytic anonymity as (re)traumatizing—they were used to constant receiving of soothing and support.

Heinz Kohut (1979) introduced the idea that this was a consequence of growing up with absent or weak fathers, based almost certainly on his own experience, as he was born in 1913, and his father was in the army for the whole four years of World War I (Strozier, 2001). While in Freud's time, fathers did not hesitate in introducing prohibitions, threatening, and punishing, the contemporary (or so-called postmodern) ones were mostly absent, insecure, and undemanding, Kohut believed. Add to this the growing percentage of dysfunctional or divorced marriages, consequently of single mothers, and you get generations with little or no experience in being disciplined or having a relationship of rivalry. You end up with, as Christopher Lasch (1991) named it, the culture of narcissism.

The basic differences between these two levels of functioning (sometimes referred to as oedipal and preoedipal) deserve to be reviewed.

- *First*, the oedipal one includes apprehension of the linear progression of time, so children start understanding the difference between (and, gradually, among) generations and that this separates them from their parents in important ways: They belong to the same group (family), yet at the same time they belong to different groups (generations). Children must learn how to live with the notion that not everything can be received "here and now," which reinforces gratification-delay and strengthens the ego. A particularly difficult task that oedipal children face is to accept that the world existed before them and will, one day, again, continue without them. One should remember here that the riddle ancient Oedipus solved was exactly about the linear time and mortality: "What walks on four legs in the morning, two legs in the afternoon, three legs in the evening, and no legs at night?"

- *Second*, the oedipal level of functioning includes the capacity to endure tension, anxiety, and mental pain. The highly unpleasant phenomenon of mental pain can be defined as "a sharp, throbbing, somewhat unknowable feeling of despair, longing, and psychic helplessness" (Akhtar, 2003, p. 5) and it is never easy to cope with. We can, nevertheless, observe differences and say that oedipal children are better in bearing with the separation and rivalry, and it may be plausible to hypothesize that the inner world develops only together with and in so far as the capacity for enduring mental pain develops. As a result, these children also take the risk of curiosity and they do not refrain from asking millions of questions. Opposite to this, children (and later adolescents and adults) who have not reached the oedipal level do whatever they can to immediately get rid of mental pain: employ developmentally primitive defense mechanisms, vent off the tension as soon as it rises, ask to be consoled before trying to overcome the problem on their own, and use various types of "pain-killers."

- *Finally*, this developmental advancement is closely connected with the capacity to tolerate the fact of life that our important others have lives of their own, filled, at least sometimes, with initiatives, wishes, or intentions that do not include us. It requires a lot of inner strength to forgive our caregivers the fact that they are independent subjects and to not succumb to temptations of sadistic over-control, pseudo-depressive self-pity, or narcissistic dismissal. This is, at the same time, a precondition for relationships in which jealousy is at least possible, for one cannot lose a loved object if this object is not a subject as well. On the opposite pole, we find those persons who choose only partners or friends who will never even dream of emancipating from them. A contemporary sociologist might also, following Lasch, decide to discuss strong current societal trends of being in contact instantly and constantly, using huge quantities of anxiolytics and/or illegal drugs, and hierarchization of the professional domain as well as superficiality of the intimate.

Based on all this, it is obviously possible to thoroughly describe one group of persons incapable of experiencing jealousy. Due to traumatic experiences in early infancy, they do not develop the capacity for coping with the risks of triangulation, but remain in dyadic relation-ships, sometimes long into adulthood. They may feel intense separa-tion anxiety and protest at any sign that they are not the focus of their partners' attention or that they will be mentally or physically moving away from them. They may also often be envious, which may be mis-taken for jealousy; their reactions, however, show more of deep anxiety and fragile self-respect than of real jealousy. Their personality structure is too fragile to withstand the experience of jealousy, of ever allowing themselves to end up in danger of the object of love being "taken away" by another person. If it ever seems to them that something like that could happen, their reaction is not that of an adult competing with a rival, but of a child abandoned by the basic source of support. For all these rea-sons, we could, especially in psychotherapeutic situations, even wish for persons of a preoedipal level of functioning to experience moderate "amounts" of jealousy, as that would be a sign of improvement and maturation. This usually takes a long time and focused work.

Repression

The clue for the second form of the pathological absence of jealousy is in the aforementioned paper by Freud (1922b), where he wrote that "[I]f anyone appears to be without [jealousy], the influence is justified that it has undergone severe repression" (p. 223). Why would jealousy be connected with repression? Is it that someone might experience strong jealousy, but then cannot admit it and thus mental images associated with it disappear into the depths of the unconscious?

Compared to what was described in the previous section, another form of the incapacity to experience jealousy is connected to the opposite problem with the oedipal constellation: having too much of it, as it were. In some families, a child starts developing a capacity for triangulation, expressing preferences and jealousy. Freudian "strong-enough father" would (in the case of a boy) then introduce some limits and boundaries. Not infrequently, one can see the pain on a youngster's face caused by hearing, for instance, "Yes, she is your mother; but she is also my wife." The pain would be that of separation, grief, anger, rivalry—of jealousy.

If the story would develop like this, we would expect the child to behave toward one of the parents with a strong rivalry. Freud thought that this included intense anxiety—specifically, castration anxiety— unconscious fear of boys that mighty fathers can take revenge by cutting off their penis. Then, suddenly to the eye of an outside observer, rivalry would give place to identification and the child would, explicitly and implicitly, communicate a strong desire to be similar to the formerly rivaled parent (in Freud's initial formulation, the opposite-sex parent). Some preschoolers can say something like: "We are completely the same: we both wear t-shirts, we both wear shorts, we both wear sneakers, we have the same last name!", or, if precociously articulated, even: "I did that because I want to be like you in everything." A psychoanalytically informed observer would find this to be (1) the child's unconscious maneuver to avoid possible or fantasized punishment by the more powerful rival, that, in Freud's opinion, involved strong emotions, particularly the castration anxiety, and (2) the introduction of social norms and prohibitions into the child's mental "apparatus," so that they would now start operating from the inside, from the personality instance named superego.

If things do not develop so smoothly, however, ensuing problems may be related to another form of incapacity to experience jealousy. On one level, some parents are very harsh in introducing discipline and may actually punish their children traumatically, in a way or at the period that make the punishment associated with castration anxiety. Other parents may find in triangulation a reawakening of their own childhood anxieties and jealousies, so their emotions may be overwhelming for their children. Or the source of the problem may be a widely applied practice, like during the nineteenth century, when many books and scientific papers were written about what was called "childhood masturbatory disorder" and thousands of children of both sexes were "cured" of it by a surgical intervention similar to circumcision or castration (Bonomi, 2015), which must have had long-lasting psychological consequences.

In line with what was briefly described in the previous two paragraphs, these parental and/or societal attitudes and actions can make some children experience high levels of castration anxiety that in some cases may be present even until the end of their lives, and to experience too restrictive instances of the superego. If this really happens to be the case, these children may put a lot of effort into presenting themselves as perfect in their parents' (and their own superego's) eyes. This means that they might behave as persons without any emotions that are not sublime, jealousy definitely belonging to this group. They may be moral, hard-working, patriotic, devoted, concerned, but they will try not to show and/or admit anything like anger, lust, envy, or, in general, losing control over emotions or drive-wishes. Their romantic or professional choices may also be directly related to this denial of socially unacceptable emotions. To briefly outline an example: Freud's famous patient, Emma Eckstein, who is the heroine of Carlo Bonomi's study (ibid.) about the influence of actual medical castration of children in the nineteenth century on the birth of psychoanalysis, was a victim of this procedure as a child, and in later life never married, wrote a touching poem, "Love did not find me," and became a prominent social worker who devoted her life to orphans and the issue of women's rights.

To admit, particularly to oneself, feelings of jealousy or of being jealous, means that one is aware of one's wishes and only moderately (or optimally) anxious that they might provoke the third person's anger and punishment, or, in other words, that one is self-confident enough to risk being involved in a relationship of rivalry. It also means that on the inside, one is in contact with one's wishes, able to experience intensive emotions, and is not too castrating toward oneself. When of a certain type and in small dosage, jealousy may even be a sign of strong ego; when it is completely denied, that is not to be respected, but should be relaxed and overcome. Again, the first signs of jealousy in persons of this kind can be considered small therapeutic successes.

Another possible explanation for this process comes from attachment theory and research. Therein, it is postulated that when parents are actively rejecting closeness, and especially at the moments of high anxiety in children, children may try to adapt to this by employing attachment deactivation (Bowlby, 1980). Although their attachment needs are always present, proximity-seeking behavior is active only infrequently. That way, they get at least some of their parents' time and attention, while, on the other hand, they suffer from their attachment needs being unreflected and remaining unconscious. They show no outward signs of distress at separation, or of comfort at reunion with attachment figures, although scanning shows higher levels of cortisol, blood pressure, and heart rate. These children are classified as "insecure-avoidant" and in most cases they will grow up to become dismissively attached adults, who describe themselves as strong and independent, denying painful attachment realities and feelings of distress (George & West, 2012, p. 137). They massively use mechanisms of minimization, normalization, and neutralization, often feel contempt for emotional issues or inner life in general, paying more attention to inanimate objects and exploration in childhood as well as to sexuality in adulthood (Beebe, Cohen, & Lachmann, 2016; George & West, 2012). This general avoidance of the emotional world, then, involves jealousy as well: When emotions are unimportant and other persons should be avoided, one feels relief and not jealousy. True emotions remain hidden and may be transformed into substance abuse or violence, but will never be admitted.

Idealization

Another form of the denial of jealousy, may, I believe, be explained as idealization. Someone may devote much time and energy to the over-enthusiastic idea of the world as a place devoid of envy and jealousy, be it as a part of a religious or an ideological framework: one day we will all live in a society of equals, who will have what they need, and there will be no need to wish for anything that belongs to our neighbors. One important issue that will, one would hope, disappear in the process is jealousy. It is plausible to hypothesize that enthusiasm, for some even missionary or revolutionary zeal, can stem from idealization as a defense against rivalry, anxiety, and admitting jealousy.

The least controversial illustration of this may come from the realm of esthetics, though not completely unrelated to religious and political domains. It is Friedrich Schiller's (1786) "Ode to Joy," most famously set to music as the finale of Ludwig van Beethoven's (1824) *Ninth Symphony*—the ultimate expression of utopian longing for a society of embraced brothers.

Schiller wrote the poem in 1785, and then slightly revised it in 1808. It was devoted to one of his friends and the idea behind it was that humanity could reach freedom only through esthetic education. Beauty should lead to joy, which should then lead to freedom.

In the "Ode," which, in fact, is a dithyramb, Schiller used the classical form: constant alteration of chorus and stanza. This is probably what made the poem so attractive for composers, so it was set to music more than a dozen times. It, or at least the parts of it, were immortalized by another artistic genius, when it became part of Beethoven's last symphony. Beethoven first considered putting it to music as early as 1794, as part of his song "Requited Love" (Lockwood, 2003, p. 424; Sachs, 2010, p. 154). The famous melody is already present in his "Choral Fantasy" of 1808 (Lockwood, 2003, p. 424), where the choir sings about the importance of beauty and the arts, although not about gods. Although Beethoven held Schiller even above Goethe (after Kerst & Krehbiel, 1964, p. 22), he adapted the verse so as to express better his own emotions. Most notably, he changed the very beginning, so that the "Ode" now opens with the exclamation "Oh, friends!", and also to make a connection with the previous three symphonic movements.

Indeed, the opening movements should show the pain of human existence. The first bars of the first movement in particular, as they have no real melody or key. In the manuscript, Beethoven wrote "despair" above this passage, and it is described as "rendering in music of the abyss that the circumstances of his life had forced him to look into" (Sachs, 2010, p. 134). From there on, all throughout three movements, some forty-five minutes of music, we follow portraits of human suffering, be it in its earthly form or when Beethoven marks it *maestoso* in order to underline its religious dimension. Then, the melody is born in double basses and cellos, moves to upper strings, to be taken by the whole orchestra, and finally given voice by baritone solo. Three more soloists and the choir will join soon, to produce, together with the orchestra, the most famous and exuberant piece of symphonic music ever.

What is it that they sing about? There are two distinct, although interconnected lines in the poem. The first of these is embracing the whole of humanity in its efforts to reach God, while the latter gives voices to friends celebrating the joy of life. Thus, the very first verse describes joy as a spark of divinity, and then it is said to be the daughter of Elysium (referring to the ancient Greek image of what Christians will have come to call Heaven), before it evokes "Heavenly, thy sanctuary!", and leading to what is the topic of this essay:

> Your magics join again
> What custom strictly divided;
> All people become brothers,
> Where your gentle wing abides. (Schiller, 1785)

The "Ode" opens with yearning for all people to be united in brotherhood and under the auspices of (divine) Joy. The verses also imply equality and reparation of all wrongdoing. This would be an ideal world, with no negative emotions. This line is continued in the third section (the second chorus), where Joy is depicted as a god-like mother, since "All creatures drink of joy/At nature's breast" and "She gave us kisses." The final part is the most openly religious, as it depicts "a loving Father," who dwells "above the starry canopy" and we should "seek him in the heavens." This thread of heavenly harmony is then intertwined with a more earthly one, focused on social relationships among humans. In the first stanza, we learn who is invited to this gathering: those who have managed "to be a friend's friend," "whoever has won a lovely woman," "he who can call his own even a single soul on this whole Earth!" Joy, thus, does not come only from the world of uttermost sublimity, but also from having close, intimate relationships. It all culminates with "Be embraced, you millions!", requesting a brotherhood of perfect social harmony.

The *Ninth* was premiered on May 9, 1824, and immediately recognized as a masterpiece. Despite occasional harsh criticisms (Sachs, 2010, p. 122) or disappointment with its optimism (most notably expressed by Theodor Adorno (see Lockwood, 2003, p. 420; Sachs, 2010, p. 131)), it exerted incomparable influence, especially on the nineteenth century's music. In the mid-nineteenth century, its political message was also very influential, as fights for equality were still not won (Lockwood, 2003, pp. 418ff.; Sachs, 2010, pp. 131–132). For the last several decades the melody without verse is the hymn of the united Europe and is very solemnly performed each May 9, which is not only the day of the end of World War II and the day of anti-Fascism, but, uncannily, the day of the symphony's premiere.

One psychoanalyst with profound insights into the fabric of music wrote about this symphony and others of Beethoven's late works that they are "inspired by or written in emulation of the great cosmological ladders of the world's sacred books and hymns" (Solomon, 2003, p. 201). For the purpose of this essay, it is more relevant that this jubilant music was written in a moment of acute personal misery and moral imperative in Beethoven's life (Sachs, 2010, p. 129). Not only was he completely deaf, which threatened to ruin his musicianship, but he was also abandoned by the last person who could have given him the experience of family life. Ill-treated by his father as a child, hurt by the sudden loss of his mother in adolescence, bachelor without hope of having a family of his own, Beethoven started a bitter fight for the custody of his nephew Karl. Although he finally won in judiciary terms, Karl tried to run away from him and once even tried to commit suicide. Beethoven was devastated. He wrote: "I haven't a single friend; I must live alone" (after Kerst & Krehbiel, 1964, p. 41). In one note he claims "friendship and similar sentiments bring only wounds to me" and then addresses himself in the second person singular: "There is no outward happiness; you must create it only within you— only in the world of ideality shall you find friends" (ibid., p. 88). And that is exactly the motif we find in his "Ode," as it presents resolution for his inner pains, but only under ideal circumstances, not in everyday life (Sachs, 2010, p. 124). As a matter of fact, its second stanza, in the only pessimistic sentence in the whole poem, contains the portrait of the composer:

> Who has succeeded in the great attempt,
> To be a friend's friend,
> Whoever has won a lovely woman,
> Add his to the jubilation!
> Indeed, who calls at least one soul
> Their's upon this world!
> And whoever never managed, shall steal himself
> Weeping away from this union. (Schiller, 1785)

When you are absorbed with hatred for your widowed sister-in-law and desperately jealous because her son prefers her to you, when you cannot "call at least one soul yours," one way to survive might be to put all your power into creating the idealized image of a world where jealousy is unknown and someone would finally embrace you instead of telling you to "steal yourself weeping away." A cunning defensive strategy, which may lead to masterpieces or revolutions, but, unfortunately, does not help psychologically in the long run.

Healthy absence of jealousy

Is it possible that the absence jealousy can be a sign of personal maturity and not of the massive employment of defense mechanisms? Freud believed, and many would agree with him, that this was impossible (1922b, p. 223). And indeed, after what has been discussed in this essay so far, it is difficult to find that option feasible: love and jealousy, be they separate or combined, are so intensive emotions, that it is difficult to even imagine relationships free of them in not just a defensive manner.

It may be possible, however, that because of his personal limitations, like pessimism and suspiciousness, Freud did not have enough experience in interpersonal relationships to be able to give a complete answer. I am aiming at a well-known issue of "whether Freud somehow needed to make his friends into enemies" (Gay, 1988, p. 242). For in the world of philosophy, the answer to the question of a healthy absence of jealousy has been discussed since its very beginnings: friendship.

Contemplating the notion of virtues, Aristotle opined that friendship was so pleasurable that "[N]o one would choose to live without friends, even if he had all the other goods." For him, friendship "is the happiest and most fully human of all loves, the apogee of life and the very school of virtue" (cited in Agamben, 2009, pp. 31–32; Appignanesi, 2011, p. 342). Why was he so enthusiastic about the topic (and experience) and Freud so disinterested?

For centuries before psychoanalysis even existed, friendship was believed to be of therapeutic value for those suffering from mental pain. Montaigne, for instance, believed that thanks to friendship, souls get purified, nourish each other and grow (cited in Appignanesi, 2011, p. 344). Shakespeare's contemporary, Robert Burton (1632), wrote in his *Anatomy of Melancholie*, which had enormous influence on the development of contemporary psychiatry, that melancholic persons should be encouraged to openness and confessing their sorrows to an empathetic friend (see Dimitrijevic, 2015). At approximately the same time, Francis Bacon came to that same conclusion: "A principal fruit of friendship, is the ease and discharge of the fulness and swellings of the heart, which passions of all kinds do cause and induce. [...] no receipt openeth the heart, but a true friend; to whom you may impart griefs, joys, fears, hopes, suspicions, counsels, and whatsoever lieth upon the heart to oppress it, in a kind of civil shrift or confession" (cited in Appignanesi,

2011, p. 346). And in full accord with this, contemporary empirical psychology has found that not only having happy friends influences our health, weight, and loneliness, but our chances of living happy lives are related to the happiness of our friends (R. S. Miller, 2014).

The reason for all this is that the nature of friendship is substantially different than the nature of family or romantic relationships. Simply put, no one can choose relatives, but we are granted the opportunity to select several close friends among masses of people we meet throughout our lives. When surveyed, people state that they get more pleasure from time spent with friends than with siblings, although it is best to be with both together (Miller, 2014). On the other hand, when we are "acutely" in love, neuropsychological studies show, our social cognition stops working, we idealize the other person, and are flooded with intense emotions (Bartels & Zeki, 2000, 2004). With friendship, this is not the case.

For friends, to return to Aristotle, you wish "what you believe to be good things, not for your own sake but for [theirs], and being inclined, so far as you can, to bring these things about" (cited in Appignanesi, 2011, p. 342). Friendship, thus, cannot include jealousy. Empirical research again confirms ancient wisdom: A cross-cultural study of the "universal rules of friendship" found that these include "not being jealous" of your friend and "striv[ing] to make him/her happy" (cited in R. S. Miller, 2014, p. 222).

In a true friendship, one's mind is not under the influence of burning, almost uncontrollably intense emotions, one should not be feeling dependent, passionate, or, indeed, jealous. It is exactly this distinction between *eros* and *philia* that makes possible deeper insights into the nature of friendship. *Philia* is affirmative desire towards the Other—"to respect the Other, to pay attention to the Other, not to destroy the otherness of the Other" (Derida, cited in Appignanesi, 2011, p. 339). As the *locus classicus* from Aristotle's *Rhetoric* (c. fourth century BC) describes, "What a good man feels with respect to himself he also feels with respect to his friend: the friend is, in fact, another self [*heteros autos*]." In probably the earliest expression of the idea of intersubjectivity in history, the friend is seen as another subject, respected and necessary for our recognition and development. If jealousy may be closely connected to *eros*, here it is unimaginable, as friendship is recognition without the wish for subjugation. You do not need your friend always available or affirming, ideal or powerful, idealizing you or being in love with you.[3]

What we cherish in friends is exactly this otherness, which should never be lost through unlimited support or passionate merger. A friend is precious for the very reason that he is the second self "through whom individual identity can be mirrored, measured and constituted" (Appignanesi, 2011, p. 345). Dialogue between friends provides food for thought that cannot be found anywhere else, for it forms a mental space in which one can discover who one is and how others experience this process of discovery and its results. This ("ideal") form of friendship is thus quite similar to the ("ideal") form of psychoanalysis. One may go as far as to claim that we cannot discover our true identities without or outside this dialogue of friends. Italian philosopher, Agamben (2009) writes:

> ... friendship has an ontological and political status ... being itself is divided here. It is non-identical to itself, and so the I and the friend are the two faces, or the two poles of this con-division or sharing ... The friend is not another I, but an otherness immanent to selfness, a becoming other of the self ... Friendship is this desubjectification at the very heart of the most intimate sensation of the self ... Friends do not share something (birth, law, place, taste): they are shared by the experience of friendship. Friendship is the con-division that precedes every division, since what has to be shared is the very fact of existence, life itself. (pp. 34–36)

Jealousy, we see, can be a challenge to many, in the form of absence and/or excess. Yet, there is at least one form of human relationships that it cannot corrode and destroy: the one between persons aware that another one's freedom is a precondition for their own—friendship.

Conclusion

Our personal and analytical experience shows that jealousy is undoubtedly among the most widespread emotions, known to persons of all life's ages, both genders, and different persuasions. At the same time, jealousy indeed may be absent from some people's behavior and conscious awareness. Searching underneath this absence, a psychoanalyst can discover various defensive strategies one employs in order to avoid facing one's own jealous feelings or traumatic memories related to it. In this essay, I have discussed three of these: fragility, repression, and idealization. All three revolve around the oedipal constellation, albeit in different ways, but cannot lead to mature ways of dealing with jealousy.

Despite Freud's claim that a healthy absence of jealousy is impossible, I hypothesized here that true friendship is a relationship that does not include this emotion. Freud did not leave us an important legacy when it comes to studying friendship, either as a scholar or as a person. Just as he himself wrote to Ferenczi, on October 6, 1910, that since the end of his friendship with Fliess, he "had no longer any need for that full opening of [his] personality" (cited in Falzeder & Brabant, 1993, p. 221), he also did not write about it extensively. It may thus be urgent for psychoanalysis to devote more attention to studying the phenomenon of friendship, especially if we take into account that currently PEP-Web shows just twenty-five hits for friendship as a title word. Therefore, we need to look for inspiration to the wisdom of philosophers and poets, who have dealt with it for centuries and in great detail.

Further psychoanalytic research of both jealousy and friendship, together with awareness of the importance of "psychopathic" motivation to provoke jealousy in someone, would help our patients as well as ourselves, privately and professionally. Many of our patients need to learn how to control their intense jealousy, but many also need to learn how to grow robust enough so that they would become able to admit and recognize it. As to psychoanalysts, we may too infrequently be aware of our jealousy toward patients and their loved ones, as well as our institutional colleagues, training analysts, and supervisors (see Dimitrijevic, in press a, b). Hopefully, it is time, for the sake of our patients, ourselves, and the psychoanalytic community, that we make a choice—*jealousy or friendship*.

PART II

CULTURAL REALM

CHAPTER SIX

Shakespeare and the "green-eyed monster" of jealousy

Richard Waugaman

This chapter studies jealousy in Shakespeare's play *Othello*, show-ing that knowledge of the true author's life experiences with pathological jealousy will deepen our understanding and appre-ciation of this unsettling play. This chapter builds on the previous Oxfordian[1] study of *Othello* by A. Bronson Feldman, the first psycho-analyst to take up Freud's call that we re-examine Shakespeare's works with a revised understanding of who wrote them. Freud (1990), who wrote to his friend Eduard Silberstein about having seen a performance of *Othello* in Vienna in 1873 when Freud was seventeen, cited *Othello* in his 1922 explanation that "projected jealousy" defends against guilt about one's actual or fantasized infidelity by attributing unfaithfulness to one's partner. In *Hamlet* (1603), Gertrude anticipates Freud's formula-tion when she says: "So full of artless jealousy is guilt" (IV, v, 21).

Freud, in 1937, wrote to Arnold Zweig that he was "almost irritated" that Zweig still believed Shakespeare of Stratford simply relied on his imagination to write the great plays. Freud explained:

> I do not know what still attracts you to the man from Stratford. He seems to have nothing at all to justify his claim [to authorship of the canon], whereas Oxford has almost everything. It is quite inconceivable to me that Shakespeare should have got everything secondhand—Hamlet's neurosis, Lear's madness ... Othello's jealousy, etc. (1968a, p. 140)

When Shakespeare scholars acknowledge Freud's Oxfordian opinions at all, they create a "straw man" as to his motives, overlooking Freud's expectation that Shakespeare's life experiences would bear a significant relationship to his plays and poetry. After all, Freud took seriously his concept of psychic determinism. Psychoanalysts who still support the traditional authorship theory seem to have a blind spot for this dimension of Shakespeare's works.

Feldman published two articles on *Othello*, in 1952 and again in 1954.[2] This chapter is also an extension of my previous chapter on betrayal in Shakespeare,[3] since jealousy is based on a fear of being betrayed. More pathological forms of jealousy lead to a false perception of betrayal when there has been none. Jealousy is intensified by projection onto another person of one's own disloyal impulses and acts.

Shakespeare offers us extraordinary insights into human psychology. The phenomenon of jealousy is no exception. From his profound self-awareness and from his penetrating observations of other people, Edward de Vere understood and explicated the psychodynamics of the "green-eyed monster" of pathological jealousy. Now, nearly a century after Freud called on us to connect Shakespeare's works with his life, it is time for us to heed Freud's call. We might emulate Freud's repeated courage in defying "groupthink"[4] as he explored controversial ideas. Freud highlighted the importance he placed on this character trait when he wrote to Ernest Jones in 1926 about "the great experiment of my life, namely to stand up for a conviction ..." (cited in Gay, 1988, p. 148).

Tomie de Paola's (1973) *Nana Upstairs & Nana Downstairs* is a classic children's book that helps young children cope with the death of loved ones. Four-year-old Tommy visits his grandmother and her mother every Sunday. The story describes the routine he follows during each visit, spending time downstairs with his nana, then upstairs with his bedridden great-grandmother. She and Tommy are both tied in chairs, and share mints. Eventually, his "nana upstairs" dies, followed later by his "nana downstairs." A work of the imagination, right? No. De Paola explains in a postscript to a later edition of his book that every detail is autobiographical.

"So what?" you ask? Well, we should not assume that every classic work of "fiction" has no autobiographical elements. Certainly not when it comes to the works of Shakespeare. We cannot fully understand a theme like jealousy in Shakespeare's works without looking at the glaring role of pathological jealousy in the life of the true author. However, a catastrophic historical blunder in attributing the pseudonymous works of Shakspere to William Shakespeare, the businessman from Stratford, has fueled a far-reaching misunderstanding of the role of all authors' life experiences in their literary works. For centuries, Shakespeare scholars have confronted an embarrassing lack of fit between their alleged author and his works.[5] This foundational error leads to an equally pernicious misunderstanding of how literary universality is achieved. If Shakespeare did not base his universally appealing works on personal experience, it is then falsely concluded that a great writer aims for universal appeal through a generalizing strategy, rather than through the far more effective means of capturing the individuality of her experience so eloquently that the writer's emotions are communicated to the reader or listener, tapping into their respective personal experiences powerfully enough that the literary work has profound affective resonance and appeal. We cannot fully understand the pivotal operation of unconscious communication between author and reader—or playwright and audience—if we fail to appreciate this crucial role of the writer's life experiences.

Rather bizarrely, the traditional approach to Shakespeare[6] is to dissociate the author and his life story from his literary works. The resulting one-sided emphasis on Shakespeare's inborn genius stems from the lack of connection between what we know about Shakespeare of Stratford and the plays and poems that many still attribute to him. Freud was the world's first prominent intellectual to be persuaded that the real author was probably the highly educated genius Edward de Vere, Earl of Oxford (1550–1604). It is said that in war, the first casualty is the truth. Similarly, in highly polarized academic debates, complexity and ambiguity often give way to circular, all or nothing thinking, with those who express contrary opinions treated as the "enemy".[7]

Mainstream explorations of the personality of Shakespeare are naturally limited by their erroneous assumption about his identity. Edward Wagenknecht (1972), for example, avers that "Unless I am completely wrong in my reading of his character, Shakespeare could not have deliberately killed any human being under any circumstances" (p. 13). As Freud observed, one attraction of the Stratford businessman "Shakspere" is that we know so little about him that we can imagine he was as perfect a human being as are his literary works. But the real "Shakespeare" killed a man when he was seventeen.[8] Thus, he knew the mind of a killer from introspection.

Once we accept the controversial conclusion that Shakespeare's *Sonnets*[9] are autobiographical, we see the poet's intense jealousy of both the Fair Youth (the Earl of Southampton) and the Dark Lady (her identity is unknown) in their notorious love triangle. We also see de Vere's jealousy of the Fair Youth's relationship with the rival poet (probably Christopher Marlowe),[10] which seems to have incited murderous literary and erotic feelings of competition in de Vere.

One of the most glaring and public instances of de Vere's jealousy was his refusal to live with his wife, Anne (1556–1583), for at least five years after he returned from his fourteen-month visit to the Continent when he was twenty-six years old. Despite the entreaties of Queen Elizabeth and her principal secretary (he was also de Vere's former guardian and now his father-in-law), Lord Burghley, that he reconcile with Anne, de Vere accused his wife of having been impregnated by another man.[11] She gave birth to their daughter, Elizabeth, in July, 1575. De Vere left for his lengthy trip to the Continent five months earlier, so he may well have been the father.[12] Venice offered legalized prostitution when de Vere lived there, and it is doubtful that de Vere resisted opportunities for sexual adventures, thus increasing the possibility that he hypocritically projected his own sexual infidelity onto his wife.

Everyone at Queen Elizabeth's court knew of de Vere's jealousy of Anne. The way he later depicted states of pathological jealousy in his plays (e.g., Claudius in *Much Ado About Nothing* (1600); *Othello* (1622); Leontes in *The Winter's Tale* (1623); and Posthumus in *Cymbeline* (1623) hints that de Vere later regretted his accusations against Anne, and performed self-deprecatory acts of literary penance through showing innocent women wronged by outrageously jealous men, who resembled de Vere in that way.

The year that de Vere spent living in Italy (1575–76) offers crucial insights into the connections between the works of Shakespeare and the life of their author.[13] For example, *Othello* has its title character rush to Cyprus to defend it from an impending Turkish attack. There was actually a Turkish attack on Venetian-controlled Cyprus in 1570, five years before de Vere's stay in Venice (Johnson, Steevens, & Reed, 1813). Further, in 1571, Venetian forces played a key role against the Ottoman Turks in the naval battle of Lepanto. Many poets commemorated that Venetian victory, and it may be part of Othello's implicit "backstory." Feldman (1952, 1954) believes de Vere hoped to gain military experience during his stay in Venice if the Turks attacked Venice itself while he was living there. Shakespeare introduced into the English language several words from "Veneto," the dialect of Venice. For example, his use of "gondolier" in *Othello* (1622) seems to be its first use in English. It is difficult to imagine how Shakspere of Stratford learned this dialect—or the detailed geographic knowledge of Italy reflected in Shakespeare's plays—without ever leaving England.

One priceless benefit of realizing de Vere probably wrote Shakespeare is that it allows us to expand the corpus of his other writings. A classic study of rhetoric probably written by de Vere, the anonymous 1589 *Art of English Poesy*,[14] contrasts the high reputation of poets in former days with the contempt that the Elizabethan aristocracy showed toward poets. Just after this observation, there is a passage highly relevant to an understanding of maladaptive emotions such as jealousy.

The author said many of his contemporaries showed "scorn and derision" toward creative writers, calling them "light-headed and fantastical" (p. 109). De Vere believed this contempt confused the creative imagination with "disordered fantasies" (p. 109). But a good imaginative writer, by contrast, is "very formal [sane],[15] and in his much multiformity uniform, that is, well proportioned, and so [sur]passingly clear, that by it, as by a glass or mirror,[16] are represented unto the soul all manner of beautiful visions,[17] whereby the inventive part of the mind is so much helped, as without it no man could devise any new or rare thing" (p. 109). De Vere then compared the creative writer's imagination to a mirror, noting that a mirror may be accurate, or may be distorted. Some mirrors beautify an object; while still others deceptively portray attractive objects as "very monstrous and ill-favored" (p. 110). "Even so," man's imagination, if unimpaired, can represent "the best, most comely, and beautiful images or appearances of things to the soul and according to their very truth. If otherwise, then doth it [the imagination] breed chimeras and *monsters* in men's imaginations, and not only in his imaginations, but also in all his ordinary actions and life which ensues" (p. 110; emphasis added). This comparison eloquently describes the monstrous pathology of a diseased imagination, such as Othello's pathological jealousy of his wife, Desdemona. The author adds that sound judgment should ideally accompany a strong imagination, not only in creative writers, but in politicians and military leaders (think of Othello).

Four paragraphs later, de Vere provides a pivotal hint of his own practice of writing anonymously (as in *The Art of English Poesy* itself), or under pen names: "I know very many notable gentlemen in the court who have written commendably well and suppressed it again [afterwards], or else suffered it to be published without their own names to it, as if it were a discredit for a gentleman to seem learned and to show himself amorous of any good art" (p. 112). This passage documenting the so-called "stigma of print" for the Elizabethan upper classes is now dismissed by scholars who are desperate to deny that a nobleman such as de Vere needed to conceal his authorship of Shakespeare's works. Such circular reasoning based on the flawed premise that "Shakespeare wrote Shakespeare" bedevils Shakespeare scholarship.

Note de Vere's phrase "their *own* names" (emphasis added).[18] There is strong evidence suggesting that de Vere may have been the actual author of some of the many literary works dedicated to him but published under "allonyms"—that is, the names of *other* known people (such as the Latin translation of Castiglione's [1528] *The Art of the Courtier* and the English translation of Cardanus's [1573] *Comforte Complete*); that de Vere put his uncle Arthur Golding's name on his own translation of Ovid's *Metamorphoses*, which Ezra Pound called the most beautiful book in English (cited in Rouse, 1904, p. 2); that he put the initials "E. K." on his commentary on Spenser's *The Shepheardes Calendar* (knowing that Edmund Kirke was Spenser's friend); and that he used the allonym "William Shake-speare" in a possibly half-hearted effort to attribute authorship of those works to the Stratford businessman and London theater investor, William Shakspere.[19]

One way to think about *Othello* is in terms of the projective identification of unbearable feelings of jealousy. Contrary to Samuel Coleridge's (1987) influential conclusion that Iago suffers from "motiveless malignity," I would suggest that we take seriously Iago's opening lines to Rodrigo, complaining that he has been passed over for promotion by Othello. In addition, Iago tells Rodrigo, "I do suspect the lusty Moor/Hath leap'ed into my seat; the thought whereof/Doth, like a poisonous mineral, gnaw my inwards;/And nothing can or shall content my soul/ Till I am even'd with him, wife for wife,/Or failing so, yet that I put the Moor/At least into a jealousy so strong/That judgment cannot cure" (I, i, 316–323).

If we assume this induces narcissistic rage in Iago, his then seeking the death of Othello is fully motivated. Similarly, Brabantio reacts with rage to the narcissistic slight of his daughter Desdemona marrying Othello without Brabantio's permission. Iago's aim of inducing unbearable feelings of jealousy in Othello is also clearly motivated. *Othello* has been described as nearly unbearable to watch. So this implies a further process of projective identification—of the playwright's unbearable feelings into the audience.

Yes, *Othello* is a play about Othello's jealousy. But it is equally about Iago's skill in provoking that jealousy; Iago is sometimes considered the play's central character. Why? Any question we might ask about Shakespeare usually has a complex answer, and we should never presume that we have arrived at the last word. For starters, we might note that Iago's skill in playing on Othello's emotions parallels the playwright's skill in playing on ours. So this play, as do all Shakespeare's plays, holds up a mirror to us, so that we might better understand ourselves, and our vulnerabilities. Further, the play helps us understand the workings of projection—and of projective identification. Iago, in his envy, wants to project onto others his own vile nature. With Othello, he cannot, because of Othello's noble character. So he now turns to projective identification, inducing in Othello the very jealousy Iago tells us he feels himself. It suggests that one of Iago's possible motives might be his intolerance of the pathological jealousy Iago feels himself.

Moments before Othello's death, he usurps the position of writing his own history; judging himself; and performing his own execution. He sounds dissociated from himself, splitting himself in two when he says,

in Aleppo once,
Where a malignant and a turban'd Turk
Beat a Venetian and traduc'd the state,
I took by the throat the circumcised dog,
And smote him—thus. (V, ii, 402–406)

What has just happened? In splitting his own identity between narrator and condemned criminal, Othello enacts the very split that allowed de Vere to tell this disguised story of his own pathological jealousy of his first wife, Anne. This moment is an excellent illustration of Harold Searles's (1979) observation that suicide often amounts to one part of the personality murdering another part. Think of the phrase quoted earlier, in de Vere's 1589 description of a good creative writer, who is "in *his much multiformity* uniform." Among other things, this may allude to de Vere's awareness of his own multiple self states, which contributed to his extraordinary skill in creating fully realized fictional characters. Further, if Othello stabs himself as he speaks the final word, "thus," it constitutes an extraordinary intersection of word and action in Shakespeare, when the past tense of "smote" becomes present indeed, suddenly making us aware that Othello is using his narration of a past event to compare his current suicide with his earlier killing of an enemy. Othello's identification with the "Turk" in this story is further enriched when we learn that Queen Elizabeth's nickname for de Vere was "Turk."

The subtitle of *Othello* is *The Moor of Venice*. In this play, Iago manipulatively warns Othello, "O, beware, my lord, of jealousy;/It is the *green-eyed monster*" (III.iii.188–189). Portia, in *The Merchant of Venice*, observes, "How all the other passions fleet to air,/As doubtful thoughts, and rash-embraced despair,/And shuddering fear, and *green-eyed jealousy!*" (III.ii.110–112). Thus, the only two instances of the phrase "green-eyed" are in the two Shakespeare plays that have "Venice" in their titles, and in the pivotal third act in each play.

Both plays use "green-eyed" to refer to jealousy; Shakespeare was the first writer to do so. Such is Shakespeare's influence that "green-eyed" to allude to jealousy is still a current usage. In de Vere's day, a green complexion was thought to reflect envy or fear. De Vere may also have been influenced by the Veneto phrase *"esser verde"* ("to be green") meaning "to be irate" in calling jealousy a green-eyed monster. Why would de Vere associate Venice with jealousy? Because he was living in Venice when he became consumed with pathological jealousy of his wife, Anne, convinced she was pregnant by another man (possibly her father).

Here is where biographical information about de Vere is invaluable for exploring such questions about Shakespeare's works. De Vere's literary work served as a sort of self-analysis for him. He was able to bring all his characters to life in unprecedented ways because he could find in himself the traits they embody, including those offensive traits that made him so controversial during his lifetime. Among these were jealousy of pathological—and possibly even murderous—proportions.[20]

The first recorded performance of *Othello* was November 1, 1604, a few months after de Vere's death. It was one of several Shakespeare plays performed at court to celebrate the marriage of de Vere's youngest daughter Susan to Philip Herbert, Earl of Montgomery (one of the brothers to whom Shakespeare's *First Folio* of thirty-six plays was dedicated in 1623). For reasons unknown, *Othello* was not published until 1622, just a year before the *First Folio* appeared. The literary source of the play is a 1565 Italian story by Giovanni Cinthio, not yet translated into English, that was in the library of de Vere's guardian and father-in-law, Lord Burghley.

Charles Arundell alleged in 1584 (cited in Peck, 1985) that the Earl of Leicester often set "the great lords of England" against their wives. Arundell singled out de Vere as one such lord. Lord Burghley wrote in his diary that de Vere "was enticed by certain lewd persons to be a stranger to his wife" (cited in Anderson, 2005, p. 115). He also wrote that de Vere's cruel treatment of his wife after he returned from Italy seemed "grounded upon untrue reports of others" (p. 120). Who were these people? Rowland Yorke, one of de Vere's trusted servants, had a brother who was Leicester's servant, and may have played an Iago-like role in telling de Vere lies about his wife's ostensible infidelity. When he served in England's military, Lieutenant Yorke more than once betrayed his country to its enemy, Spain. "Iago" as a name does not appear in Cinthio's source story for *Othello*. But "Iago" is the Spanish word for James, Spain's patron saint.

Shakespeare scholars have been slow to discover Shakespeare's veiled commentary on events at the Elizabethan Court. They know that Elizabethan playwrights were often arrested, tortured, and otherwise punished for arousing the ire of powerful court officials for appearing to offer critiques of contemporary politics. For example, nineteenth-century Shakespeareans knew Polonius in *Hamlet* is a spoof on Lord Burghley. But current Shakespeare scholars such as Jonathan Bate say that's not possible, because there is no way Shakspere of Stratford could have gotten away with it. Precisely. Shakespeare scholars are thus depriving us of one of the most fascinating levels of the multilayered meanings of Shakespeare's works. This view of Shakespeare's writing as lacking any political dimension was perhaps stated most bluntly by Northrop Frye (1986), when he wrote,

> [One] thing seems clear in Shakespeare: there is never anything outside his plays that he wants to "say" or talk about in the plays ... [I]n his day nobody cared what Shakespeare's views were about anything, and he wouldn't have been allowed to discuss public affairs publicly ... his plays merely present aspects of social life that would have been intelligible to his audience ... Even then he would deal only with those aspects that fitted the play he was writing. (p. 2)

However, the plays of de Vere cannot be fully understood without considering the fact that the most important member of his audience was Queen Elizabeth I. He wrote with her in mind. When he was in his early twenties, a court insider wrote to his father that de Vere was one of the queen's favorites. Much of his classic work on rhetoric and courtly behavior mentioned earlier, the 1589 *Art of English Poesy*, is addressed in the second person to the queen. And consider for a moment some of the central facts of the queen's background that de Vere pondered as he wrote. Her father had her mother executed. It was the most prominent dysfunctional marriage of the land. Due to religious and political struggles over the succession, there were widely known efforts to have Elizabeth declared illegitimate, and therefore ineligible to succeed her father on the throne. This fact was likely to have had special resonance for de Vere, whose older half-sister Katherine went to court to have *him* declared illegitimate when their father died, in 1562, when de Vere was twelve. Alleged or actual illegitimacy is referred to in nearly every Shakespeare play, and is a prominent theme in several of them. Yet these plays depict male bastards, not illegitimate women, probably in deference to the queen's sensibilities about the accusations against her.[21]

Many of our blind spots for overlooked contemporary allusions in the plays reflect our failure to ponder what the queen's reactions to Shakespeare's plays would be. It is falsely claimed that *Henry VIII* was written after the queen's death. Yet it includes an eloquent reenactment of her christening, with Cranmer saying of her, "This royal infant .../ Though in her cradle, yet now promises/Upon this land a thousand thousand blessings,/Which time shall bring to ripeness" (V, iv, 17–20). It is likely de Vere wrote that scene partly to flatter his queen.

Some theater history context will be helpful. The queen became exasperated with court entertainment that included transparent attempts to influence her decisions, such as whether and whom to marry. She tried to put a stop to this by creating an Office of Revels, which passed judgment about which plays could be performed. John Lyly (1564–1606) succeeded in evading censorship with several plays set in ancient times, offering a thicker level of disguise for any court commentary. Several of his plays were performed for the queen in the 1580s by a theatrical troupe sponsored by de Vere himself. As early as 1579 and into the 1590s, Lyly was employed as one of de Vere's literary secretaries.[22] It is likely that de Vere collaborated in writing the plays attributed to Lyly. For example, during Lyly's lifetime, anonymous printed editions of his plays omitted lovely lines of poetry that may have been written by de Vere; those lines were included in a 1632 edition published years after Lyly's death. R. W. Bond (1902) called Lyly "Shakespeare's only model" for writing plays, unaware that the work of Lyly may have been written by de Vere. Lyly wrote no more plays after he left de Vere's employment.

When de Vere writes about jealousy, he is not only alluding to his notorious streak of pathological jealousy, but also to salient events in the queen's life. For example, Brabantio, the father of Othello's wife, Desdemona, claims that Othello must have won Desdemona's love through *witchcraft*—"She is abused, stol'n from me, and corrupted/By spells and medicines bought of mountebanks;/For nature so preposterously to err …/Sans witchcraft could not" (I, iii, 68–72). De Vere would have known that such an accusation would remind the queen of the fatal downfall of her mother, Anne Boleyn, after her father, Henry VIII, similarly accused Anne of winning his heart through "*witchcraft*." Anne had given birth to a stillborn and possibly deformed son. Witchcraft was commonly thought to cause such tragedies at that time. King Henry needed to make Anne the scapegoat to preempt the alternative explanation that the stillbirth reflected divine disfavor of Henry for divorcing his first wife, Katherine of Aragon. Thus, thinking of that piece of her family history, Queen Elizabeth I probably took comfort in Othello's eloquent reply that Desdemona fell in love with him not because he used any witchcraft, but because she heard him tell the story of his heroic life, after her father asked to hear it—"She loved me for the dangers I had pass'd,/And I loved her that she did pity them./This is the only witchcraft I have used" (I, iii, 181–183).

Further, Queen Elizabeth I showed possible signs of jealousy when de Vere impregnated one of her ladies-in-waiting, the fifteen-year-old Anne

Vavasour, in 1581. The day after Vavasour gave birth to Edward Vere, she was imprisoned in the Tower of London. De Vere was caught trying to flee England, and thrown into the Tower, too, for two and a half months. There is suggestive evidence that some of the poems signed "Anomos"[23] were written by de Vere in the Tower. One of these anonymous poems ("Two His Muse") alludes to one of the motives for de Vere's anonymous authorship—"The honor great which Poets wont to have [are accustomed to have],/With worthy deeds is buried deep in grave,/Each man will hide his name,/Thereby to hide his shame." De Vere repeatedly used his poems and plays to try to influence the queen. De Vere's 1593 long poem, *Venus and Adonis*, may hint at an earlier affair between him and Queen Elizabeth I, further suggesting that he provoked her jealousy with his other affairs. After de Vere married Anne Cecil in 1571, Cecil's mother apparently objected to de Vere's intimacy with the queen, but the queen sent word that she should mind her own business.

The astonishingly universal appeal of Shakespeare allowed de Vere to write plays that spoke on one level to the queen and to court insiders; while speaking to everyone else on many other levels. For example, commentators have puzzled over Katherine's seeming submissiveness toward her husband by the end of *The Taming of the Shrew*. Among other meanings, this echoes an event in the life of Henry VIII's last wife, Katherine Parr. She brought all of Henry's children into the royal household, and became a warm stepmother to Elizabeth. So Elizabeth would have been familiar with a conspiracy to remove the evangelical Katherine by religious conservatives. Henry had warned her that she would be tested the next day for her loyalty to him. When she was duly questioned, she completely abandoned her past pattern of debating with him on controversial matters, and told him that Eve was created to submit to Adam, and so did she submit to Henry. She said she had debated religion with him in the past only to distract him from his physical ailments and pain.

In conclusion, psychoanalysts are wise to emulate Freud in using a close study of Shakespeare's works to expand our understanding of human psychology, including Shakespeare's analysis of pathological jealousy in *Othello*. If we are willing to explore Freud's controversial belief that Edward de Vere wrote Shakespeare's works, we will be richly rewarded by an even deeper understanding of these priceless literary treasures, and the connections between life and great literature. I hope other colleagues will be emboldened to join me in this exhilarating project.

CHAPTER SEVEN

Race, sex, jealousy, and power*

Joël Des Rosiers

Psychoanalytical studies on Shakespeare's (1622) *Othello* have mainly focused on the morbid nature of denial within the delirium of jealousy, where the subject's emotional reactions are imbued with hostility and aggressiveness and likely lead to attacks on either the self or the other.

This study of a tragic play tries to demonstrate that the cumulative effects of oppression on human subjects of Afro-Caribbean origin lead to a much larger complex, based on the return of the oppressed. "Internalized aggression" is the splitting and projection mechanism that allows the self to survive precariously against a background of systemic violence. Fakhry Davids (2011) posits a remarkable psychoanalytical

*The author wishes to thank Ms. Susan Altschul for her translation of this manuscript from French into English.

concept of internalized racism like an intense function of disconnection from the still inaccessible object, a sort of *radical decathexis* that undoes the unity of the self and endangers life itself. Survival is often manifested in the form of pseudo-stupidity, by which the oppressed subject sabotages machines and production tools, disables itself by self-mutilation and pretends not to understand instructions in order to delay the process of submission and dehumanization. In the words of Christopher Bollas (2015),

> The repressed refers to the elimination from consciousness of specific mental contents. The oppressed refers to the suspension or distortion of human thinking. The repressed returns through the rerouting of ideas. The oppressed refers to an alteration not of the *contents* of the mind, but of the *capacities* of the mind—the way one forms thoughts. When discussing the course of oppression, we note a cumulative degradation of the *forms* of perception, thought and communication. … The oppressed *is* to be found in the unconscious but as a *failed effort*, the trace of what might have been ideationally created (even if banished) and linking up to other forms of such failure. (p. 539, italics in the original)

The Tragedy of Othello, the Moor of Venice is the Shakespeare play that relates to contemporary issues. *The Tragedy of Othello* enlarges on notions of place, race, and sexuality, class, ethnicity, and gender. The emotional contagion sparked by jealousy evolves amid the social ideals that reveal and reflect the tensions of all multiracial societies. Women's sexuality as an object of racial desire can cause terror.

Othello: in the name of the father of the horde

The fact that Freud did not comment on *The Tragedy of Othello, the Moor of Venice,* should not be a surprise, even though the play reflects the resemblance between the tragedy and his own family romance: like Othello the general, Freud's father, Jacob, an elderly man with two grown sons, married Amalia, a nineteen-year-old beauty. It is also notable that Freud never commented on the erotic dream that Iago attributes to Cassio, despite its exemplary character as the imaginary acting out of a homosexual desire. It is worth examining Freud's remarks on parricide.

It can scarcely be owing to chance that three of the masterpieces of the literature of all time—the *Oedipus Rex* of Sophocles (429 BC), Shakespeare's (1603) *Hamlet*, and Dostoevsky's (1880) *The Brothers Karamazov*—should all deal with the same subject, parricide. In all three, moreover, the motive of the deed—sexual rivalry for a woman—is laid bare.

Can *Othello* be legitimately added to this list of universal works? Is Othello just a jealous husband, or is he also a father, the true father of humanity, the fatherless father, the father of all fathers, the prehistoric father, the black father of humanity, the father of the primitive horde threatened by the fraternity "explicable only by repressed homosexuality" (Freud, 1928b, p. 184) of Iago, Cassio, Roderigo, Lodovico, and Montano? The tavern scene (Act II, Scene III) where a drunken Cassio injures Montano and is then punished by Othello resembles the brothers' totemic feast after killing their father. Castration anxiety, guilt, and ambivalence are the elements that lead Cassio to seek Othello's affection with the help of Desdemona. From his all-powerful position, Othello then abases the public interest to his emotions.

Othello, whose introjected and projected primitive personality characteristics have been distorted by jealousy, is the primary object, that is, the Moor—the Negro—hidden under the wood, the rejected cornerstone of the theoretical construct, the un-father figure in psychoanalysis. The Freudian invention of parricide among primitive hordes (1912–13) is supposedly based on the recognition that the origins of humanity, religion, ethics, and civilization are African. Prehistory and history are lumped together, just as the psychic and the cultural go together. This interconnection becomes clear when Iago warns Desdemona's father that his daughter will be "covered with a Barbary horse" (Act I, Scene I, 111, p. 204) or "an old black ram is tupping your white ewe" (Act I, Scene I, 88–89, pp. 203). The phylogenesis, precursor to the murder and its transmission, has as a fundamental prerequisite an essential concordance between prehistoric man, primitive man, perverts, neurotics, and psychotics: the transformation of the original impulse into *action*, the absence of inhibiting factors. Everything starts with the action. In Shakespeare's interpretation, even honest Iago holds back at some point:

> Though in the trade of war I have slain men,
> Yet do I hold it very stuff o' the conscience
> To do no contrived murder: (Act I, Scene II, 1–3, p. 208)

This is where civilization starts, just the way Freud (1912–13) develops the missing link in *Totem and Taboo*. However, Freud (1900a) cites *Othello* for the first time in *The Interpretation of Dreams*, treating Desdemona's handkerchief as an example of psychical displacement: "… in *Othello* a lost handkerchief precipitates an outburst of rage" (p. 177). That means that the focus, interest, intensity of a representation can be detached from the object and attached to other, less intense representations, linked to the first one by a chain of association (Laplanche & Pontalis, 1967). That kind of phenomenon, where satisfaction is limited to just one detail out of the whole libidinal complex, can be found in dream analysis based on psycho-neurotic symptom creation and more generally in all creations of the unconscious. Desdemona's lost handkerchief—white material embroidered with strawberries that was Othello's wedding present to her and that Othello's mother gave to him after receiving it from Othello's father—thus becomes the hymen of chastity in which he invests all his emotion.

Freud cites a second passage from *Othello*, "Desdemona's song",[1] in a chapter devoted to neurotic mechanisms in jealousy, paranoia, and homosexuality (1922b, p. 224). The jealous person projects his own unfaithful impulses onto the person to whom he himself should be faithful. Consider the following analysis from Brusset (2011):

> Jealousy is widely prevalent. But, in addition to the rivalry based on the object of desire being coveted by a rival, homosexuality and also unconscious identification are part of the picture. Othello kills his beloved Desdemona because he thinks she loves Cassio: "With mine officer!" But he is the one who loves Cassio, which implies a feminization by identification with Desdemona. He desires Desdemona's desire for Cassio. The unconscious homosexuality is imputed to the other person and rejected as intolerable. The projection of self onto the other, who has become an unacceptable version of that self, can only lead to murder and suicide. (p. 682)

Othello thus joins Desdemona in the incestuous sheets of death.

As a black man in and from Venice, sold into slavery and converted, Othello parades his foreignness: he exorcises himself into a false self (Winnicott, 1960), adopting the psychological behavior that consists of responding to the accommodations and demands of his social environment. In his defense against accusations of witchcraft, Othello seduces the Council by recounting his extraordinary adventures "strange, passing strange" that moved Desdemona so: "And of the Cannibals that each other eat,/The Anthropopagi, and men whose heads/Do grow beneath their shoulders" (Act I, Scene III, 144–145, p. 224). Othello had been a child soldier, confronting dangers "even from my boyish days" (Act I, Scene III, 132, p. 223), "That my youth suffer'd" (Act I, Scene III, 158, p. 224) since he was seven years old. Now a soldier who is respected and appreciated by the Duke and Senators, this senior officer is a frequent guest in Brabantio's house. Racial prejudice only surfaces when he secretly marries his host's daughter, knowing he will never get her father's consent. By turns "sorcerer," "abuser of the world," "foul thief," "thick-lipped beast," "sooty bosom," "such a thing as thou," and "diabolical monster," a sensual animal that overwhelms the young, virginal Desdemona: "Transported … To the gross clasps of a lascivious Moor" (Act I, Scene I, 125, p. 205), black devil, Othello is revealed as the false object whose fall Iago provokes through intense intrapsychic and interpersonal maneuvering (Akhtar, 2009). The Duke, more rational but affected by the discourse of the Moorish general, defends Othello when Brabantio interrupts a Council meeting for family concerns:

> I think this tale would win my daughter, too …
> If virtue no delighted beauty lack,
> Your son-in-law is far more fair than black (Act I, Scene III, 287–288, p. 233)

Brabantio has to take a back seat to official policy, since the Turks are converging on Cyprus and threatening the supremacy of the Republic of Venice, a Mediterranean colonial power. He reluctantly agrees to give his rebellious daughter to the Moor after she declares that she will submit not to her father but to her husband: "So much I challenge that I may profess/Due to the Moor my lord" (Act I, Scene III, 188, p. 226). The oedipal desire for the father is thus shifted onto Othello, "an old black ram" seduced by the erotic appeal of a young virgin. While Desdemona adopts a counterphobic attitude toward the race difference, that same color difference is Othello's weakest point, his Achilles' heel. Brabantio retreats in bitterness, but first makes a prediction to the Moor:

> Look to her, Moor, if thou hast eyes to see:
> She has deceived her father, and may thee.

To which Othello replies without hesitation:

My life upon her faith! (Act I, Scene III, 290–293, p. 233)

Trust has been corrupted by doubt. The external object remains real, but a real object is transformed into a false one. From being an idealized object, Desdemona becomes the same as all those venal Venetian women who hide their sexual prowess from their husbands. Shakespeare's tragedy is thus the symbolic display of an intrapsychic episode (Bishop, 2004). The story arcs from the schizoid-paranoid position to one of depression and narcissistic love. The projection of parts of oneself into another person, yielding to an interpersonal love object, is obstructed and finally destroyed by the omnipotence of a morbid element. The split personality, whose traits are masochistic and self-destructive and vulnerable to internalized racism, is represented by Iago. It is the most violent, raucous, and unsolvable tragedy, still today evoking the most psychic turbulence in theatres.

Othello is a man who is proud of being a soldier; he is aware of his military successes, of the services he has rendered to the state, of his warrior-like bravery. He is also a raconteur, an African "griot," a poet, and it is his storytelling talent that has seduced Desdemona, fascinating her with his world of amazing and monstrous creatures. He is made up of an internal object, imperfect but honest and resilient but at the same time torn into several parts: African, black, Moor, *morisco*, Venetian, Muslim, Christian, child soldier, nobleman sold into slavery, mercenary, hero, but a man who has killed other men. No one could accuse him of being unworthy. Thus the trouble, Brabantio's quest for vengeance after being betrayed by his daughter, enters Othello's soul. For that time on, vulnerability appears in a personality whose defensive position of grandeur is not enough to block the narcissistic injuries. Iago has an impressive arsenal of motives—and no doubt unconscious homosexual desires that Shakespeare will exploit indirectly—to take Othello down with a fear of being cuckolded by Cassio; with his sexual desire for Desdemona; with his need for revenge against Othello who promoted Cassio to lieutenant instead of him …; all added to "a daily beauty in his [Cassio's] life" that makes Iago himself "ugly" (Act V, Scene I, 20, p. 364). The triumph of Iago entangled in his desires for Othello, Cassio, and Desdemona is in the final analysis that of absolute evil, because everyone who dies is innocent. This absolute evil is the epitome of jealousy—Othello and Cassio have what Iago wants—love and power and his jealousy evokes murder. The ultimate victory of the old senator Brabantio, who was the first to cast doubts on his daughter's fidelity, centers the Oedipus complex in this tragedy: Why would Desdemona be faithful to her husband if she was not faithful to her own father?

The Moorish sons of Othello: General Alexandre Dumas and Alexander Pushkin

Dumas's (1846) *The Count of Monte Cristo* is one among many examples in literature whose authors perpetuate the race, sex, jealousy, and power theme. This is the quintessential story of a Caribbean Othello, worthy son of the French Revolution. His cloak-and-dagger adventures are featured in *The Three Musketeers* (1844), and his triumphs and tribulations inspired *The Count of Monte Cristo*. Dumas was a dark-skinned mulatto, son of a French refugee nobleman, le Marquis Antoine Davy de la Pailleterie (born in 1762 in Jérémie, a town in Santo Domingo, now Haiti) and a Creole slave called Césette Dumas. Ruined after the slave uprisings that burned down the colonial plantations, the marquis was forced to sell his son and concubine in order to pay for his ticket home. When he got back to France, the aristocrat married the housekeeper of the family château. He inherited some money and brought his ten-year-old son to the capital, giving him the best education in the great fencing and music schools reserved for the French aristocratic élite.

Tall, handsome, and endowed with prodigious strength, the young Dumas joined the army at the time of the French Revolution. Although he was the son of a marquis and bore the rank of count, he dropped the aristocratic title in favor of his mother's surname—Dumas—and joined the lowest ranks of the army after separating from his father. Unanimously praised for his military prowess, Dumas was made a major-general in 1792. At the age of thirty-one, he commanded the 50,000-strong Italian army. Leading his men, he distinguished himself in military campaigns so that even his enemies considered him the greatest soldier of all time. Although covered in glory, Dumas continued to live by the sword and eventually became a threat to Napoleon himself.

Bonaparte's admiration for General Dumas, who had taught him the art of war, turned to rivalry during the French expedition to Egypt (1798–1801). The two men, who were ideological opponents, came to detest each other. Dumas, while returning to France after conquering Egypt, was shipwrecked. He was captured by the Italians, thrown into a dungeon for two years, tortured, and slowly poisoned. Ill, handicapped, and disgraced upon his return to France, he was decommissioned in 1802. The military pension of one of France's greatest military heroes was never paid, on Bonaparte's orders. Abandoned by those in power, General Dumas died in poverty at Villers-Cotterêts in 1806. His wife and two children were left destitute. The career of General Dumas must be viewed against that of his son, the novelist Alexandre Dumas, author of the famous *Count of Monte Cristo*. Alexandre's literary fate was symbolically inspired by the tribulations of his father's life. A moving literary testimony emerges from the permanent love connection between father and son.

Alexander Pushkin, poet of Russia, is yet another literary example. In his classical novel *The Brothers Karamazov* Fyodor Dostoyevsky wrote a magnificent tribute to Pushkin's insight: "Jealousy! 'Othello is not jealous, he is trusting' Pushkin observed, and that single observation alone bears witness to the extraordinary depth possessed by our great poet." Pushkin's observation is based on Othello's own opinion of himself as being "not easily jealous" although not denying that, like any human being, he could be prone to oedipal jealousy. When he starts to feel ensnared by Iago's convincing lies he demands motives and proof. Othello is afraid of his own madness, afraid that Iago's toxic allegations of Desdemona's adultery could transform him into a murderer (the ultimate destructiveness of jealousy). At this point Iago turns to elaborate deceits and constant lying, and the manufacturing of 'evidence' like Cassio's erotic dream with Desdemona:

> I lay with Cassio lately …
> In sleep I heard him say, *Sweet Desdemona,*
> *Let us be wary, let us hide our loves;*
> And then, sir, would he gripe and wring my hand,
> Cry, *O sweet creature!* and then kiss me hard,
> As if he pluck'd up kisses by the roots,
> That grew upon my lips; then laid his leg
> Over my thigh, and sigh'd, and kiss'd, and then
> Cried, *Cursed fate, that gave thee to the Moor.* (Act III, Scene III,
> 420–427, p. 308)

"O, monstruous, monstruous!" laments Othello as, prompted by Iago, he unconsciously experiences a homosexual attraction to Cassio. The irony of this is the transformation of a hero, an honest man, into an almost psychotic one possessed by Iago's emotion: murderous jealousy (S. A. Mitchell, 2000). In the tirade on the folly of man attributed to the cycle of the moon, we can appreciate the richness and the multiplicity of Shakespearian poetics:

> It is the very error of the moon;
> She comes more nearer earth than she was wont,
> And makes men mad. (Act V, Scene II, 111–113, p. 380)

When Othello yields to Iago's malevolent power, he feels desperately damned as he has lost both the good object and himself to a satanic figure. The play's cruel implication is that the discourse of redemption is futile:

> I do believe it, and I ask your pardon.
> Will you, I pray, demand that demi-devil
> Why he hath thus ensnar'd my soul and body? (Act V, Scene II, 300, p. 393)

"That demi-devil," Bradwood remarks of Othello's reference to Iago, and "blacker devil," Emilia's characterization of Othello, reveal that "to Iago have been transferred all the qualities normally associated with black men on the English stage" (cited in Pechter, 1999, p. 162). In Act III, Scene III (pp. 91–280), the dialogue between Iago and Othello shows the chiasmata mirroring of Iago's and Othello's status: both men split into internal and external selves are afraid of jealousy; Othello, asking to be exchanged for a sacrificial animal, a goat, is conscious of the deleterious effects on his soul of "such exsufficate and blown surmises." He tries to resist Iago's inferences about the sexual nature of Desdemona:

> 'Tis not to make me jealous,
> To say my wife is fair, feeds well, loves company,
> Is free of speech, sings, plays, and dances well;
> Where virtue is, these are more virtuous; (Act III, Scene III, 186–189, p. 294)

Shakespeare imagines a dramatic situation where Iago is not alone; he is supported by his tribe.

> Poor and content is rich, and rich enough;
> But riches fineless is as poor as winter
> To him that ever fears he shall be poor:—

> Good God, the souls of all my tribe defend
> From jealousy! (Act III, Scene III, 175–179, p. 293)

If Iago is guilty, so is the audience. Even after being stabbed by Othello, Iago does not properly act the scapegoat. We are left with the immortality of our transgressions: "I bleed, sir, but not killed" (Act V, Scene II, 287, p. 392). Othello and Desdemona are dead. The Bard suggests that Iago will not simply die for our sins; indeed he will never die.

The Moor's image haunted Pushkin. He referred frequently to his own African blood and his "Negro" temperament; his mother, Nadezda Osipovna Gannibal, was known as "la belle Créole." The poet perceived the tragedy of the Moor very personally by identifying with an ego ideal, his great-grandfather. When his own wife, beautiful and flirtatious, Natalya Pushkina, was courted by a handsome French officer from Alsace named George d'Antès, Pushkin, known for his jealous nature, challenged the man to a duel. Each of them was wounded. Pushkin received a gunshot in his abdomen. The greatest Russian poet died two days later, on February 10, 1837, at the age of thirty-seven.

Desdemona: from Shakespeare to Pushkin

"Othello was not jealous. On the contrary, he was trustful."

—A. Pushkin

> Ask Desdemona why her whim
> Did on her dusky Moor alight,
> As Luna fell in love with night?
> Like wind and erne, it is because
> A maiden's heart obeys no laws.
> Such is the poet: like the North,
> Whate'er he lists he carries forth,
> Wherever, eagle-like, he flies,
> Acknowledging no rule or owner,
> He finds a god, like Desdemona,
> For wayward heart to idolize.

—A. Pushkin, *Egyptian Nights, ch. II*

A literary character, Tcharsky is a thirty-year-old poet, heir to a small fortune, having had the misfortune to write. He is the alter ego of Alexander Pushkin, taking the lead role in the posthumous unfinished novel *Egyptian Nights* written by the Russian poet, two years before his death. An intertextual sign points out that in Shakespeare's *Othello*, Desdemona's lost handkerchief was given to Othello's mother by an Egyptian prophetess. Undoubtedly, the fatal duel for a mundane story of jealousy where Pushkin died from two bullet wounds in the groin resembles a worldly trap in which he was pushed by social class enemies. "*A poet has perished,*" wrote the poet Lermontov on the day of his passing. The tragic death of Pushkin at dawn on January 29, 1837, at the age of thirty-seven, is added to the martyrology of Russian poets who disappeared at an early age in massacre or riots or killed in a duel.

Tcharsky, a somewhat bitter figure, unhappy at the derisory appellation of *a man of letters*, proposes to an Italian artist traveling to St. Petersburg a meditation on the romantic theme of the freedom of creation. Inspired by his gradual social isolation, Tcharsky offers the aristocrat a literary manifesto: "*The poet himself should choose the subject of his songs; the crowd has not the right to direct his inspirations.*" (Pushkin, 1916). Responding to Tcharsky's incitement, the Italian wanderer improvised an ode to the fragile majesty of poetry in which he portrays Shakespeare's Desdemona as a muse. Upon listening to the verses recited by the Italian, Tcharsky took them from memory to have them translated by a friend and then remained "speechless, surprised and moved."

The incomplete novel is written under a constant change of register, poetry and prose entangled. Stylistic variations indicate an indefinite genre conducive to the potentialities of redoubling as a psychoanalytic figure of representation. Indeed, the couple Tcharsky–Italian improvisator, introduces other persona pairings: Desdemona as the Moon while the Moor personifies the night. An unexpected unconscious occurrence associates Desdemona with Natalia Goncharova, Pushkin's young wife, both unblemished teens at the time of their marriage with men much older who were avid for their immaculate purity and afflicted by the sensuous possession of a feminine figure. Although it has sacred, symbolic, and social constructs, virginity is conceptualized by contemporary scholars as a paradigm of sacrifice and mystery. In Roman antiquity, the transgression of virginity by a Vestal virgin was punishable by burial alive: "Remaining 'intact' before engaging in sexual activity reserved the full force of erotic energy for this anticipated event" (MacLachlan & Flechter, 2007).

The young nubile princesses ignite our perverse desire to witness their loss of sexual innocence, as they are ambivalent figures, in transition from *partheneia* (virginity) to *gyne* (female maturity). So powerful is the insight of great writers like Shakespeare and Pushkin that they continue to shed light on our human infirmities beyond the theater. Once fantasies of idyllic innocence are lost, we may declare: "I will not yield to sorrow."

In Pushkin's poem, the freedom of creation is entirely absorbed by the feminine transgression. *"A maiden's heart obeys no laws,"* a verse of the poem crystallizes the resistance of Desdemona metamorphosed into a new Antigone. The author's reflection leads to Desdemona because she manages to be inhabited by a passion so strong for the Moor that her whole being is exalted at the price of strong symbolization. Pushkin's literary thought is prolonged in two directions: the freedom of the artist posited as an absolute and the idealization of a polymorphic cosmic feminine object, but feared:

> *Every moment a vain object*
> *Makes your torment and seduces you*
>
> (ibid.)

The wind, the eagle, and the heart of the beautiful Desdemona powerfully open the way to the dynamics of subjectivation. *Self as the other* testifies to the loss of the configuration of the subject and opens up the possibility of observing other esthetic management of self-constitution. Desdemona's decomposition/recomposition as a moon or idol parallels the loss of identity. It is this self stylization that is offered as a model, or an obstacle to the poet. The reading of the poem confirms the discomforts felt in a round-trip between human and nonhuman characters which represent different ego-states, treasures from the wreck of the unbelievable, even if they are nonhuman.

Poetry abandons the safety of the mother tongue—in the novel, the poem is the object of a translation—like material beings transformed into timelessness. The poem creates thresholds, spaces of tension, intimate metamorphoses by organizing a network of associations. Desdemona has a plurality of beings. Now, these living mutations blend into the depth of the night, finding an image just right to represent Othello by the allegory that matches the color of his skin. Thus, these images of wind, moon, eagle, skin, or idol constitute transitional objects proposed to our senses under the effect of a slight "narcosis" as noted by Freud: "Nevertheless the mild narcosis induced in us by art can do no more than bring about a transient withdrawal from the pressure of vital needs, and it is not strong to make us forget real misery" (1930a, p. 80).

Representations participate in the process of differentiating between self and non-self, ego and non-ego. They possess the quality of a tangible anti-traumatic presence. While Desdemona embodies the virtues of gentleness, continuity, and consistency, she incarnates the firmness of her desire and the violence of her love for the Moor. She is the hostile object, the idol, the other, yet she is "the only power that helps" (Freud, ibid.). Now a poetic fragment has discreetly intercepted her desire and dictated to the reader the oceanic feeling (Romain Rolland) that invades Desdemona:

> Ask Desdemona why her whim
> Did on her dusky Moor alight,
> As Luna fell in love with night?

Pushkin uses the black night metaphor based on the conventional stereotype of the color of the ego-skin assimilated to moral darkness. In this passage, Desdemona's self-perception is expressed through the connection of the feeling she bears for the Moor, that "face" she sees in her thoughts. It is as if by writing the poem, Pushkin had completed his self-analysis through which he perceived the obscure key of the tragedy: Desdemona is not a traitor; Othello is not jealous; love is immortal.

The essence of fictional beings is to seduce us, to seduce our senses and our sense. They make us believe in their existence. In the theater more than elsewhere, since their representation is incarnated in the actors, they persuade us to lend them life. The being which we feel in ourselves is like every member of the human race; it asks to be understood. These beings, we judge them, we love them or hate them. However, they have another thickness, another texture, another density than the men with whom we trade, because they are poetic creations, truer than the creatures of the world.

The Othello complex: theorizing Shakespeare, from Desdemona's ego-skin to Othello's self-abjection

The *Othello complex* refers to a whole range of amorous and hostile desires that a black man feels for a white woman, the love of his life but of whose sincerity he is never sure. Positively, the black man arranges his personality into a false self in order to survive in white society at the price of a hysterical conversion. "I am not what I am," says Iago in Act I Scene I, underlining the difference between what he is and what he seems to be.

The line "I am not what I am" is a parody of the Lord's response to Moses's query on God's identity: "I am that I am" (Exodus 3:14). Iago's twisting of the words represents a subversive enactment of identity, in a sense the subject's uncertainty over its own identity, and one that applies paradoxically to its target, Othello. Honest Iago, master of language, shows us just how much words can wound as he uses them to transform the noble Moor into a blacker devil.

Shakespeare's *Othello, the Moor of Venice* (1622) displays the black man in all his glory, but the black man remains alienated, a stranger to himself. He cannot assimilate, no matter what he does. He may have been superficially converted to Western values that mask the archaic elements of his self, but yet he is acknowledged for his abilities as a vessel of Western hubris and the services he renders to white society. After making use of his talents as a military strategist the Council recalls him to Venice:

> Your power and your command is taken off,
> And Cassio rules in Cyprus. (Act V, Scene II, 330–331, p. 395)

While this rehabilitation by the political power of Venice is really a coronation for Cassio, for Othello it is a wound to his pride that can only lead to death. Negatively, the complex manifests the other way round, shaped by the two destructive modalities of totemism and traumatism. Paul Ricoeur (2008) had this comment on the Freudian theory of totemism and exogamy:

> In order to fill this gap, Freud posits at the origin of mankind a real Oedipus complex, an original parricide, of which all later bear the scar. The last essay, *Totem and Taboo*, works out a theory of totemism whose elements are borrowed from various sources and held together by an Oedipus complex projected into the prehistory of mankind.... According to Freud, the savage's belief in actual descent from the totem is the reason why he must not kill the totem (or what stands for it) or marry women of the same group; we recognize here the two major prohibitions of the Oedipus complex. (p. 205)

Freud's (1955c) memorandum on war neuroses, written after the end of World War I at the request of the Austrian government, formed the cornerstone of the scientific research that has lent so much support for classifying the concept of PTSD (post-traumatic stress disorder), that, at least since the Vietnam war and up to the present day, is underscored by the globalization of terrorism and human debris scattered by bombs in cities, airports, and streets. Freud's thinking had a profound impact on psychoanalytical theory. In *Beyond the Pleasure Principle*, Freud (1920g) introduced the concepts of "repetition compulsion" and "death drive" to account for the overwhelming trauma on the mind. For Freud,

> ... the immediate cause of all war neuroses was an unconscious inclination in the soldier to withdraw from the demands, danger-ous or outrageous to his feelings, made upon him by active service. Fear of losing his life, opposition to the command to kill other people, rebellion against the ruthless suppression of his own per-sonality by his superiors—these were the most important affective sources on which the inclination to escape from war was nourished. (pp. 212–213)

Like Othello, father of the horde, the black man is vulnerable to vic-timization, premature aging, and psychic and mental illnesses includ-ing epilepsy, drug abuse, schizophrenia, paranoia, and depression, due to the frequent antecedents of repeated physical and psychic traumas (chronic PTSD and multiple microaggressions) suffered since early childhood. Always battling to defend himself against another clan or against himself, he confronts feelings of impotence, imperfection, and incompetence which are only partially compensated by the grandeur that does not quite glorify him. He draws on his powerful but enslaved body, while at the same time rejecting it by an abomination process that might be called self-abjection (Kristeva, 1982). His savagery[2]—showing metaphorically that he is not quite human—can surface at any moment.

Despite power, authority, or success, black men with higher social status are vulnerable to hostile introjected objects relating to envy and sexual jealousy. Melanie Klein (1957) distinguishes jealousy from envy. Jealousy involves projection mechanisms and requires the presence of a third party who wins the favors of the object of desire, favors that the subject fears he will lose. Envy, on the other hand, results from a destructive introjection of hostile forces intended to destroy the object of desire. Jealousy is addressed at the object, while envy is primarily a kind of death narcissism. These affects inherited from the progress of negativism lead to self-rejection and a self-destruction which leads to an incomplete "integration" of antagonistic aspects of the object and of the ego. In the paranoid-schizoid position, the ego is vulnerable to anni-hilation by the bad object(s). The Kleinian (ibid.) concept of integration has theoretical and social applications as it stands at the basis of human destructiveness. Othello starts as a good integrated ego-object, a noble and honest hero, close to his men, generous and valiant, but through active disintegration turns back into the bad object, the absolute Other, the questionable origin that he has never stopped representing.

Because there is no consummation, the sexual frenzy he promises the white woman makes her willing to sacrifice and betray the patriarchal status. The aim to save him from himself in exchange for sexual grati-fication is an illusion. The black man, incapable of keeping this prom-ise of gratification, cannot escape from his tragic destiny. His body is a powerful fetish that allows the white woman to displace her incestuous sexual desire for her father onto a black body, more exotic and less guilt-inducing. From that perspective which is not related only to skin color, a black woman, who has acquired the values of white society, plays the same role as a white woman. But the cleavage between sexual desire and amorous desire is perfectly well perceived by an omniscient Iago. Although Desdemona's amorous desire is fixed on Othello, a clone of her father in terms of rage, violence, and age difference, her sexual desire actually settles on Cassio, who she keeps trying to rehabilitate even at the expense of her marital intimacy and at the risk of provoking Othello's wrath.

Didier Anzieu (1989) relies on Freudian principles in stating: "Every physical function develops by supporting itself upon a bodily func-tion whose working it transposes on the mental plane" (p. 99). If the ego is initially formed by the experience of touch, the original form of communication is direct, unmediated from skin to skin. In the cases of faces where the histology of both touching skins is different or where the softer, finer, suppler black skin leaves a trace, what happens to the white infant and the black maternal object represented by his nanny? Desdemona's nanny was called Barbary.[3] She was a black woman, an African servant who surrounded Desdemona with hugs, song, lan-guage, generous and intimate ways, evident from the way she held and rocked the child. The charm of black skin, for her, therefore, has a whiff of melancholy and abandonment. Encrypted feelings and emotions, conducive to maternal reverie are equivalent to the "container" according to Bion (1962) and to "holding" according to Winnicott (1960).

The black woman, Barbary, had been in love with a man and her love had driven him mad and made him leave her. Thus abandoned, Barbary died. When Desdemona sings the "Willow Song," a lullaby she learned from Barbary, Desdemona identifies with the nanny who was her dead mother and thus prepares herself for death. We can understand the story of Desdemona partly as a morbid repetition, but also as a hyper-cathexis of the black skin of her nanny, the preoedipal primary maternal object whose loss she tries to subsume into the masculine black skin of Othello. She is no less than the warrior asking to leave for the front for her honeymoon, the idealized prophetess. "Oh my fair warrior," Othello describes her (Act II, Scene I, 178, p. 252), "our great captain's captain" says Cassio (Act II, Scene I, 74, p. 245). She has become the sacred icon, object of worship, the immaculate receptacle of an embalmed adoration.

Desdemona is the essence of pure ecstasy, unpossessed by Othello. Like a priestess, Desdemona is the Vestal Virgin of Ancient Rome (MacLachlan & Fletcher, 2007) who transgressed chastity so she can become the sacrificially perfect victim, the scapegoat of a social conflict of race, power, and sex. Heiress of a lost handkerchief given to Othello's mother by a gypsy and which symbolizes the hymen, Desdemona knows things about memory and desire. The drive theory—the libido is withdrawn from the object and available for the death drive—allows us to conclude that the sexual consummation with Othello is a moment of impossibility. Othello is in spiritual thrall to a phallic mother who gave him a magic handkerchief, a talisman woven of silk and the blood of virgins. This sexual moment, incestuous for both Desdemona and Othello, constantly interrupted by the war between the Turks and the Venetians and the fighting between the Venetians themselves, is one where idolatrous adoration should give way to desire and its object. The impossible embrace (the wedding night that we are never sure took place) dampens Othello's raging desire and strips away the fantasies of deflowering, rape, prostitution, and murder that plague him. Descending from the heavenly angels and virginal creatures to the hollow of the marriage bed, the loved one becomes a demon and a whore.

Othello's hell is the only one that is sure, as he is impelled "to a purity that the posture of *death* guarantees" (Kristeva, 1982, p. 27).

The Othello complex plays a fundamental role in our understanding of the worldwide phenomenon of racism against blacks, negatively cathected as the receptacles of primitive aggression and repudiated aspects of the ego. Paleontology, genetic biology, and modern anthropology are all in agreement that African blacks are the fathers of humanity; this is the widely accepted theory of humanity's first diaspora, called "Out of Africa."

As a result, racism can be understood as compulsive repetition, marching through history from the murder of the father of the primitive horde by his sons who then spurn the parricide, guiltily renounce the women who belonged to him, and become homosexuals. To paraphrase Freud's comment on the Oedipus complex that inspired it, we say that "Every new arrival on this planet is faced with the task of mastering the 'Othello' complex," a complex that is more archaic, original, but just as intelligible and structuring. The issue then becomes one of the universality of the psychoanalytical discourse. Although the Jews have managed to survive and dominate certain spheres of human activity despite anti-Semitism, the blacks have internalized racism and continue to self-destruct in a world dominated by "matriarchs with balls" and absent pseudo-fathers. It is worth noting the continuity between the first manifestations of racist fascination for the play, *Othello*, and the modern and postmodern versions of that same fascination that contaminate the critics and influence the way we read it now—reducing it to a domestic affair of a missing magic cloth and murderous conjugal jealousy.

Thomas Rymer, historiographer in the seventeenth century, called Shakespeare's tragedy "a bloody farce without salt or savour" (1693, p. 146) and thought it was unbelievable and scandalous that a black man could become a general in the army of the Most Serene Republic of Venice and marry a young noblewoman, daughter of a senator, without her parents' consent. Blinded by racism, Rymer ignored the fact that the Moors were the civilizing light of medieval Europe due to the culture, art, translations, and science they helped disseminate throughout the continent, starting in Andalusia. And the historical truth is that for over four centuries, over two million Europeans were raided by the Moors—from the Italian coasts to Ireland—and taken as slaves to Mauritania, which is the land running from Egypt to Morocco and the south of Spain.

CHAPTER EIGHT

Portrayals of jealousy in cinema

Greg Zeichner

Within schools of psychoanalytic thought, jealousy is described as either a delusion or normal and inherent in all people. Either way, it is a dysfunction that everyone is confronted with in their lives and can resist or succumb to it. Because we all identify with this problem, films about jealousy, even if they are badly acted or made, will usually resonate in some way with viewers. Most good films about jealousy portray it as an irresistible force. Owing to this narrative purpose, viewers can see characters act in ways they might not in real life and even take a guilty pleasure in watching the characters being affected by situations and consequences that they themselves would not get into. Four films are covered here for the complex and interesting methods and results of the way they tackle the subject. Several schools of thought have impressions of what jealousy is, but most take the view of Klein (1957) in that jealousy is based on envy (a relation between two people) yet involves a relation between three or more people, where the jealous person feels deprived of the second person by the third person. They can show up together frequently as situations become more complex. These phenomena are believed to be rooted in unresolved childhood trauma. Kaplan and Saddock (1985) define jealousy as something every child suffers from when a third person (father or sibling) intrudes between the self and the mother. The occurrence of pathological jealousy in adult life is related to the lack of resolution of this early childhood attachment.

Films with a jealous female protagonist

Play Misty for Me *(1971)*

This movie was actor Clint Eastwood's directorial debut. An atmospheric thriller, it is filmed in the quiet seaside town of Carmel, California, which is a key element in setting the film's mood. Eastwood plays Dave Garver—a philandering disc jockey at a local radio station. While hosting his show, he receives frequent calls over time from a female listener requesting he play the jazz song "Misty," by Earl Garner. While having a drink at a bar with his friend the bartender (played by veteran Hollywood director, Don Siegel, who directed Eastwood in *Dirty Harry*, also released in 1971), he meets a woman named Evelyn Draper (played by Jessica Walter), who claims she was stood up. She then reveals this is not true, she was really waiting for him and she has been the caller who always requests the song, "Misty." They have a one night stand that evening—business as usual for Dave until she shows up the next day at his place with groceries—obviously expecting a serious relationship with him. He tries to draw boundaries, but continues to sleep with her even though she continues to exhibit obsessive and clingy behavior that reflects her great fear of abandonment. Dave starts to grasp the seriousness of the situation when Evelyn displays abrupt mood swings. We don't know what type of psychosis she suffers from and why, but it is clear that the trigger for it is jealousy: When others vie for Dave's attention, even in trivial matters, such as a neighbor complaining to Dave to keep the noise down, Evelyn's mood shifts to one of extreme anger and she screams profanities at the person who is the source of the intrusion. He can tell that she suffers some type of mental disorder but since it seems for the moment to be a simple love

PORTRAYALS OF JEALOUSY IN CINEMA   133

obsession (and he enjoys the sex), he does not take any drastic measures. Meanwhile, he learns that his ex-girlfriend, an attractive and intelligent sculptor named Tobie (played by Donna Mills) is back in town. She had left him because of his philandering ways, and had been avoiding him since returning to town. They talk and she admits that she left because she was jealous of the other women he was seeing. This is the complete opposite of Evelyn and the way she deals with her jealousy. Tobie even tells Dave that she hated being jealous, therefore she was aware and had enough consciousness to see that jealousy is dysfunctional and creates a painful state of being. Dave wants to commit to her and agrees to end his philandering, and though she is not yet ready to get back together with him, he agrees to wait until she is. Meanwhile, Evelyn continues to stalk and harass Dave, even stealing his car keys at one point. He has had enough and breaks up with her. Upon hearing this, she begs and pleads, "You don't love me anymore," and then says, "It's about that bitch in the photo on your dresser" (referring to Tobie). He says he never lied to her. They then scream at each other and he leaves. She immediately calls him, frantically apologizing. He hangs up. Next day, as he's hanging out with Tobie in the park, we see, as the camera pulls back, that Evelyn is standing up on the hill in the woods.[1] Now Tobie is the object causing Evelyn's jealousy; the movie now turns into a straight-up horror/suspense film. In a big plot twist, Evelyn shows up at Dave's expecting him to be with Tobie, but Dave is alone. She frantically apologizes, talks about love, to which Dave says, "You don't have the vaguest idea of what love is." This so greatly shames her that she attempts suicide in his bathroom. Tobie makes plans over the phone with Dave but then Evelyn awakes from a nightmare in which Dave watched her drown and didn't help. She is terrified of being alone. He stays with her, thus standing up Tobie. He must feel guilt at her suicide attempt and fears that she will try it again. This goes unappreciated as the next day she shows up at an important business meeting Dave is having with an elderly lady who is runs a radio show in San Francisco. She accuses the woman of being a tramp and sabotages Dave's planned career partnership. From here she ransacks Dave's home, stabs his maid, tries to kill him, and then murders a police sergeant while holding Tobie hostage in her home. She uses Tobie as bait for Dave while threatening to mutilate the parts of Tobie's face that she thinks Dave likes. She also destroys a painting Tobie made of Dave. Once Dave arrives he kills her in self-defense while rescuing Tobie.

Play Misty for Me is a classic story of jealousy being an irresistible force. Adler (1928) says jealousy can be recognized in the mistrust and preparation of ambushes for others, the critical measurement of one's fellows, and in the constant fear of being neglected. This is shown from Evelyn's behavior at the beginning of the film and scattered through-out. Once the love triangle is established with Tobie, Evelyn's jealousy escalates into murderous acts. What makes this film even more inter-esting is that Tobie is shown to be jealous as well. She admits it as the reason for leaving Dave, though in doing so, she shows that she is a mature person. She has what Freud (1922b) refers to as "grade-one jealousy" which is normal since she acknowledges and deals with it, whereas Evelyn exhibits "delusional jealousy" which is grade three. She also shows envy as well (generally described as being between two people), when she destroys Dave's objects and also destroys him in a symbolic manner, in the form of the portrait painting she cuts up in front of Tobie, when she reveals her identity to her. The filmmaking is top-notch and proved Eastwood's talent as director. The suspense is created from the contrast of the beautiful seaside locations coupled with dark lighting and lack of music during the tense scenes—it relies mainly on location sounds and abrupt editing.

There is even a scene filmed at the 1970 Monterey Jazz Festival featuring prolonged footage of jazz greats Cannonball Adderley and Joe Zawinul. It's different in tone from the rest of the film—almost like the director understood the strong effect the subject matter has on the viewer and was giving them a rest period before escalating the third act towards the denouement. The inability of Evelyn to resist her jealousy is frightening to watch and makes her a great film villain. We see her rapid mood swings—from joy to fury and then to begging. While the film does not explain the origin of Evelyn's condition—surely some type of psychotic disorder like bipolar disorder or schizophrenia—it notes that her condition is brought on by her jealousy and fear of abandonment.

Disclosure *(1994)*

Disclosure is a film containing both sexual jealousy and workplace jealousy. It is a suspense drama film directed by Barry Levinson—of *Diner* (1982) and *Rain Man* (1988) fame—and based on best-selling author Michael Crichton's novel released earlier the same year. Starring Michael Douglas, it capitalized on Douglas's smash hit *Basic Instinct*

(1992) released two years earlier, which also portrays sexual jealousy. In the film, Michael Douglas plays Tom Sanders, a chauvinistic chief of manufacturing at the large technology company, DigiCom, headquartered in Seattle. He is expecting a promotion, but there are technical problems with the company's new product—a computer hard drive—which may delay the release date, for which he will be held accountable. Due to this and other internal politics, he is passed over for the promotion and the job is given to Meredith Johnson (played by Demi Moore). It turns out that Meredith was his ex-lover with whom he broke off before he got married to another woman. Almost immediately upon starting the new position, she summons him to her office after hours and attempts to seduce him. He mentions that he has settled down and shows her pictures of his family, to which she reacts by offering disparaging comments about his wife's appearance. She then escalates the situation and through reenacting their mutual history of enjoyment of aggressive sex, she succeeds in the seduction though he stops it before they are about to have intercourse which insults her. Angrily spurned, she threatens him and the next day she tells the CEO, Bob Garvin (played by Donald Sutherland), that he sexually abused her. Garvin offers Tom relocation to an office in Texas, but this will cause him to lose his stock options and career advancement. Tom refuses and to everyone's surprise, he counterattacks by suing Meredith for sexual harassment and bringing in a notorious muckraking reporter to attract publicity to the case. Tom thinks Meredith will be forced by Garvin to retract her accusations as the company is in the process of a merger and IPO and negative publicity from a court case such as this will jeopardize the deal. Once this back and forth happens, instead of backing down, Meredith uses her new power at the company to fight back. The case goes to mediation and while Meredith continues to lie about what happened, Tom ends up looking bad. It is brought up and proved that Tom is chauvinistic and touchy-feely with his female subordinates and also did not tell his wife that he was meeting Meredith late at night. His wife is present at the mediation and jealousy is first mentioned explicitly when Tom says that his wife is jealous regarding the subject of his past girlfriends. Lucky for Tom, he is able to receive from a friend a voice mail recording made at the time of the incident that proves that Meredith's accusations are false. With this battle lost, Meredith tries to sabotage Tom's career by locking him out of the computer system and plans to blame him for the technical faults of the new hard drive at an upcoming press conference which would guarantee his dismissal. It turns out that Meredith is really to blame. She was previously an executive in DigiCom's operations department and ordered reductions and cut corners on the making of the hard drive in order to slash costs. She deletes the files that contain this information, but Tom is able to obtain a backup of the files from a friend in another office. At a press conference he exposes them, exonerating himself and getting Meredith fired in the process.

What makes *Disclosure* such an interesting film is that it portrays an admixture of career jealousy, romantic jealousy, and gender jealousy. When the film came out in 1994, critics and viewers alike were polarized by the issues of gender rights covered in the story, especially that of role reversal: a woman being chosen to head a technical department over a man with many years' experience on the subject, also a man suing a woman for sexual harassment. Issues of gender rights are on the surface, but the film is about romantic jealousy, plain and simple.

Meredith is jealous of Tom's wife and son—his family is the obstacle to his sexual attention. When Tom admits to his lawyer that the reason for not telling his wife that he was meeting Meredith after work is because sometimes she is jealous about his past relationships, it adds the element of the third person. This is the love jealousy. The triangle is Tom, and his wife, and Meredith, who is jealous that this wife has her ex-boyfriend and has gotten him to settle down. She cannot resist being jealous and retaliates by insulting the wife in and outside of her presence.

The career jealousy has the triangle of Sanders and Meredith and Garvin. He is jealous of her for her career position—she is the obstacle between him and Garvin's attention. This could also be seen as envy on his part in the sense that the promotion is an object that he feels he should have gotten. But Tom has been rejected by Garvin, and Meredith was chosen. His previous sexual history with her, coupled with the aforementioned love jealousy makes this instance of jealousy compounded and complex for Tom and drives him to take massive action and adopt a strategy in order to avoid total career annihilation if he loses this battle. The gender jealousy takes place in the realm of societal norms. Menninger (1938) says unconscious hate shown by people towards one whom they think they love can be caused by unconscious envy. In the case of women, it is the unbearable humiliation they feel in having to play the societally passive female role.

In Meredith's case it is both: she loved Tom and he rejected her. In the meantime, she has advanced in her career, but she is a female executive in the male-dominated tech sector. While there have been advances in the twenty-one years since the film's release on the issue of having more women in upper management at corporations, it has not been resolved enough to make the film appear dated today.

Films with a jealous male protagonist

Possession *(1981)*

This film was directed by the Polish filmmaker, Andrzej Zulawski, and stars Sam Neill as Mark and Isabelle Adjani as Anna. They play a couple who have a young son but suspect each other of cheating; the relationship is in trouble at the start. This is a very interesting film as it blends the genres of drama with supernatural horror but does not pick one exclusively. The film is very well made and the actors give histrionic performances, coupled with wide handheld shots that create a setting of claustrophobia. *Possession* was shot in the Kreutzberg area of Berlin in 1980 which, at that time, adjoined the Berlin Wall. There are many burnt-out and abandoned buildings on display from the communist era adding to the bleakness of the film and giving it a frightening sense of decay and despair. The film has had a polarizing effect on viewers over the years and still enjoys a cult following thirty-four years later. Jealousy is the cause of nearly all the bizarre events and behaviors from the characters.

The film opens as Mark, who is employed as a government spy, quits his job to spend more time with his wife, Anna, and their young son, Bob. This was not a good idea, as he finds out that Anna has a lover; he tries to find out who it is. As Mark is cuckolded, his jealousy greatly affects his ego: He wants to know graphic details about the affair, like where they have sex, and if she prefers the lover to him (she says she does). He meets her in a café and tells her he will agree not to see their son anymore, and physically attacks her when she tells him she wishes they never had a son together. He demands that she leave the lover or he will kick her out of the apartment. He cares for her and the family as a unit. Later, the lover calls and tells Mark that Anna will be staying with him for good. Mark drops his son off at school and notices that his son's teacher, Helen, looks just like Anna (also played by Adjani). We, the audience, are unsure at this point if this is a hallucination on his part. He confronts the lover, an older German man named Heinrich, who immediately tries to befriend him. He says that he suffers too, and reveals that the affair has been going on for a year. Mark looks around every inch of Heinrich's apartment, his jealousy driving him to size up and understand why this lover was chosen over him and therefore changed Anna. In the bedroom, he stares at the bed where the sex takes place. Heinrich asks Mark whether at that point in time when they first spoke on the phone, sex was good between the two of them, because at that time, Anna and he had achieved great sexual harmony. Heinrich's elderly mother shows up and Mark quickly learns that this woman is ever-present in the apartment, even when Heinrich and Anna have sex. Mark attacks Heinrich when he learns this but gets beaten up. Heinrich is very affectionate towards Mark at this point—almost mothering him. It is most likely a combination of pity and his own jealousy, as Mark was the original lover, has been with Anna longer, and they have a son together.

Back at his apartment, Mark learns that Anna has been lying to him about where she has been. She said she was with her friend Margie, but she wasn't, nor was she at Heinrich's; she has been lying to both Mark and her lover. She is offended and slaps him, to which he says, "You care!" He then slaps her around, and she runs out of the house and attempts suicide by trying to get hit by a car. Anna seems to do everything out of anger and not sadness—seemingly in a way to punish Mark or herself. Mark needs to know where Anna has been going; he hires a private eye to follow her. He feels shut out because she won't tell him things. She claims she's afraid he won't like her if she does tell him and then she cuts herself with an electric knife, perhaps wanting to be rescued by him. He cuts himself as well.

Later, the private eye tracks her to a dilapidated building on Sebastianstrasse, where he finds her with a bloody inhuman-looking monster in one of the rooms. Unique to this film, this creature is a physical manifestation of Anna's own anger and jealousy. She then kills the private eye for viewing it. At this point, the film is clearly in the horror genre and mostly stays so until the end. Heinrich confronts Mark and says he wants to discuss their love triangle and have a sexual contest between the three of them. He is clearly jealous and feeling despair that Anna is now shutting him out and not talking to him either. Mark begins an affair with Helen and they argue about their interpretations of what freedom is. He is envious that women have freedom to do what they want sexually with anyone. She says, "To you, freedom seems evil," at which he reveals that he is angry with women and feels at war with them. Clearly he resents how easy and quick it is for women to find sexual partners and wishes it were the case for him. They sleep together but it is not passionate.

Meanwhile, the private eye has a homosexual lover who notices he is missing, finds out the address of Anna's other apartment from Mark, and goes there to find Anna. When he gets there, Anna shows him the monster and tells him that she has been having sex with it. He sees his lover's dead body, and tries to shoot her; however, she kills him with his own gun. Later, Anna is with Mark and she tells him that she had a miscarriage. This accident is shown in graphic detail in a flashback where she is in an empty subway station and screaming and bleeding out various colored fluids. She says she "miscarried" faith and what was left is chance, making that past event one of symbolism. Heinrich is looking for Anna and gets the Sebastianstrasse address from Mark. He goes and finds the monster and body parts that Anna has hidden in the refrigerator. She stabs him but he escapes. He contacts Mark and meets him in a nearby bar. Mark doesn't believe the story about the monster and kills Heinrich in the bathroom stall, making it look like an accident. He then goes to Anna's apartment and burns it down. Coming home, he finds Margie murdered, possibly by Anna. He has sex with Anna who tells Mark that Margie was trying to take their son, Bob, away and that Bob needs protection. He tries to cover up the murder and then later finds Anna at Margie's apartment having intercourse with the monster which he has never seen before. She says "Almost, almost" while having sex with the creature, possibly to make Mark more jealous by letting him know that the monster is bringing her close to orgasm which he has not been able to do. The monster is a symbol of her unattainable orgasm in addition to her jealous ego. While returning to Margie's apartment they encounter Mark's former employers and also a police team who engage in a shootout with Mark. He is now in a high speed chase and ends up at the top of a staircase in a building where Anna is. The monster has now evolved into a double of Mark. Mark tries to shoot the double but the police are at the bottom of the stairs and shoot all of them, though the monster is unhurt. Anna then shoots herself and the double says to Mark, "So hard to live with it, eh brother?" The monster escapes and Mark jumps to his death.

The final scene in the film is with Bob at home with Helen. There is a knocking at the door and he says not to open it. He then runs upstairs and drowns himself in the bathtub. Helen is standing with her back to the front door and it is shown that Mark's double is on the other side. There are sounds of thunder and her eyes glow. In this final scene, it is vague how much of it is actually taking place in grounded reality so one can assume the characters and events here are symbolisms of jealousy and envy.

Possession is a very interesting film as it is all over the place, combining elements of different genres making it complex and difficult to pin down in terms of genre and explicit meaning. It asks more questions than it answers, and confounds most viewers. Yet when understanding that this is a film about jealousy, all these seemingly disjointed elements actually make a lot of sense and the more cryptic situations and characters in the film can be seen as symbols even though this is not explained outright. For example, the monster really is a physical manifestation of Anna's rage. The fact that it exists in the real world is interesting because we see how it affects the other characters. While Heinrich, Mark, and the private eyes acknowledge that it is a supernatural unexplainable horror phenomenon, their behavior in its presence indicates they understand that it is a representation of Anna's inner psyche. While Mark is clearly the most jealous character, the film also sets up several jealous love triangles and then throws and layers in extra characters and situations to make it more interesting. For example, the jealousy triangle between mother, father, and child (Mark threatening to take Bob away and also Bob being taken away from Mark) is compounded by the introduction of the character of Helen—the lookalike of Anna who is Bob's teacher. She exists in the narrative because of Bob and serves the narrative purpose of a more docile version of Anna once Mark starts an affair with her. When Mark's former bosses (whom he rejected at the beginning of the film to spend more time with his son) appear at the end chasing him, it shows that they are jealous that Mark was taken away from them because of his son. While it's questionable that this even takes place in reality (more likely it takes place in Mark's mind as projected jealousy), it is up to the viewer to decide whether it is or not, which makes for a more enriching viewing experience.

The Room *(2003)*

This is an independent film written by, directed by, and starring Tommy Wiseau. It is a drama concerning a love triangle between an engaged couple and the groom-to-be's best friend that takes place in San Francisco. It portrays the jealousy and tragic events following the infidelity of the bride-to-be. The main character is Johnny (played by Wiseau) who has a moderately successful career in finance. The film opens with Johnny buying his fiancée Lisa a dress. He gives it to her and they are about to have sex when Denny (a teenager who Johnny knows) wants to watch the couple have sex, but is sad when they don't let him. It is explained that Johnny had at one time wanted to adopt Denny once he turned eighteen, but couldn't, so he pays Denny's rent and acts as a father figure to him. Afterwards, Lisa's mother shows up. Lisa tells her that she doesn't love Johnny because he is boring. She arranges to meet with Johnny's best friend Mark and seduces him. Meanwhile, Johnny is passed over for an important promotion at work. Denny gets involved with a drug dealer, then confesses to Johnny that he loves Lisa. There is a definite theme of oedipal jealousy in this aspect of the story. Lisa makes up a lie that Johnny hit her in order to justify her guilt about not wanting Johnny anymore. Johnny overhears Lisa telling her mother about the affair she just had with Johnny's friend, Mark. Mark begins to feels guilty. A psychologist friend who is told about the infidelity figures out Mark is the cheater. Lisa is really selfish and unable to love. She sleeps with Mark again. Lisa's mother tells her daughter to stay with Johnny. Her mother has the old-fashioned attitude that men and women abuse each other, and financial security is what matters in marriage, not love. Lisa lies to Johnny and tells him she's pregnant. A birthday party is thrown for Johnny during which he happily announces the pregnancy to the guests, without knowing it is untrue. Lisa then fools around with Mark at the party in front of Johnny. Spurned, he gets in a brawl with Mark, who says Lisa wouldn't have cheated on Johnny if he was able to satisfy her. Mark has gotten attached to Lisa though previously he rejected her, not wanting to betray his friend. Later, on the phone, Mark tells Lisa to ditch Johnny—that he doesn't like him anymore. Afterwards, Johnny plays a secretly recorded tape he made of this conversation to Lisa, confronting her. He cries that he treated her like a princess when they first got together seven years earlier. This is a brutal scene: The audience reacts to the jealousy and betrayal aspects even though the acting is overdone. Johnny destroys the room while remembering good times with Lisa, then he shoots himself. Mark and Lisa find his body and Mark rejects Lisa, blaming her for Johnny's death. A really dark ending.

The Room is a typical jealousy story with a love triangle. The sub-plot with the teenager Denny is interesting as it shows he is jealous of Johnny, because he is in love with Lisa. Because of his youth and naiveté, he asks them if he can watch while they have sex. Goleman (1995) says jealousy is a negative comparison between oneself and others. This results not from some external event, but from the emergence of a cognitive skill—comparing oneself with others, which occurs when one enters the social world of school around age five, where multiple qualities of people such as popularity, height, appearance, talents are seen for the first time. This is what makes *The Room* sustain its popularity to this day after languishing in obscurity for years. It now enjoys a huge cult following. The budget for the film was several million dollars, some of which was spent on a billboard advertisement that stayed on Sunset Boulevard in Los Angeles for several years. Eventually, a few Los Angeles residents saw the film out of curiosity because of the billboard (it was composed of a bizarre picture of director Wiseau) and its notoriety spread through word-of-mouth. The acting is overdone, and the dialogue and writing is bad as well—to the point of unintentional humor. These days the film plays midnight screenings around the United States with the actors in attendance. Those in the audience frequently know the lines by heart and interact with the film. It is touted as one of the worst films ever made and this has brought it endearment. The question is: Why is this film so popular? There are hundreds of films made every year with bad acting and poor technique, and they are forgotten about or never seen. It is most likely because of its theme of jealousy that it so resonates with the audience and propels this film into its own experience and genre.

Synthesis and conclusion

In addition to their narrative styles, these four films have their own unique cinematic methods by which they depict jealousy on the screen. Typically in cinema, when a character is shown to be suffering or dealing with a strong emotion (jealousy in this case), more unusual techniques for placement of the camera, editing, and score will be employed to heighten the emotion in order to resonate with the audience's personal experiences and provoke empathy. In these films, the directors' choices in settings, cinematography, editing, and musical score / sound design are used to give life to the characters' sufferings from jealousy and stimulate the audiences' knowledge and realization of their own dealings with jealousy. The characters in these four films are trapped by the force of jealousy, and in the narrative their surroundings are made into arenas of suffering. Each film has a certain technique in the way it goes about showing this.

Play Misty for Me is nearly devoid of non-diegetic music, using mostly silence and natural sounds to build the suspense of the narrative. The sweeping aerial views of the Carmel landscape, its parks, and Pacific coastline would in a different film appear as images of joy and beauty, but in this context create a wide open empty space of despair and fear which the three major characters (who all suffer in some way) are trapped within. None of them escapes the town—the one chance is when Dave gets interviewed for the job in San Francisco but that opportunity is sabotaged by Evelyn. Evelyn is the character who suffers the most from jealousy as the force she cannot conquer. Over the course of the film, as the events escalate, this force becomes greater. Cinematic techniques like "choppy" editing and use of the zoom lens show how her behavior transitions from seeming acts of affection into sociopathic acts and murder, towards the film's denouement.

Disclosure uses a similar technique of space. In a different film, the setting of the historical Pioneer Square neighborhood of downtown Seattle and the rustic beauty of nearby Bainbridge Island would be pleasant, but not in this portrayal. Instead, the ferry commute from his family home on the island to the city is used as a tool of suffering for Tom—it isolates him from his home; he can easily miss the ferry and be late for work, and when onboard it he is stuck listening to peers and coworkers who are jealous of him and warn him of approaching retributions. In the case of Meredith, who is the most jealous character in the film, the beautiful historic building in which she is now a boss has wide open modern windows where one can see everyone at all times. There are few shots if any where the camera or contents of the room are not placed in a diagonal position where they are covered on the top and sides by other workers, hallways, doors, and other windows all able to look in. It's a deliberately intrusive non-private workplace where all emotions and doings are exposed, in a way somewhat similar to Hitchcock's *Rear Window* (1954). Meredith, with her new power, is enabled to keep a close watch on people, and take action against them as she pleases, especially Tom, who is the object of her jealous rage. The musical score by Ennio Morricone is scary and suspenseful and uses both orchestra and electric guitar elements blended together. It is a throwback to some of the high emotions in his "Spaghetti Western"[2] scores in some parts. Its effects are subtle and it is one of the maestro's more underrated film scores.

In *Possession*, the cinematography utilizes wide angles shot with a fast and smooth moving camera, following actors through large rooms and sometimes handheld or moving from a car. These shots are even more intense than those in *Play Misty for Me*, as they give the impression that the characters are constantly trying to escape their surroundings. It shows the emotional affects of jealousy on Mark as he paces or runs around different ugly surroundings and is essentially helpless as Anna has no intention of giving up her infidelity. Adding to this effect is the great creative decision to shoot in the Kreutzberg area of Berlin. When the film was shot there in 1980, the landscape was still war damaged, burned out, and the Berlin Wall covered with graffiti was frequently in view. This scenery adds to the bleakness of the story and pretty much guarantees the viewer that there will not be a happy ending to the film.

The Room, while not a great example of cinematic technique, seems to have the bleakest ending of all these films as the main character cannot overcome his jealousy and commits suicide. The progression of the narrative is unsettling: You don't really see the suicide coming—it seemed like he would still be able to somehow move on even after all the trauma. At least in the other films there was some slight degree of hope or transcendence at the end in some way.

These films all show jealousy as an irresistible force. Whether it is overcome at the end of the stories or not, it controls and destroys the lives of the characters while it is present. A normal and ubiquitous emotion, as noted by Freud (1922b) and others after him, it has been experienced by everyone at some point and most can empathize with the tragedy that it is one of the most destructive human emotions. Therefore, when translated to cinema, the result, desired or not, revered or not, is usually memorable in some way.

PART III

CLINICAL REALM

CHAPTER NINE

Retroactive jealousy

Jack Novick and Kerry Kelly Novick

We were introduced to the term "retroactive jealousy" when a patient, whom we will call John, said in his first session that he was suffering from it. He had looked it up on the internet and found many links addressing this predicament in men and women of all ages. John described several examples of his retroactive jealousy. The most vivid involved his first sexual experience at the age of fifteen, when his parents had taken the whole family to another country on their sabbatical journey. John became involved with a schoolmate. After they became sexually active, she told him that, a year earlier, she had been assaulted in a date rape situation. Young John reacted with rage and wanted to find her assailant to beat him up. Twenty-five years later, John still thought of this girl and her assailant numerous times daily, and was filled with jealousy and rage. He realized that this was irrational but he couldn't stop himself.

A different man, "Bill," described a similar preoccupation about a coworker who talked of her promiscuous adolescence as something she was now leaving behind in view of her upcoming marriage. He was plagued with imagining what her new husband would feel when he learned of his wife's past; he knew that he would find it unbearable.

"Zeb's" wife admitted to him that she had been attracted to another young man before they were married (Novick & Novick, 2004). We didn't have the vocabulary of "retroactive jealousy" when we wrote about Zeb, but the term fits his experience of torment and turmoil about something that never eventuated in action and took place fifty years earlier. Zeb also showed "prospective jealousy" in his compulsive fantasy that he would predecease his wife and she would take up with another man, preferring the new man to Zeb.

The obsessional flavor of Zeb's thinking is reflected in material from another patient with an unequivocal obsessional neurotic diagnosis. "Walter" ended a two-year relationship with a young woman, then didn't even try to meet anyone new for over a year. That year's psychoanalytic work facilitated his resuming dating and he soon found a very nice girlfriend. But progress and pleasure in the new relationship were impeded by his near-constant anxiety over his sense of responsibility for his old girlfriend's feelings, specifically his worry that she would be jealous, even though she lived far away and they had not communicated in a year.

The internet descriptions of retroactive jealousy all attribute it to "insecurity" or "low self-esteem" and prescribe methods of boosting self-confidence. A psychoanalytic examination, however, reveals much greater complexity in the etiology and dynamics of these feelings. I asked John if his compulsive thoughts related to past experiences of inadequacy or insecurity.[1] He assured me that this had never been an issue, that his sexual partners had always appreciated his consideration, potency, and skill. Similarly, Zeb, a highly successful and prominent member of his community, had no doubts about his sexual prowess with both men and women.

But they were both deeply insecure about their capacity to fend off trauma. They experienced this inability as an intense, panicky fear of helplessness. A major contribution of psychoanalysis was to recognize the ego's experience of helplessness as traumatic. In the discussions on her *Ego and the Mechanisms of Defense* (Sandler & A. Freud, 1983), Anna

Freud asserted that fear of helplessness underlies all the other anxieties in the classical sequence.

What is the nature of the helplessness referred to by Anna Freud and/or of the defense against it in these men? In all these cases, we notice that the jealousy is not in the present, but in the past, the future, or thousands of miles away. John and Zeb had mixed feelings about their wives, but no current jealous feelings. Walter had no jealous feelings about his new girlfriend, but could not shake his belief that his current pleasure would harm his old girlfriend and evoke her overwhelming and dangerous jealousy.

Two-systems responses to helplessness

In ordinary work with couples, we often hear complaints like "He's married to his work;" "He'd rather watch football with his friends than be with me;" "She spends more time talking to her mother on the phone than with me;" "She seems less interested in sex—is there someone else?" and so forth. These jealous feelings can serve as a signal affect for exploring any friction or difficulty. What is significant is that the feelings are current; they are experienced in the present reality of the relationship and practical solutions are available. In our two-systems model, we would consider the experience of this signal emotion of jealousy as a choice point that challenges an individual to address the situation. The person can respond in an open-system realistic way, thinking about the issue and seeking solutions to the problem, or in a closed-system way, that leads him into the omnipotent sadomasochistic cycles we saw in John, Zeb, and Walter.

The patients mentioned above presented themselves as helpless victims of their thoughts, but in fact, they had made themselves very powerful, because they rendered everyone around them, including the analyst, helpless to convince them of the unreality of their jealous beliefs. They had created an omnipotent defense. What defines it as omnipotent is their belief that they can obliterate time and space and the reality of separateness. This magical, hostile defense protected them against trauma. The need to protect oneself against trauma is fundamental and legitimate for everyone. Helplessness in relation to inner and outer forces has to be mastered at each stage of development. We, along with Freud and all other subsequent developmental psychologists, see mastery as a basic motivation in human functioning.

But we differentiate between a closed, omnipotent, sadomasochistic system of mastery and an open, competent system. The aim of self-regulation is the same in both systems. In the open system, the maximum use of one's genuine mental and physical capacities to be realistically effective and competent is the method of mastering inner and outer forces. In the closed system, the basis for mastery is omnipotent belief in the power and necessity to be a perpetrator or victim in order to survive (Novick & Novick, 2002, 2006).

In the course of development, people grappling with overwhelming challenges may find realistic, adaptive open-system solutions. Some, however, create a "vicious cycle" (Wurmser, 1996, 2007), where masochistic suffering entitles the person to be an exception to the rules of society, reality, and biology, and justifies acting on a sadistic omnipotent belief in the power to control the lives of others (Freud, 1916d). But to satisfy and assuage feelings of guilt from a sadistic, closed-system superego, such behavior has to be continually justified by seeking out masochistic suffering and then finding victims for renewed sadistic attack.

John and Zeb reported the torment of sleepless nights filled with jealous thoughts and the daily distraction of the jealous thoughts intruding on their work. Walter suffered from his worries about his old girlfriend's well-being. All three experienced intense psychic pain.

Developmental roots

As we have described in earlier work on sadomasochism, the active pursuit of psychic or physical pain serves functions of attachment, defense, and gratification at every level of development. We noted that:

> Within a month from birth, it can be observed that such failures [real failures to meet infants' needs] produce signs of discomfort or psychic pain and are soon followed by signs of anger such as gaze aversion. This is followed by denial of the source of pain and denial is maintained by the transformation of pain into first a sign of attachment, then additionally a sign of specialness and unlimited destructive power, then a sign of equality in every way with oedipal parents and omnipotent capacity to coerce parents to gratify all infantile wishes. By school age, the magic omnipotent system has been established and the possibility of an alternate system of competent interactions with reality is undermined by the child as

each realistic achievement is experienced as due to omnipotent magical behavior. During latency, this delusion of omnipotence can be maintained, but in adolescence, it becomes increasingly difficult to deny, avoid, or distort reality without resorting to escalating self-destructive behaviors, which adolescents may use to shore up the crumbling omnipotent fantasy. (Novick & Novick, 1996, p. 61)

Each of our patients had suffered neglect, or disappointment, or betrayal, or lack of attunement from important people in their lives from the beginning. Each of them was denying the essential separateness of individuals from birth on because to them separateness signified separation and abandonment, the ultimate experience of loss, death, and helplessness.

John's congenital eye defect interfered with his vision in infancy and ultimately required surgery before his first birthday. Eyes bandaged, he was left alone in the hospital for ten days without parental visits. His terror of abandonment, desperate reactions to any threatened helplessness, and compulsive need to make sure others were all right became predominant features of his developing personality.

Zeb's father was frequently absent. As a boy, Zeb regularly slept in his mother's bed until well into school-age, only to be kicked out beyond the closed door when his father intermittently returned. He vigorously defended against overstimulation and rejection, even while seeking out dangerous sexual situations that he kept secret from his wife and his public persona.

Walter's mother was a very sensitive person, frequently unavailable because of illness. She was hospitalized and treated for a serious cancer when Walter was twelve. His helplessness in relation to his mother's physical and emotional fragility established an omnipotent belief that he was responsible for the well-being of all the women in his life.

We would note here that, for these men and all other patients we have seen, omnipotence did not represent a "normal" way of thinking, but constituted for them a hostile defense against trauma, layered and consolidated at any point in development.

As a defense against experiences or threats of helplessness and the rage that inevitably follows, they had devised the omnipotent belief that important people, starting with their mothers, were not separate, but objects under their omnipotent control. The idea that Zeb's wife, unbeknown to him, had a sexual thought about someone else, or

John's teenage girlfriend had been sexually abused by someone else, or the reality that Walter's old girlfriend did not know and might not care about his new relationship—all this felt like an unbearable attack on their omnipotence and threatened the trauma of helplessness and uncontrolled, unending rage. Zeb described it succinctly, when he said that what he couldn't bear was his wife's "separate sexual existence."

These men were insecure, but this was the anxiety that, if they were not omnipotent, they were completely helpless. Omnipotence was validated when they could be aggressive and sadistic and get away with it. Zeb exploited his younger sister sexually in adolescence, then his college roommate and the roommate's girlfriend, then a mentee, and a business associate, without apparent compunction. John thought of himself as a very caring and respectful person, but was addicted to sadistic internet porn and frequented prostitutes to spank and debase them. Walter was drawn to women who seemed fragile and damaged, making them completely dependent on him; he masturbated to snuff films. The pain of their jealousy justified to them their sadistic disregard of and attacks on others, giving these men an omnipotent sense of license to do whatever they pleased. This is the familiar vicious circle of sadomasochism that we have characterized as omnipotent, closed-system functioning, organized according to a closed-system conscience. Then the circle is completed by suffering and victimization.

The omnipotent denial of time that we discern in retroactive and prospective jealousy appears to be predicated on a terror of and denial of separateness, in its catastrophic meaning to these men. The internet descriptions relate to both men and women, but it is mostly men we have seen clinically who display this phenomenon.

Jealousy and omnipotence in women

There is, however, a group of women in whom a similar dynamic appears in a different form. Many years ago, we described the "negative therapeutic motivation" of parents who bring their child or adolescent to treatment in order to make the analyst and the analysis fail (J. Novick, 1980; Novick & Novick, 1996). We described the "defensive need of both patient and parent to maintain an idealized image of a loving, loved, and omnipotent parent" (Novick & Novick, 1996, p. 268). In that same paper, we attributed some roots of this motivation to the effort to maintain a purified pleasure dyad, where all safety and gratification resided in the delusion of symbiotic union between mother and child.

We now understand this to include the wish to deny separateness, and see manifestations at every stage of development, in both clinical and other settings. At our psychoanalytic preschool,[2] for instance, a mother of a three year old cried piteously each morning, saying, "I can't understand why she would rather spend her time with ten other kids than with me." This mother, who had suffered a loveless and difficult childhood, was desperately determined to be the best mother she possibly could be. But this drive, so central to her own identity and psychology, left out her child's needs and individuality. When her child later entered treatment because of oppositional and defiant behavior, the mother undermined the treatment relationship by creating exciting competing attractions and eventually terminating the analysis prematurely when the child began to develop strong loving feelings for the analyst.

Another example is of a sixteen-year-old boy, "Ben," who was referred because of severe psychogenic chest pains and his fear that he would die. The family was intact middle class and everyone seemed cooperative and eager for treatment. Ben came to his first session with his shirt unbuttoned down to his waist, lolling over his chair, seeming to expect a sexual response from his female therapist. He soon said he was bored, and, by the second session, declared he was feeling much better. During the third session, he presented what turned out to be his mother's assessment and solution of the problems. Ben did not come for his fourth session, but his mother telephoned, saying to the therapist, "You must be so disappointed."

In a parent session, Ben's mother spoke of herself as the only one who understood and could meet his needs. He had been a difficult and unmanageable child from birth, but she was the one who could always handle him. Right before the referral, she had felt that she could no longer manage him and his increasing anger. She said he had also been making his sexual needs more noticeable at home. Both mother and child dealt with feelings of failure and helplessness in the face of Ben's growing adolescent separateness by externalizing the failure on to the therapist. Ben and his mother found relief by making a joint plan for her to supervise his schoolwork at home, which represented a retreat into a closed-system omnipotent delusion of union, with overtones of sexualized sadomasochism.

There is a group of children and adolescents in whom the degree of disturbance is such that the parental role in a negative therapeutic motivation initially remains hidden. These are the wildly "out-of-control" youngsters who often receive diagnoses of PDD or borderline pathology, or, increasingly, bipolar illness. If they enter psychoanalytic treatment, they present serious management problems, often trashing the office and trying to hurt the analyst or themselves, seeming almost to be striving to make the treatment impossible and unbearable. When this is dealt with therapeutically, the children begin to see the analyst who has survived the unceasing attack as someone separate from themselves (Novick & Novick, 2015). As they gradually perceive the analyst as a separate and valued person, they can begin to have a transference relationship. We can then see that the negative therapeutic motivation on the part of the child reflects, in part, a defense against positive feelings for someone outside the family. This is when the maternal negative therapeutic motivation often becomes visible and operative. Parents may summarily remove the child from treatment, or one or both parents may become depressed or show other signs of severe disturbance resulting from disruption of the pathological family balance predicated on the omnipotent delusion of fusion of mother and child.

Our clinical experience with mothers who could not bear to allow their children a separate existence contributed to our developing a model of concurrent parent work, described in our book *Working With Parents Makes Therapy Work* (2005) and subsequent papers (J. Novick & K. K. Novick, 2013a; K. K. Novick & J. Novick, 2010, 2013a; Dowling, Lament, Novick, & Novick, 2013). It often took years of work to help parents regain their primary parental love for their child, recognize their symbiotic enmeshment and soul blindness as destructive, and help them find an alternative in open-system authentic love between two separate individuals.

Similarly, John, Zeb, and Walter took many years of analysis to set aside their closed-system omnipotent delusions of controlling others by being a jealous, aggrieved victim who was then justified in being sadistic. Alternatively victimhood can be achieved by externalizing the jealousy defensively and seeing the other as a potentially pathetic, jealous person who would then attack. The contrast we drew earlier between an open-system constructive response to the signal affect of jealousy and the psychic constructions of the three men we described makes clear that their jealousy was embedded in a lifelong closed-system omnipotent defense against helplessness.

Open- and closed-system techniques

Detailed description of the techniques that were useful in addressing this pervasive pathology and long-standing character structure is beyond the scope of this chapter, but we have written extensively about techniques that elucidate the closed system and foster growth of open-system responses (Novick & Novick, 1996, 2000, 2002, 2003, 2004, 2012, 2013b, 2013c).

The three men sketched in this chapter were very different, but each saw himself as very caring, loving, and self-sacrificing. John was in a helping profession; he sought treatment because he was consumed by the needs of his wife and his clients. He prided himself on "always being there" for everyone else, but felt unable to make the slightest demands to meet his own legitimate needs. Zeb felt responsible for all the poor people in the world and gave vast sums to charity, but still felt consumed and tormented by guilt. Walter, a young man in a challenging job, devoted all his energy and much of his time to taking care of a series of fragile, disturbed women. He worried constantly that any independent action was selfish and would hurt them. All three hid the hostility in their retroactive or projected or externalized jealousy from themselves. The underlying aggression that became part of their character defenses, including their obsessive jealousy, emerged in the transference relationship where each of the three men seemed unusually anxious about hurting or damaging me. Techniques addressing their closed-system, sadomasochistic beliefs, fantasies, and functioning included all the usual ways of engaging with transference dimensions of attachment, gratification, desire, and attack.

But real change only began with the impact of simultaneous work on their open-system capacities to protect themselves and respond to others in more realistic and genuine ways. The jealous obsessions abated only when these men could own the hostility of their jealousy and come to terms with their real limitations, finding dependable pleasure from their real powers. After years of work on both systems of self-regulation, these men could experience the full gamut of emotions as signals in authentic interactions with separate others.

At the core of the pathological belief that mother and child are one is a denial both of separateness and of the inexorability of time, where growth and change make ever more evident the individuality of each person. Mothers who struggle with these issues seem desperate to hold back the tide of reality. They cannot allow their children to have a will of their own, separate desires and thoughts, or make relationships with others. They are fiercely jealous of anything that threatens to come between them and their children.

Here is where we perceive a commonality between the men grappling with retroactive or prospective jealousy and the women who disrupt and destroy their children's friendships, or their love for their teachers or therapists. John, Zeb, Walter, and others could not find fulfilment and mutuality in the reality of their present relationships, while the mothers gave up the chance for a constantly transforming and generative ongoing real present relationship with their children. Our sense is that these pathological forms of jealousy are useful clinical markers of underlying closed-system sadomasochistic functioning, with its core omnipotent beliefs.

Coda

As we were thinking about the topic of retroactive jealousy, we found ourselves humming a song from long ago.

> I wonder who's kissing her now,
> Wonder who's teaching her how?
> Wonder who's looking into her eyes,
> Breathing sighs!
> Telling lies!
> I wonder if she's got a boy,
> The girl who once filled me with joy,
> Wonder if she ever tells him of me,
> I wonder who's kissing her now.
>
> (Frank Adams, Will Hough, Joseph Howard,
> Harold Orlob, 1909)

This song, written for a stage play of 1909, remains current as a standard in popular music and film. It was much recorded and played in the late 1940s, when singers used only the above chorus and conveyed the sentiments in a wistful, nostalgic tone. For our purposes here, we note that the song describes a jealous reaction to loss and separation from a loved person.

"I Wonder Who's Kissing Her Now," with the lyrics quoted above, is actually only the chorus of a song that has two verses. In 1909, the verses were sung as a reality counterpoint or internal dialogue with the wistful nostalgia of the chorus. In the first verse, we learn that the abandoned, jealous lover is actually a serial seducer. He has loved many women, has vowed affection and fidelity to each one in turn, and then has left "to hunt new game." This verse ends with the lines:

> Does it ever occur to you, boy
> That she's probably doing the same?

So the aggrieved, pained lover is confronted, just as he would be by an open-system superego or a therapist, with the reality that the woman he abandoned is a separate person, not under his omnipotent control, who has her own will and desires (Novick & Novick, 2004).

The final verse confirms the reality limitations on the jealous lover, and makes clear that he cannot control the woman, time, or even his own future.

> If you want to feel wretched and lonely and blue,
> Just imagine the girl you love best
> In the arms of some fellow who's stealing a kiss
> From the lips that you once fondly pressed;
> But the world moves apace and the loves of today
> Flit away with a smile and a tear.
> So you never can tell who is kissing her now,
> Or just whom you'll be kissing next year.

After World War II, possibly as an echo of the uncertainty many young people felt about relationships when millions of men had been away for years, the verses of the song were omitted in recordings and crooners like Perry Como, Bing Crosby, and Ray Charles, among many others, made the chorus into a song of longing and loss.

The song was written in the year Freud published the case of the Rat Man (1909d). The patient was Dr. Lorenz, about whom Freud first used the phrase "omnipotence of thought." This was a case of successful psychoanalytic treatment of OCD; among the many obsessions Lorenz suffered from was the thought that his own private sexual pleasure with his girlfriend would hurt his father, make him jealous, and in fact kill him. As Freud noted, Lorenz's father had in fact been dead for a number of years. But Lorenz's omnipotent sadomasochistic thoughts obliterated the reality of time and held him in a suspended jealous universe, much like John, Zeb, and Walter, and the mothers who tried to stop their children's development.

CHAPTER TEN

Jealousy betwixt envy

Judi B. Kobrick

Remembering a Scottish ballad

I have struggled to find words where feelings prevail in the maelstrom
of confusion as well as understanding the realms of jealousy and envy.
I have been asked to write about the analyst's encounters with "jealousy,"
a protected domain sequestered away, in contrast to envy that arises in
a more conscious realm.

The medieval Scottish ballad, attributed to the 1700s, *Get Up and Bar
the Door*, comes to mind. Memories return of its presence in my analysis
and earlier years as a student. Remarkably, this ballad of an unknown
author, I interpreted as it related to my own subjectivity that does not
coincide with traditional thinking. The ballad unfolds as a husband and
wife enter into a battle of wills as to who will get up to bar the door
blown open by the wind. They agree that the first to speak will close

159

the door. Two thieves arrive at midnight and steal in in the dark, first declaring they will eat the woman's carefully prepared food and then rape her while holding a knife at the husband's throat and cutting off his beard. The husband is the first to speak and the wife informs him that he is now the one to get up and bar the door. The stubbornness of each has surpassed invasion and violence from outsiders with ill intent. Has the envy of the intruders whetted their appetite? Has the jealousy of the husband hearing their intentions directed at his wife given him a voice, albeit perhaps too late? Why has this ballad remained so etched in my memory with associations of both envy and jealousy?

The words had been a metaphor for the invasion of my mother's family, both envious and jealous of all that we possessed and the relationships we enjoyed. My mother, the youngest of eight children and known for her stubbornness and determination, was favored by her own parents. When she married and had three daughters, she did not "get up and bar the door" and catered still to her extended family's needs and demands. Their ill will was palpable, and my mother's subservience to their omnipotence was without comprehension. She feared their envy and jealousy would destroy her intimate relationships and needed to keep them at a distance by her "acts" of caring and generosity. My sisters and I were the recipients of red ribbons pinned to our undergarments by our mother and her mother to ward off "the evil eye" that embodied both superstition and magical thinking. The Yiddish chorus chanted "*kennehora*" that translated to "Let it be without the evil eye." I too became adept at navigating and avoiding anticipated attacks of envy and jealousy, whilst experiencing a sense of loss and at times a sense of humiliation. I kept valued belongings, accomplishments, and relationships hidden and out of sight from the intruders.

I reflected on these musings and promptly returned to verify my recollections and associations. The ballad that came back into focus, recalled from my adolescence, actually existed and had spurred associations in my analysis more than thirty years ago. In addition, I discovered two illustrations, one created by Alexander George Fraser (a Scottish painter) in the late nineteenth century and another by Arthur Rackham (an English book illustrator) in the early twentieth century. Inspired by this very same ballad, each artist had his own interpretation.

Fraser depicted the couple sitting at a table, with one intruder caressing the wife by candlelight and the other intruder a dark and menacing silhouette by the door, with a dog posed upright at his side. Rackham

Figure 1. *Get Up and Bar the Door* by Alexander Fraser (1786–1865).

portrayed the wife as animated with rosy cheeks, fiercely posed, standing with a pot in her hand and looking at her husband sitting on a chair, who in turn is grimacing at her, with a cat complacently lying on the ground near the couple. The intruders for Rackham are illustrated by two dark shadows behind the couple. The desire to interpret the illustrations is tempting and would only serve to escape and distance myself from my own struggle.

Then, into my psychic realm entered Nancy Friday, accompanied with memories of her book, *Jealousy* (1985). I searched and found it on a dusty and damp shelf, waiting to be reopened and read again, thirty years later. She regarded envy as the most destructive of all the elements of jealousy. As the reader, I believed she was searching for freedom from the malevolent grip of jealousy that held fear of loss and threatened self-esteem. Friday dedicated her book to her mentor, Richard C. Robertiello, a psychoanalyst, who appears throughout in her odyssey as her sparring partner in attempts to unlock the essence of jealousy. Robertiello was closely connected to the contributions of Kohut (1971, 1977). Her book is replete with interviews with brilliant psychoanalytic

Figure 2. *Get Up and Bar the Door* by Arthur Rackham (1867–1939).

minds that include James Grotstein, Daniel Stern, Hanna Segal, and the paediatrician, Berry Brazelton, as well as interviews with men and women she encountered. The backdrop is the early writings of Freud (1922b) on jealousy, and Melanie Klein (1957) on envy and gratitude. At the time of my encounter with Nancy Friday's book and her cast of characters, some of whom I had met, I was ensconced in training as a psychoanalyst. The work and clinical relevance of Melanie Klein had been foremost in my previous training as a psychologist; Daniel

Stern had been most generous in sharing his work and in inspiring my doctoral dissertation. In her book, Friday queried: "Why do I hear more about jealousy on the street than therapists do in their office?" (p. 27). I wondered about my own avoidance in the complex and multifaceted tensions of jealousy as it may reside and disguise itself both within my patients and myself.

The etymological approach regarding envy and jealousy leads both to clarification and confusion, words used interchangeably at times as well as being distinguished from one another. Jealousy is from the Greek word *zelos*, meaning emulation or rivalry, and envy from the Latin word *invidere*, that is referenced to coveting.

Psychoanalytic writers have made the distinction that jealousy, embedded in a relationship, involves three persons, with one real or imagined rival, posing as a threat to the loss of connection between the other two. Envy is highlighted as the desire to have what the other possesses that is deemed valued and important.

Freud (1922b) believed that jealousy was a normal affective state akin to grief and that its absence from the psychic landscape indicated severe repression and a presence in unconscious mental life. He also indicated that abnormal intense jealousy could be revealed "and constructed of three layers ... 1. competitive or normal; 2. projected, and 3. delusional jealousy" (p. 232). Jealousy was inevitable and emanated from the demands of early life for exclusive relationships with important others (Freud, 1931b).

Klein (1957), borrowing from Crabb's English synonyms expressed that "... jealousy fears to lose what it has and envy is tortured by seeing what another has and wants for itself" (pp. 7–8). Klein referred to the baby's earliest and exclusive relationship with the mother and the breast that is envied as a precursor to later object relations and jealousy associated with the oedipal situation. Jealousy was accompanied with rivalry when a new object appeared on life's stage that threatened the fear and loss of the mother as a primary love relationship.

Riviere (Klein & Riviere, 1964) reflected:

> ... jealousy derives from that first experience of sexual rivalry in our childhood ...
>
> ... jealousy is a reaction of hate and aggression to a loss or threat of loss ...

... one special feature in jealousy is the sense of humiliation which invariably accompanies it, owing to the injury it entails to one's self-confidence and sense of security

... unconscious feeling of unlovableness and unworthiness in oneself

... dangers of loss, loneliness and helplessness. (pp. 41–43)

Klein (1957) commented that in Shakespeare's *Othello*, jealousy was symbolized by "the green-eyed monster" and that one was also confronted in the play with a lack of differentiation with envy. Is this monster akin to the evil eye encountered in the Old Testament and embedded in the folklore of many cultures? The dread of the evil eye, a destructive look, without words, to be feared was considered an "uncanny" and widespread superstition that could destroy all that was valued (Freud, 1919h). Evans (1975) aptly reflected: "... the eye of jealousy is passive in that it seeks not to possess, but rather to torture itself with the danger of being dispossessed" (p. 490). The malevolent glance, as a link between jealousy and the sense of sight, embodies the potential threat of a rival disrupting the relational matrix and contributing to a profound sense of exclusion. The eye of envy focuses on the possession or accomplishment of the other that one desires while feeling lacking and diminished. In turn, when the focus of rivalry shifts from persons to possessions, envy appears as a definition of jealousy (Spielman, 1971). The talisman or red ribbon was created as a protection and shield from unbidden assault and potential destruction whether emanating from jealousy or envy.

Sullivan (1953) had viewed jealousy as "... much more poignant and devastating than envy; in contrast with envy it does not concern itself with an attribute or an attachment, but rather involves a great complex field of interpersonal relations" (p. 348). "In the everyday conception of jealousy, a man or a woman feels deprived of the loved person by somebody else" (Klein, 1957, pp. 7–8).

Morrison (1989) importantly viewed shame, one's self-contempt and perceived lack of accomplishment, as generating envy that shifts the preoccupation from one's "... meager state of self to the powerful state of the object" (p. 109). The analyst's avoidance of feelings of shame with regard to feelings of inferiority and lack of accomplishment may be expressed in the envy of one's colleagues. If envy is a failure in unconscious identification and the patient experiences too much of a felt difference with the analyst, anxieties associated with dependency and vulnerability fuel the pain of exclusion that widens the gap for potential connection (Gerhardt, 2009a, 2016). Jealousy enters the stage when one is preoccupied with the painful feeling of being the excluded third (Wurmser & Jarass, 2008a) from the relational closeness and intimacy of others whether it be colleagues, patients, family, friends, strangers, or even imagined others. The analyst's narcissism and dissociated destructive envy and jealousy may be heightened as the desire to bask in the acclaim, achievement, and manic energy of important others, and is countered with states of vulnerability and felt inadequacy (Hirsch, 2011, 2014). Friday (1985) considered envy as being "additive" (p. 157), and jealousy as being "subtractive," masking fears of loss, abandonment, exclusion, betrayal, and humiliation. Phillips (1994) posited: "If there is envy of the desired object in the earliest relationship, there is rivalry for the desired object in the later three-person relationship" (p. 56).

Lewin (2011) made the distinction between normal and traumatic jealousy and the important contribution in detailing "parallel identification," a primitive form of identification that inhibits conscious jealousy, "as a manic defence that blocks the acute suffering brought on by consciously experienced jealousy arising from the loss of a beloved yet sadistic object" (p. 551). Parallel identifications create an experience and illusion of merger, whilst obliterating the intrusion of jealousy or the rival, and eventuate in a stasis in the therapeutic encounter. The protective cloak of these identifications, akin to the red ribbon talisman, wards off unbearable jealousy that needs to be formulated and give way to the possibility for "penetrating identifications" between self and other creating an enriched and cocreated psychic landscape. "Identification … begins from the wound of jealousy" (Carnochan, 2011, p. 583).

Clinical encounters

There are many encounters, not only in our practice as psychoanalysts, but also in our everyday life and buried histories, when envy and jealousy are exhumed, at times dissociated and at other times in plain sight. The memories of my mother and her family erupted alongside her fears that envy and jealousy could destroy important and intimate relationships. Her acts of caring and generosity to the intruders bearing malevolent glances and destructive forces were baffling. The red ribbons of protection and her reluctance to "get up and bar the door" marked a trail of confusion and a fragile sense of safety. Ophelia,

Horatio, and Hawk deeply touched me, as they brushed against and into my early family narrative and the presence of envy and jealousy in the clinical encounter.

Ophelia: looking into the mirror

Ophelia, a thirty-four-year-old black woman, appeared on the psycho-analytic stage, distraught and despondent. She was the youngest of four siblings and had immigrated to Canada when she was seventeen years old with her parents, brother, and two sisters. When I first saw her, I was struck both by her glamorous appearance and childlike demeanor. Her eyes widened as she approached the couch and then placed herself slowly and deliberately on the edge and haltingly began to lie down. The prospect of analysis was both frightening and exhilarating. She related a recent dream about watching herself lie down on the couch only to find herself shrinking until she was invisible. This scene fore-shadowed her fears of being colonized, devalued, and abandoned as she had been by her family. She embodied the competent, effective, and mature woman holding the lost, frightened little girl, waiting for a sense of vitality and presence to be exhumed. She ultimately believed that she would be viewed "as a peasant girl, a disappointment and not a glamorous and accomplished woman."

Her mother, a successful businesswoman, shared with her a hor-rific narrative of taking "a potion" to abort a pregnancy; that memory constantly lingered profoundly in her damaged sense of self as being unlovable. She created a rich fantasy life to combat her night terrors as well as a shrine in her bedroom with a small, blue and white porcelain Virgin Mary as her protector. Her early education was in a convent where she suffered physical and verbal recriminations for not express-ing herself in Standard English. She remained self-conscious about the choice and intonation of her words. Ophelia eventually garnered stellar academic and professional accomplishments that she under-valued, as she feared that it would become the target of her family's and interlopers' envy and destruction. Her mother had a dream that Ophelia's career accelerated and that she found her daughter shak-ing and unstable on the top of a pile of boxes: "My mother's dream could have been my dream." Women in her life were idealized and despised as she searched to find her "glitter" away from the shadows of her life. She struggled with attachments with both men and women that she envied, wanting to crawl inside and enter into an idealized merger while fearing the erosion and disappearance of her bodily and psychic self.

Ophelia spoke of her envy and jealousy and her idealized version of me as having "perfect punctuality, intactness, ability to organize a perfect life which is never disrupted and a perfect marriage." I could not resist wondering who was she talking about and how hard the impact would be when I fell from the pedestal she created; I would be black and blue and most certainly not the Virgin Mary.

Ophelia proclaimed:

> Envy might come up, if I feel you've got things I don't have. I want things; I want to be like you. One thing might happen, I don't feel I can get what you have, seeing us as different … the process of separateness. I admire your capacity of blending sides … you could be active, quiet, nurturing … where it fits where I'm at … if stuck, you say something to pull me out of it … I admire many sides you can be. I see you as being analytical and serious, and have fun and let go … there is a vitality about you that I like … how might envy or jealousy come into that experience … at times when I feel I can't acquire something you might have, there is a separateness from you, a hint of anger which turns into acceptance … I am alone … you have a husband … not part of a visible minority.

I noted sadness and longing in her tone, her voice subdued and I had thoughts of hiding under a rock, disappearing so as not to loom so large. I thought about my own struggles with envy and jealousy and furtive attempts to shrink myself to protect what was valuable and who was valued. I did not bask in the sunlight of the admiration and I did not fear malevolence: I felt awkward and "shaking on the top of a pile of boxes." Ophelia profoundly experienced her family's expressed view of her as inadequate and incompetent and "too slow." She was left alone a considerable amount of time as a young child and reflected that her slowness, when others were impatient, was her way of engaging others and pushing back. It was poignant that the needs of the other family members were paramount and superseded her own. The family myth was a loving and attentive atmosphere while the experience was cloaked in envy, and denigration of her accomplishments and jealousy of her relationships beyond the family perimeter.

Ophelia dreamed:

> I arrived late for my appointment, your office was crowded with other
> people as if it was a television talk show, and you ask me if I want to see
> someone else. In the centre of the room, there is a little girl in psychoanaly-
> sis in front of all these people being televised.

The dream made an appearance immediately prior to my attendance
and presentation at a conference of which she had become aware. She
kept abreast of my whereabouts and involvements albeit as a result
of her own research. Would I, like her mother, become involved with
personal pursuits, leaving her neglected, abandoned, and unable to
compete for affection and attention? She needed to see and be seen, to
be recognized and revered. She alluded to jealousy of my relationships
outside of the analysis with those she regarded as important others
and viewed herself as the "little girl" attempting to find her way as
"a little child in a long tunnel with a candle, not knowing, trying to
go to the end of the tunnel, careful how I walk." She then connected
with her anger and frustration as her "inner candle had blown out." In
another dream, she walks out of an analytic session as I am preoccupied and engaged in a press conference and in the dream retold anger
is rekindled.

Ophelia imagined that I could provide her with a script that
would fulfil her primary needs, offer containment of her affective
storms, and protect her from fears of being abandoned, left alone, and
depleted. I wrestled with her desire for something that she believed I
possessed and that I was potentially withholding. I could not "get up
and bar the door" from her needy family and intruders that disrupted
her stability. I found myself in reverie with a memory of sitting at the
kitchen table with my mother and grandmother as a young child, feeling that nothing could disrupt the peaceful and intimate ambience and
savoring the rich aroma of the food cooking … until the phone rang.
It was the "intruder" … it was as if I no longer existed … the room
filled with angry voices … I remained silent and alone … envious of the
power of the intruder and jealous that my mother's and grandmother's
relationship with the intruder, my rival, took precedence. I then could
join Ophelia without a script as the affective storms arrived and a door
blew open.

Ophelia had oscillated from sitting on the edge of the couch and lying down, connecting and disconnecting, with me following close behind. She yearned for and was terrified of an archaic merger that would erase and resolve all tensions of envy and jealousy, thereby rekindling her vitality at times of vulnerability. Ophelia's desire for merger and sameness may have been akin to the parallel identification described by Lewin (2011), obliterating the experience of jealousy and negating the perception of rivalry or asymmetry in our relationship. There were occasions when I was with Ophelia, in my reverie, that I experienced myself looking into a mirror and finding a black woman, dressed similarly with an identical hairstyle and familiar mannerisms apprehending her attempt to join with me and I with her. This cocreated ambience left us cocooned, protected, and in search of creating a psychic space to think together (Davies, 2004). However, it limited the dialectic process of mutual recognition and complementarity in discovering differentiation of self and other within connectedness. Benjamin (2002, 2004) and Aron (2006) elaborate the "rhythmic third" as creating a new "third-ness" that emerges from the space of the dyad rather than in the mind of one or other of the participants alone. The sense of merger needs to be penetrated in opening a space for the disruption accompanying envy and jealousy that has previously been dissociated and that needs to be brought to life in the relational matrix.

Disappointment and disillusionment entered the stage. She ruminated about her expression of anger, envy, hostility, and jealousy that could potentially lead to annihilation and destruction. Ophelia viewed her emotional needs as too intense to communicate to another person and as she appeared intact, she experienced her "insides falling out." She imagined herself as the greedy baby with insatiable needs. She entered the consultation room bristling with anger, as I was late for her appointment: "You have forgotten me … the other patient is probably more important … the aggression I feel … who can I trust, let close … I am defending my territory."

Later, Ophelia had a dream in which I appear and share personal and intimate details, reflecting less than an idealized existence that includes problems with a teenage son, an eight-year-old daughter who has psychic abilities and suffers from insomnia, and an imperfect husband. She then fantasized about a teenage daughter with whom I share my vitality, and associates this to "the bond between us."

Ophelia:

> There was the analysis at the beginning. As I benefit, change, grow, I look at what some of the excitement was ... my attraction to the ideal was represented by you ... perfection in total control ... I am going to be like that ... no one is like that ... dealing with what has to happen for me to grow ... own my inadequacies ... you sharing your inadequacies with me and not feeling alone.

Ophelia had tended to devalue her very being and hid what she valued and feared would be destroyed by others that touched upon my family narrative of envy and jealousy. The trauma and terrorizing encounters with her family were initially dissociated as she focused on her solitary imaginative encounters in her world of fantasy that could not be invaded and were only controlled by her. She desired closeness and intimacy while fearing that she would be swallowed up by the other. The retelling of her dreams became the gateway of discovering, albeit at a safe distance, that she had a voice, feelings, and a veritable presence that could be heard, in what she had previously experienced as an inimical and threatening world.

Jealousy is betwixt envy; when I consider the ramifications of when one is idealized and hated and while being thrown from a pedestal is humbling, it is also human. I needed to bare Ophelia's envious and jealous attacks opening a safe expanse where together we could navigate rather than avoid the unbearable. My personal family narrative and my desire for my mother to "get up and bar the door," if reenacted in attempting to fortify against the jealous intruders, needed to be abandoned and the ghosts of the past needed to be confronted.

Ophelia sojourned on a journey imbuing the *sweet sparkling eyes* of the engaging and forgotten baby that she wished to reclaim; the *nasty glaring eyes* of the greedy child's envy and jealousy that she preferred to disavow and the *avoidant eyes* of the childlike woman that begin to look and explore. She did not become, as she had feared, Shakespeare's Ophelia who is tragically lost and unknown.

Horatio: a tale of two men

I call him Horatio, as Horatio Alger foretold his narrative from rags to riches. Horatio, a single man in his late forties, entrepreneur and inventor, presented as bereft and severely depressed, lost in a morass of confusion and fear. His life had become unraveled and, in the past, he had turned to alcohol to anesthetize his pain. He came from humble means and over the years had amassed a fortune. He looked to older aristocratic mentors when he was young for recognition as well as his desire to identify with their wealth and accomplishments. His own father had abandoned him at the age of three, eventually resorting to an alcoholic stupor and bankrupting the family. His mother was resilient and determined to care for the family emotionally and financially. Horatio ingratiated himself with the upper social echelon, craving status and a sense of importance. He was unaware of underlying feelings of depression and inadequacy.

Horatio returned to treatment following a ten-year hiatus, a period of time that reflected a sense of well-being, accomplishment, and sobriety. He had come to the realization that although he presented to the outside world as carefree and competent, a storm of sadness had been brewing within him for many years. He reflected that he felt like a fraud recreating himself in others' images. He became preoccupied with intrusive thoughts that others saw his incompetent and "false self," the vulnerable and fragile one behind a facade of strength and decisiveness. He had worn a borrowed cloak, merging and identifying with powerful others, and had lost a sense of what belonged to him. He spoke of his envy of others' possessions and "grandness" and jealousy of the relationships they enjoyed. He experienced himself as an outsider playing the part of an insider on life's stage. Horatio sequestered his envious and jealous feelings to the back stage, also carefully diminishing his own accomplishments fearing they could be stolen by the very same envious and jealous attacks he disavowed. There was never enough love or money … never enough happiness. His bon vivant lifestyle was enviable as well as his relationships with important others. He imagined me as having a seamless and wonderful life without the presence of sadness, pain, and conflict.

I imagined myself in his world feeling free and without restraint, indulging and being indulgent, without responsibility and financial constraint. Paradoxically, he expressed a sense of shame regarding his jealous fantasies of my life and relationships with caring and important others. He found it difficult to imagine that others could *really* regard him with respect and admiration although his accomplishments were considerable. It was as if he had two personas … one full and vital, the other depleted and barren. The persona that appeared robust and generative received acclaim and significant recognition fuelled by the manic excitement of challenges to be surpassed. The empty and lost persona, the one that remained hidden and not recognized was in search of nourishment and a sense of fulfilment. His mythological rival, his "internal saboteur" (Fairbairn, 1944), haunted his success with the ghost of inevitable failure. His appetite for acquisition and appearance had been propelled by envy and jealousy and he feared destruction lurked close behind. In the earlier phase of Horatio's treatment, he was battling the immobilization of depression alongside alcoholism that had left his upward mobility and financial and personal security in the dust. He returned a decade later, sobered that although his star had soared once again, he felt bereft and empty of the intimacy and energy he craved in a relationship. In Winnicott's thinking, he was resilient in being able "to do" and at a loss at being able "to be" (1971) having erected a "false self" (1965) that he no longer experienced as enlivening and sustaining. He created an interpersonal and intrapsychic castle that was constructed with complex elements of being recognized but feeling profoundly unknown both to himself and to others. I queried the enactment that I had participated in ten years earlier, recognizing and appreciating his "doing" and not paying close enough attention to approaching the depths of his "being" and the signposts of jealousy and envy. We were now standing in the same place with a different landscape and a new depth of life's tapestry to explore.

Hawk: the devil is looking

Hawk, a man in his fifties, had been hospitalized after an unsuccessful suicide attempt, charged with possessing a firearm, and had travelled a considerable distance and knocked on my door. He was curious about psychoanalytic treatment, filled with derision and distrust following previous relationships with a parade of mental health professionals. I felt myself as a target the moment he walked in the door, for his hostility and a trajectory for powerful feelings that could not be contained. Hawk described his mother as having been emotionally and physically abusive and the venom he projected came directly from her chastising him as worthless, inadequate, and lacking intelligence. He had never met his biological father, and his stepfather and half-brother had both recently committed suicide, followed by the death of his half-sister. The world was a dark place, and there was nowhere safe to hide or be protected from the maternal gaze. Would he survive? Would I survive? It is now several years later in the treatment and we have survived together.

Hawk had been traumatized and excluded from his mother's narcissistic kingdom that included his stepfather, a kingdom that he had attempted to enter as he was repeatedly cast aside psychically and physically. I redoubled my efforts to connect and recognize his resilience, to which in turn he responded with the perception that he was lacking and that I contributed to his shame and humiliation in a psychoanalytic process he did not understand … fearful to engage and submit and be subjugated. I was relegated to a role of entrapment, to be dismissed, deprecated, and destroyed, unable to have an impact, while he experienced himself as deficient and disadvantaged. His attacks against linking (Bion, 1959) protected him from what he envisioned as the painful and the inevitable place of exclusion.

He echoed his version of a refrain from a Bare Naked Ladies' song, "You treat me as I'm never there." There have been occasions when I experienced his questions as penetrating and unbearable, framed in the third person, as if I could not possibly provide him with what was right and just. He raged and I retreated. He, in turn, experienced me as not present and deliberately withholding, reifying his sense of inadequacy and lack of intelligence. In this enactment, he feared abandonment as well as connection. As I attempted to connect, he retreated, as he believed that I must certainly have seen him as flawed, unlovable, and untouchable.

Hawk expressed jealousy of my close and intimate relationships, both real and unreal. One day, he alluded to my supposed secure attachment to my parents as if they were present and alive in the room. I raised my voice in a peculiar and angry tone, without thinking, and stated that my father was dead. I was jealous of the very illusion that he had created and the profound loss that I had mourned. It was the thirty-fourth anniversary, the very day of my father's death, of which I had not been consciously aware in the moment. The next day, I told Hawk what I had realized following the session, that my anger and tone belonged to me and my loss, and that it pierced his idealized narrative of my life and relationships. This was profoundly embedded in his experience of a lack and absence of a sense of belonging and of attachment. I had indeed withdrawn, in my attempts not to reenact the role of the angry and narcissistic mother that had abandoned him. It was at that moment that I had become human to him and he then expressed that, perhaps, trust could be possible. I had barred the door, carefully not allowing my rage, hostility, and narcissism to enter and inhabit the persona of his traumatizing mother until it was no longer possible in the face of his penetrating attacks and my own feelings of anger that I experienced as destabilizing. I had got up and barred the door, unwittingly, from his envious and jealous attacks of all that I garnered valued and valuable.

Exclusion: an insider standing on the outside

Ophelia: till death do us part

I was in a crowded room of mourners, bereft and alone. Ophelia's death was sudden and unexpected, and family, friends and colleagues had gathered to mourn the loss. It had been most incredible that I recognized those who were important and challenging in her life by her past detailed and emotionally charged verbal descriptions. It was as if they had stepped out of the narrative of her life, living and breathing. I was the ghost in the narrative and unknown to others. They embraced each other, tears rolled down my face and I sobbed … the loss of a beloved patient, a unique and very special person with whom I had spent many hours, traversing both the most painful and joyful terrains. I recalled the humiliation and shame I experienced as I mused about how jealous I was of those left behind, as they would have the opportunity to connect and speak of Ophelia. My sense of loss of a life snuffed out prematurely would need to reside privately in my own inner sanctum. I had a similar experience several years earlier when another patient died from a terminal illness and I was on the outside looking in. I took a pause to consider the intimate relationship between patient and analyst that for the most part may be hidden or obscured from the patient's relationships on the outside while paradoxically we share up close and personal, on the inside. We are excluded from our patients' daily lives *in vivo* while we are privileged to share and participate in their lives in ways that cannot be adequately expressed in words. It was startling that "*until death do us part*" I realized how I would viscerally experience being an insider on the outside.

The distinction between normal and traumatic jealousy (Lewin, 2011) alongside libidinal and destructive envy (Gerhardt, 2016) could be thought of as affective storms between close relatives, with family members perhaps not in agreement. The early need to inhabit and feel like the ideal other (Benjamin, 1995) resides in the normal states of both envy and jealousy. The fear and consequent trauma of losing that important other to a real or imagined rival inhabits the emotional states of jealousy. Destructive envy takes the stage when the threat of difference between self and other is unbearable and untenable in the face of feelings of inferiority, defectiveness, and shame. Could jealousy as the rival of envy be related to the profoundly lost object beyond the landscape of the stand-in substitute that one desires to acquire?

Jealousy betwixt envy had made an unbidden entrance onto the stage of my personal landscape and paradoxically I needed to open the door to differentiate self and other, and sameness and difference within relatedness. The ghosts of jealousy needed to be met in the darkest corners to find light and understanding.

Epilogue: Dedicating a Scottish ballad

Get Up and Bar the Door

It fell about the Martinmas time,
And a gay time it was then,
When our goodwife got puddings to make,
And she's boild them in the pan.
The wind sae cauld blew south and north,
And blew into the floor;
Quoth our goodman to our goodwife,
"Gae out and bar the door."
"Hand is in my hussyfskap,
Goodman, as ye may see;
An it shoud nae be barrd this hundred year,
It's no be barrd for me."
y made a paction tween them twa,
They made it firm and sure,
That the first word whaeer shoud speak,
Shoud rise and bar the door.
Then by there came two gentlemen,
At twelve o clock at night,
And they could neither see house nor hall,

Nor coal nor candle-light.
"Now whether is this a rich man's house,
Or whether is it a poor?"
But neer a word wad ane o them speak,
For barring of the door.
And first they ate the white puddings,
And then they ate the black;
Tho muckle thought the goodwife to hersel,
Yet neer a word she spake.
Then said the one unto the other,
"Here, man, tak ye my knife;
Do ye tak aff the auld man's beard,
And I'll kiss the goodwife."
"But there's nae water in the house,
And what shall we do than?"
"What ails ye at the pudding-broo,
That boils into the pan?"
O up then started our goodman,
An angry man was he:
"Will ye kiss my wife before my een,
And scad me wi pudding-bree?"
Then up and started our goodwife,
Gied three skips on the floor:
"Goodman, you've spoken the foremost word,
Get up and bar the door."
(unknown author, 1700s)

CHAPTER ELEVEN

Treating jealous patients

Susan Kavaler-Adler

Is jealousy really a green-eyed monster? Under what psychological conditions does jealousy become a personified monster? Under what conditions is it just a very intense instinctual and affective feeling experience that can be talked about, contained in symbolic psychic fantasy, and be understood? Under what conditions is jealousy not only a "green-eyed monster," but a monster that enacts murder, as in Shakespeare's (1622) play *Othello*, and in the Verdi (1887) opera version of that play, *Otello*? How did Iago know how to push Othello's buttons, to turn a civilized man into a murderer? What role can we play as psychoanalytic clinicians in transforming potential destructive aggression, in the form of the green-eyed monster of jealousy, into the more benign experience of symbolized hostile fantasy, where self-reflection can be employed to tame the monster? How is jealousy different from envy? How is jealousy more primitive, and

177

protosymbolic rather than symbolic, when primal envy is perpetuated by a primal developmental split in the psyche: preoedipal developmental arrest or Michael Balint's (1968) "basic fault"? These are the
questions I enter this chapter with. As I continue, I hope to address
some of them.

Shakespeare's Othello

The viscerally acute and terrifying drama portrayed in Shakespeare's
Othello, despite being fiction, is mythic in portraying the potential corruption of the human soul by the green-eyed monster of jealousy. Othello is
from Venice, which is east from England, and his military commitment
is in Cyprus, which is further east. So, from the Shakespearian English-
man's point of view, these lands might be considered less civilized. Yet,
Othello is supposed to be a military man who has reached the highest
ranks of society through his military feats. He is welcomed at the level
of aristocracy, and in fact was welcomed in the home of Desdemona's
father, who is a nobleman. It is there that Desdemona heard Othello's
vivid tales of adventures and triumphs over strange creatures like cannibals, and was drawn to him as both a hero and a raconteur. Othello
has much reverence from varying levels of society in Venice. Yet, it is
the ordinary military man, Iago, who is to bring him down, and turn
him into a murderous villain towards a young bride who was presumed to be the most innocent of creatures, inciting the unconscious,
and perhaps archetypical green-eyed monster part of Othello. And by
the way, it is Iago himself who first speaks of jealousy as a "green-eyed
monster." Iago declares to Othello:

> O, beware, my lord, of jealousy! It is the green-ey'd monster which
> doth mock the meat it feeds on … Good heaven, the souls of all my
> tribe defend from jealousy! (cited in Neilson & Hill, 1942, p. 1115)

It is also an ordinary military man, Cassio—although a man promoted in
rank by Othello himself (the reason for Iago's intense envy/jealousy)—
who is to become the specter of tyranny in Othello's eyes. This only
can occur when Iago succeeds at awakening the green-eyed monster
from the personal unconscious of Othello, and perhaps from the
Jungian "collective unconscious" depths inside of Othello. In fact, Iago
sashays around Othello with a cunning art of dropping innuendoes and

implications. Iago's hints of marital wrongdoing escalate—but only in Othello's mind—into a full-blown case of betrayal by Desdemona. The full-blown case implied by Iago advances his innuendos of Desdemona having taken Cassio as her lover. However, such implied—not spoken—accusations come so soon after Desdemona's marriage to Othello that the fallacious case—building only in Othello's mind—defies all reason. What makes Iago such a successful demon, and what makes Othello so vulnerable to his demonology?

First of all, we have the insidious art of Iago, as he proposes implications. He is cunning, and armored with salacious gestures, which are crafted to confuse and perplex Othello beyond all rational thought. Second, we have Iago's brilliant, though demonic, psychological acumen. Iago not only mocks and mimics the salacious gestures that are by implication reflections of Desdemona's womanly wiles with Cassio. He manages to provide Othello with "ocular proof" of betrayal, with the supposed concrete evidence of betrayal seen in Cassio possessing Desdemona's handkerchief. Iago also mocks a conscience for himself! He pretends—again, through the most subtle of hints—that he is distraught by his own accusations towards Cassio.

Performing his evil art to a tee before Othello, Iago stops to repent his own suspicion of Cassio before Othello. He hesitates to advance to a full-blown accusation. He implies that these kind of dangerous thoughts of another man's or woman's guilt must not be thought nor voiced lightly. He does a dance of undoing himself with doubt that only the Devil himself would envy. He is a master of planting the seed of jealousy in Othello's mind, and then of letting it grow to full fruition—but only there, in Othello's mind—not in any overt way being fully formed as an accusation by himself. In this artful manner, Iago portrays, even for himself perhaps, his own mock innocence. He performs a dance of reluctance. Iago: "In the mean-time, Let me be thought too busy in my fear I am-And hold he free, I do beseech your honor" (cited in Neilson & Hill, 1942, p. 1116). And Othello, in response, in his own mind: "This fellow [Iago] is of exceeding honesty" (p. 1115).

So there we have Iago. But what of Othello's vulnerability? What makes Othello such a fertile target for Iago's Machiavellian maneuvers? Of course, like Icarus, Othello has a long way to fall ("The bigger they are, the harder they fall"). Othello had been elevated to an aristocratic status by military feats and triumphs, and not be any preordained category of birth, the latter being generally a characteristic precedent for aristocratic aura in his own society (Venice/mock England). This in itself leaves Othello vulnerable. In fact, Othello was a black Moor in a brutally racial society in Venice/mock England in 1604, the early fifteenth century. Africans in that region were usually musicians or entertainers at that time. Since Othello was being sent to fight a war in Cyprus, a land further east than Venice is to England, he could probably have been accepted to have a noble military status. However, such status may only have been viable as long as Othello was being used to fight those considered to be the "primitives" "over there"—as long as his status only reigned in the no-man's far-off land of Cyprus.

Beyond all this sociology, what can we infer might have been the preparation for the disaster of the green-eyed monster of jealousy in Othello's mind? Did Othello secretly believe that he was unsuited for the lofty status to which he had arisen? Did he secretly feel like a fraud? Did he secretly believe that he was unworthy of all he had earned, not only in terms of status, but particularly, in terms of winning Desdemona to consent to be his wife, especially when she was willing to be disowned by her father to marry him? If so, could Othello's lack of self-worth stem back to primal trauma in Othello's preoedipal childhood, which would inevitably compound oedipal stage jealousy in his psyche? Did Othello suffer early mother loss that would evoke primal envy in an intense pre-symbolic form, and thus could compel his psyche into a particularly violent form of oedipal level jealousy—as the triad of mother, father, and child follows the earlier primal attachment dyad with mother? Did Othello suffer maternal abandonment, in addition to the usual oedipal child's sense of betrayal, when he can't marry "mommy," or have mommy all to himself?

As readers of Shakespeare, we can never answer these questions, since we have no history of Othello's life or childhood. Yet, such questions have psychological conundrums related to early splitting and dissociation, and related to primal narcissistic injury, annihilation anxiety, and developmental arrest. Such psychological phenomena may hide under courageous valor, and even under a spirit of generosity, which may survive without requiring a false grandiose self-exterior. In fact, Othello was never seen as a figure of arrogance, narcissistic false pride, and contempt. It is quite possible that Othello was primarily authentic, but nevertheless he could have believed himself to be a fraud. This would make him highly vulnerable—vulnerable to all deceptions that challenge his self-confidence—and vulnerable to jealousy in particular.

In jealousy, there is always the haunting belief that the rival for the conquest of a dame is actually the more worthy one. For jealousy to have its full sway of tyranny, however, that belief must remain unconscious. The mind of the one obsessed with the tyranny of jealous rage is fundamentally plagued with fears of an unbearable loss. In the mind of Othello, if he were deranged with an obsessive fear of a primal loss at the level of maternal abandonment in infancy or toddlerhood, the only way of stamping out the murderous offense of betrayal is to murder the one who is believed to have committed the betrayal—in this case Desdemona. Yet, in responding to the betrayal that is unconsciously interpreted as murder, the prized and desperately needed loved one must be murdered, and so ironically (unconscious irony) the man creates his own dreaded loss, and actually repeats his own probable maternal abandonment (whether emotional or actual). We see then the denouement of a Greek tragedy. We see the self-fulfilling prophesy becoming fatal self-sabotage, as the rejection of self-abandonment is provoked unchecked by the authority of a reality related ego/self (Fairbairn's "central ego," 1952).

Perhaps we can even relate this to suicide bombing today. However, suicide bombing seems more related to primal level envy, which perpetually destroys those identified as "other." This contrasts to the higher level murderous hate in jealousy. In oedipal level jealousy, there are three whole object figures, who are also differentiated in terms of gender characteristics, as well as in terms of other personality characteristics.[1]

Differentiating jealousy from envy

Following Freud's view of jealousy as a competitive dynamic in the oedipal triad of two parents and a child, Melanie Klein (1957) spoke of how such jealousy had a narrative distinct from that of envy. This narrative of jealousy is separate from the narrative of relentless, perpetuated destruction towards the needed Other in the oral stage envy, where one always self-sabotages by "biting the hand that feeds you." Klein points out that in jealousy, there is love involved, not just hate, whereas in oral envy, the narrative is of compulsion to destroy what the other has, because at that level, all is polarized in a primal split of: "He has it. I don't." So, with no dialectic in the binary, only polarization, one can only want to destroy with hate what the other has that you think you can never have. However, in jealousy, there is love because the object of desire is loved. This is despite there being trenchant hate directed at the rival. Further, the man (or woman) possessed by jealousy threatens to possess the loved third other, threatening to deprive the subject of all that is loved and desired in the third party, the desired object. Subjectivity is only experienced in the oedipal level depressive position, and not in the oral level paranoid-schizoid position dynamics. So, the narrative of true jealousy, as opposed to envy, encompasses love, as well as subjectivity, along with the hate of destructive and perhaps murderous intent. Also, jealousy always involves three differentiated personalities; and is not like envy, which is reductive to one wanting what a second undifferentiated part object other has. With envy, not having what the part object other has is experienced as a severe narcissistic insult, or as the devaluation, and spoiling, of the self as object. Envy contrasts with the jealousy of a higher level self, as subject, who can eventually develop depressive guilt and grief, which leads to concern and to empathy.

However, Klein also implies that when one has unresolved, un-symbolized, and un-interpreted envy, the oedipal stage dynamic of jealousy is poisoned by the more primitive envy. So the preoedipal stage dynamics, and the paranoid-schizoid position psychodynamics of each individual, affects the nature of the unconscious, as well as the conscious, experience of jealousy, even when the oedipal stage triadic constellation of human relationship is reached. Especially in patients who have preoedipal trauma and developmental arrest, oedipal level jealousy is often enacted in a highly undifferentiated and highly polarized form, which can extend to the act of murder. Those who have a good-enough level of contact and connection with mother during the preoedipal phases, particularly during the separation-individuation phases, can internalize relatedness and attunement to a significant degree. In this way, primal trauma and psychic developmental arrest are avoided, despite primal disruptions and disappointments. With such adequate internalization (Mahler, Pine, & Bergman, 1975; Masterson, 1976, 1981), development of the subjective self, and of the internal psychic structure of relationships and dialogue, and of all forms of psychic dialectic and self-reflection can develop. The capacity to mourn object-loss also develops, since loss is then at a tolerable level of grief affect, and can be processed by a psychic structured ego. Thus, what I have termed "developmental mourning" (Kavaler-Adler, 1992, 1993, 1995, 1996, 2003b, 2004, 2006b, 2007, 2013b) can emerge organically, from the affect on whole object connections within the internal world (mostly repressed). Consequently, the subjective self evolves throughout life, with an open system in which love and creativity can continually emerge from a sufficiently integrated self Jealousy can then become symbolized and contained internally through symbolization. Then it can be processed as murderous fantasy, or as a hungry desire to have what the other has in a third person, a differentiated and loved other/ lover. Thus, contained as murder in psychic fantasy, actual fatal murder does not have to be committed!

Clinical vignette: 1

Primitive envy misnamed jealousy

Every time I attempted to speak to Vivien of her problems with her boyfriend, which she would parade before me, she would lash out instantaneously with a sharp, enraged, and vulgar attack: "You're just an envious bitch!" That would be the end of it. There would be no discussion of what she or I thought was going on with her and her boyfriend. She implied that I would be out to make critical attacking judgments on what she and her boyfriend had, but she never actually said this. She warded off any projected and feared judgments by assaulting me with "You're an envious bitch!" Sometimes she would throw in "My boyfriend thinks you're a dog! You're just jealous because no man would ever look at you!" (hardly my experience, but reality was irrelevant). When I once suggested she might be envious of a niece of her boyfriend's who was getting a lot of attention and gifts when graduating from high school, she erupted with accusatory rage (no reflective thought possible when her own sense of narcissistic injury and insult was aroused), exclaiming: "I got all the attention from all my teachers and family when I graduated. Everyone said I was brilliant, and my older sister cried non-stop at my graduation because nobody gave her any attention when she graduated! I know what 'jealousy' is!"

Then Vivien continued her assault on me: "You're just jealous because nobody ever went to your graduation, and you didn't have any boyfriends in high school." Vivien said this without any knowledge of my life. Vivien didn't even posit her paranoid theories as "probably." To Vivien, her view of me was a fact because she chose to say it. "And," she continued to spit and spout, "and now you're old and no man would look at you!" "And," she ejected again, expelling her venom, to get rid of the rage and self-hate inside of her, "you think you're a doctor just because you're a PhD," which was said with belittling, sarcastic, mocking slurs. "You're not a doctorrrrrrr. You're just a bitch!"

This woman had a mother who would exclude her from any interactions with her father. But even more, on the gross level of the envious family dynamics, her mother would sit on her father's lap in front of her, and would exhibit her body intimacy with the patient's father, while proclaiming, to her daughter, "I'm really good in bed! I'm the one who won your father!" Given this behavior on Vivien's mother's part, it is easy to see the birth of the cumulative trauma of exclusion and humiliation that led Vivien to ram her relationship with her boyfriend down my throat, while simultaneously warding off any comments I could make to help her with problems in that relationship. It was as if I only wanted to tear what she had to shreds because I didn't have it. Vivien assumed in me (or projected) the primal oral envy that Melanie Klein (1957) and Otto Kernberg (1975) talk about repeatedly. Yet, Vivien often flung out the word "jealousy" in her interactions with me. She would play the role of her mother, and put me in the position of the excluded and inferior child she had felt herself to be when she had been faced with her mother's farcical displays of superiority. There were no differentiated people involved in Vivien's spit-out cannonball blasting comments. This didn't mean that Vivien couldn't be capable of seeing people as more differentiated at other times, reaching towards whole object and subjective self-experience. However, the minute her envy and profound shame was triggered, just as it had been when her mother practically undressed and had sex in front of her with her father, she would instantly regress to the pre-symbolic paranoid-schizoid level of psychic reactivity, rather than sustaining any capacity for reflective thought.

Sometimes an analytic comment of mine would provoke this. Vivien would experience any analytic comment as pointing out a lack in herself. Consequently, Vivien would fight to the death to annihilate me as a separate presence at that point. Since she could not digest my words at a symbolic level of meaning, she would polarize her internal part objects—now projected out onto me—in an envious display. Her envious attack would masquerade as jealousy, in the way she used language. She would imply that I was jealous of her having her boyfriend, as her mother had taunted her into extreme states of envious hungry craving for her father. She might use the word "jealousy," but then would say I was an envious bitch, revealing her own state of unconscious envy. Vivien had to deny her hunger at any cost, as if it proved a lack in herself. She conveniently externalized and placed all her starving envy into me. Although she implied jealousy, I would hardly have been able to be jealous of her having her boyfriend, given the problems she told me about in that relationship.

It seems that Vivien was repeating, through her projections, her primal envy. Yet, there was also jealousy. Vivien had been deprived of her father's attention by her mother, which probably made her jealous of her mother for having her father. Yet primal oral envy could take over the psychological realm of jealousy. Then, Vivien's jealousy could be intensified by hard-core starving hunger, impulses to destroy whatever I, the other, had. This was not just a compulsion to destroy a differentiated woman who she saw as having the attraction of another man, or of men (as characteristic of oedipal dynamics). Vivien seemed to want to destroy me for having anything at all, at times when I was the "bad object" for her. It was as if unconsciously Vivien was saying, "If I can't have your breast, neither can you!"

Vivien knew I had a husband, which was the only thing she knew about my life. She would devalue this at a total level of destructive spoiling (Klein, 1957) by reducing my marriage to: "You have to bring home the money, Susan, or your husband will leave you. You better bring home the money, Susan!" Vivien always said this in a mocking sarcastic voice, splitting out her venom as her mother had often done towards her. Earlier in the treatment, Vivien had used the word "venom" to describe her mother's attacks. She said she had been the target of this kind of assault from her mother throughout her life. Given this, I could not use any of my analytic skills with Vivien. Despite having told me about her history with her mother, Vivien would protect her mother's image, and displace her retaliatory rage attacks onto me. In this place of split-off rage, she did not operate on a symbolic level. Absolutely no analytic comments could be made about how Vivien was repeating what her mother had done to her by doing it to me. Vivien would cut me off at the pass. She would override my words, so that their potential meaning was aborted. Then she wouldn't shut up until I was silent. Although there were more times in between these kinds of envious assaults, as she psychologically grew and developed her external life, there could be no alteration of this envious retaliatory reenactment with me, which eventually became only with me, as she sustained her outside life and relationships in a much better way. Her primal envy remained evident. Her envy of me for having a PhD, husband (or male tango partners attracted to me—I don't think she knew this), or books and publications, could never be felt as a differentiated jealousy, where she actually verbalized the value of what I had, or verbalized any real distinguishing characteristics of whom and what I had. Vivien reduced all to part object stereotypes.

I experienced being with Vivien in her hungry envious place as if I was constantly being reduced to absurdity. Nevertheless, increasing developmental growth, and internalization of the therapeutic relationship has seemed to space out the time between those envious attacks. More transitional space has developed in between these seizure-like states of paranoid rage, which I see as related to envy, as well as to primal hunger for a better object.

At what level can jealousy be played with? At what point can guilt over betrayal become modified into spontaneous play and real concern? At what point can jealous rivalry be thought about, rather than being enacted, and thus be played with? (Winnicott, 1971). In the case of Helen, below, we see a predisposition to jealousy, which sets her up to be suspicious. Her own self-worth becomes the issue in working this through, and helping her value herself as a woman that could actually inspire jealousy in another woman.

Clinical vignette: 2
True jealousy (as opposed to envy)

Helen had never had a long-term, truly committed boyfriend. She had never formerly had a boyfriend with whom she lived, or one with whom she could share intellectual interests and creative activities. When she found a man she could have this with, she began to imagine that he would be lured away by some other woman, who would seem more interesting and less boring than she. Helen could set up a self-fulfilling prophesy with this mindset, and was, therefore, in danger of pushing her boyfriend away. Whenever she shared with her boyfriend her fears about one woman or another being her rival for her boyfriend's attraction, her boyfriend would dismiss her thoughts as her own neurotic fantasies. He would not engage with her in any speculations about his actually wanting to be involved with another woman. Then one summer her boyfriend stayed for a few weeks with Helen's family, at their country home, and Helen's two sisters were there. Her younger sister, who was always envious of what Helen had, tried to copy everything she did, and then would parade her hyper-valued imitation before Helen's boyfriend. In fact, Helen's younger sister would read books that Helen liked. Then she would compete with Helen by discussing the meaning of these books with Helen's boyfriend. Even though Helen's sister was far less sophisticated in her intellectual discussions than Helen was, Helen felt she was faced with a rival in her younger sister for her boyfriend's attraction and affection. What was envy of Helen in the psyche of her younger sister became jealousy in Helen towards her younger envious sister, who she then experienced as a rival for her deeply valued boyfriend.

Helen's sister only wanted to have whatever Helen had, and to destroy Helen's enjoyment of what she had, as in envy. However, Helen actually valued her boyfriend (the third in the jealous dyad) and so love was involved. This was clearly characteristic of jealousy; as opposed to the hate and murderous destructiveness seen in envy. Eventually, Helen talked to her boyfriend about her feelings, having contained them enough to speak about them with symbolic meaning in her three times a week psychoanalysis (later four times a week). As usual, her boyfriend was initially ready to dismiss her suspicions, but Helen fought to articulate how seriously hurt she was by him joining her younger sister in all these discussions and activities that mimicked her own interests. Her boyfriend listened then and began to judiciously distance himself from Helen's sister.

Helen, in turn, began to value her boyfriend more, and to be less suspicious of him. Someone who never had the background of oedipal level jealousy with her father and mother that Helen had, might have been less likely to have the ongoing jealous suspicions that Helen had. This relates back to how Helen took pride in thinking herself an oedipal victor in relation to her mother. She had always thought her father found her company more enjoyable than that of her mother. Given her own wish to be a victor of the man's love in a love triangle, Helen could easily be vulnerable to feeling that another woman—even her sister— would lord it over her, and leave her in the dust, with the male prize. Her mind was set up for this level of haunting jealous suspicion that poisoned her love life.

Helen was able to contain her instinctual impulses and affective feelings in the situation, to keep them contained in fantasy, and to talk about them in her analysis, and eventually with her boyfriend. This is quite a contrast to an Othello or a Vivien. Eventually, Helen could even play with her own preoccupations with jealousy, when she spoke to me in analysis, lessening the despair behind her fears, and gradually came to sustain internal world whole object relations for longer periods of time.

Clinical vignette: 3
In the transference: on the couch a man

Leonard was an oedipal level neurotic, who had been in psychoanalytic psychotherapy with me for several years. He was capable of seeing me as a symbolic transference figure, having attained representational parental introjects in his internal world—as opposed to those who can only act things out with the therapist, since they have not formed symbolic representational forms of their parental objects.[2] Leonard could therefore contain his affect life in symbolic fantasies, which he could convey to me with words. His transference fantasies revealed his oedipal stage jealousy, and also revealed his Kleinian "depressive position" capacities to feel and process existential guilt, as opposed to "paranoid-schizoid position" level "persecution" with urges towards retaliatory enactment. Therefore, Leonard could feel and mentally process the grief of loss. This was in contrast to somebody who is psychologically operating in Melanie Klein's (1946) "paranoid-schizoid position," who cannot contain guilt, but who suffers persecution with powerful instinctual urges towards retaliatory enactment.

Leonard was aware of his jealous feelings and desires. For example, when he saw my husband bringing me a café latte at my office before his session, Leonard suspected the man he saw was my husband. Then Leonard would have fantasies of what kind of husband my husband was for me. He would be glad that my husband seemed to be taking care of me, but he would also be conscious of feeling jealous about the relationship he imagined between me and my husband. This would remind him of things he experienced with his parents in childhood. However, he would also imagine the other side of the oedipal triangle. He would think of my husband being jealous of him, whenever he would share intimate and sexual thoughts about me. He would fear a rivalry with my husband, in which he would feel small and inferior, or a rivalry in which my husband would feel inadequate, due to the degree of intimacy he shared with me. In many ways, Leonard had been an oedipal victor with his mother and father. In fact, his mother would share her confidences, feelings, and dreams with him, when she could not speak about such things with her husband, Leonard's father.

Leonard was seen as the "sensitive one" by his mother. However, this left him vulnerable to not being seen as being as much of a man as his father. His mother would use Leonard to express all her anger towards her husband, and then she would be purged of her rage, so that when her husband returned home, she was friendly and even solicitous to him. This would provoke feelings of betrayal and of jealousy in Leonard. He would be angry at his mother for treating him as so special during the day, and then catering to his father at night, having rid herself of her anger by expressing it to Leonard. Instead of just feeling used by his mother, he would feel betrayed, due to his oedipal level of unconscious fantasy.

Leonard would also be provoked into sexual interest towards herself by his mother, when she would seem to intentionally undress with her bedroom door open, so that he could see her bare breasts. Then when his mother succeeded in provoking him into looking at her, she would turn everything around on him, by glaring at him and saying "What are you looking at?" He felt tricked by his mother's seduction, and then humiliated by his mother's guilt-provoking accusatory attacks. However, later, in analysis, he also wondered why his mother needed him to be aroused by her, especially when she would walk around the house in fairly sheer nightgowns at night. When young, he had been stimulated to think about his mother's sexual relationship with his father. Then he would feel jealous, but also would feel convinced that his father was jealous of him, when his father would get punitive, arrogant, and harsh towards him, challenging him to be a man, as if his father was facing a rival for his bride. All this made Leonard angry at both his parents, but he often masochistically turned his anger into guilt, and self-condemnation, blaming himself, so as to avoid feeling alone and to avoid feeling threatened by hate towards his parents. Leonard would protect the image of his parents, by telling himself that he was bad for peeking looks at his mother's body, or for thinking that he was the superior "sensitive" man in the triad of father and son relationship with his mother. Leonard would imagine taking his "punishment" of being put down with sarcastic and contemptuous comments by his father, which implied that he wasn't a "real man." When his mother turned all her attention to his father at night, Leonard would also feel that he was being seen as the inferior man by his mother, thinking that his sensitive and empathic understanding of his mother's feelings only made him more "feminine" in his mother's eyes, and therefore in his own. In the extreme dynamic of this triadic oedipal relationship, he would feel castrated by both his parents. Then he would identify with their aggression by condemning and castrating himself in his own mind. As he belittled himself internally, he would feel more vulnerable to jealousy towards his father in relation to his mother, and towards his mother in relation to his father. He felt like a third wheel, losing the feeling of being the special son to his mother or to his father.

In the transference, Leonard would imagine me at the window, with no blouse on, baring my breasts at the window, as if he would see my bare breasts as he came towards my office. He would seek erotic stimulation to make him feel not only instinctually stimulated, but also psychologically puffed up to feel like a man, a man who was capable of being attracted to his transferential mother on an adult sexual level. Leonard would also feel guilt. He would try not to look at me if I wore a summer dress, in which there was any hint of cleavage showing. He was, however, able to talk about all this in his psychoanalytic therapy sessions, and he became less anxious about telling me his thoughts. Gradually, Leonard's persecutory guilt lessened, and we could have a playful conversation.[3]

Leonard's existential guilt (as opposed to his neurotic guilt), in relation to jealousy, would be seen when he feared he would provoke his wife into jealousy. Leonard also feared provoking the husband of the woman he was flirting with into jealousy. He would feel that he couldn't have enough intimacy and sexual desire with his wife. So he would turn to the affections of a former professor, who shared his needs, despite her own marital status. He and this professor would share their mutual attraction on the phone, mostly thoughts of sexual acts and confessions of love and desire. In the back of Leonard's mind was always the fear that he would provoke his wife into jealous rages, and that she would then divorce him. He feared such retaliation in the paranoid-schizoid psychic position, but he also felt actual existential grief within guilt, since he loved his wife and didn't want to hurt her. Further, he had fears of humiliating castrations from his ex-professor's husband, which would interact with Leonard's fears and jealousies related to my husband. Both my husband, and the female ex-professor's husband, became transference father figures in Leonard's mind.

Sometimes Leonard would imagine that God was punishing him for his psychological and enacted transgressions by creating new losses in his life. He had early-life sibling loss, and remained very vulnerable to deep feelings of grief as new losses brought up associations to his old primal losses in his mind. He tried to ward this off by avoiding thoughts of sexual interest or desire with me in the transference, or by not facing consciousness of the depth of pain he felt with new losses that always encompassed the old losses. In a sense, God became the castrating and punishing father who was jealous of his erotic relationships with women, as his father had been experienced in relation to his erotic desires and sexual curiosity in relation to his mother.

As Leonard spoke about all his provocations of jealousy in others, and also became less resistant to talk about his jealousy of others whom he saw as rivals, some of whom were rivals for me in the transference, he became more accepting of all his feelings. As guilt and fear turned to play and empathic understanding of the frustrations and conflicts he was dealing with, Leonard was able to increasingly relax about the impact of the triangles with men and women that existed in his life. He gradually stood up to his wife when she was provoked into jealousy, and he found that she actually became kinder and more attentive to him, although she was initially upset. His wife also stopped asking him about his analysis with a woman analyst in a perpetually intrusive and disapproving way. Further, his own jealousy became increasingly tolerable as he could put the emotion into words. Then he could have all his feelings, so that the dangerous aggressive instincts that accompany jealousy (even in those at the oedipal level) would not threaten his psyche and his relationship.

Leonard also accepted that he had once punched a guy who he caught having a sexual affair with his wife, when he and his wife were very young (decades ago). With self-reflection, Leonard decided that he was entitled to take a swing at the guy, when he found him in his own house, in the middle of some sexual episode with his wife. As he came to accept his own jealousy, he became less frightened of retaliation in relation to his possible provocations of jealousy in others. Then Leonard's existential guilt could be felt and processed as just being human feelings. Leonard began to value that he could feel grief with poignant acuteness, even when losses were related to things he may have done to hurt the ones he loved, rather than to major bereavements that he had suffered. His actual bereavements were much more monumental, due to the tragic level of loss involved, and particularly the sibling loss. Gradually, Leonard began to see that this capacity to feel and tolerate guilt made him more of a man (and not just his mother's sensitive son). This, in turn, lessened his taunting and castrating attacks on himself in his internal world. He became less jealous of himself as the sensitive son in his internal world. He became less identified with his father in his father's jealousy towards him, since he was separating from a father who defined manhood entirely differently.

Leonard became less afraid of provoking jealousy in others, and became increasingly free. Our playful interchanges in more recent analytic sessions are a testimony to this. In a period before "play" in his psychoanalysis was possible, Leonard had much painful grief, as well as angry resistance to sharing. He had suffered much self-hate. But now we play! I say, "You are so much more spontaneous!" He says, smiling as he gets up from the couch at the session's end: "That's what I come here for." This spontaneity came after a long period of time in which he was questioning, "What am I here for?"

Clinical vignette: 4
In the transference: a case of a woman who could express jealousy dramas in fantasies in analysis

Amy came into psychoanalytic treatment (three times a week) with a full-blown homoerotic transference towards me, her female analyst (Kavaler-Adler, 2003a, 2003b). She had adopted a lesbian lifestyle years ago, having been married to a man earlier on. Her attraction to the analyst became multidimensional in all kinds of playful scenes of triadic jealousy. Sometimes she would play the masculine role in these sexual scenes, and sometimes she would be identified with me in the feminine role. However, there was always an oedipal triangle, despite all her bisexual modes of expression, with altering gender identities, and altering sex object choice.

Some of Amy's fantasies were of having a sexual affair with me in my office. She said that she would "take my pearl in her mouth," "drown in my come," and then would "wrap me up in a blanket afterwards," holding me tenderly. Aside from the fact that she saw me as representing her, up to then unconscious, child-self, as I regressed into the state of a tender child, wrapped a blanket, Amy also had the oedipal triangle, in which my husband was imagined banging on the outside of my office door, as my husband came to jealously "defend his territory!" Amy obviously projected her own jealous rivalry towards my husband onto the fantasy figure of my husband. She also attempted to disown her own jealousy by becoming, in her fantasy, part of the sex scene between me and my husband, that which traditionally would be seen as the primal scene, with the parental couple in the internal world having sex in front of her. When I went away for a vacation, Amy told me of her imaginings about my vacation when

I returned. She said she imagined me and my husband having sex in a hotel, where I would get excited to the point of orgasm by my husband beating me. She said she imagined that I loved being beaten, and imagined me reaching the heights of sexual excitement and ecstasy through surrendering to this erotic beating. She then imagined that she was in the background the whole time, watching the sexual scene, while she cheered me on to my orgasms. So she managed to avoid feeling excluded from the parental couple; she imagined other scenarios in which she and I were being penetrated by a man side by side, one after the other, so she avoided jealousy and exclusion in this way. She was then in the feminine receptive role along with me. Other times, she was in her masculine side, and somewhat in a false masculine persona. She herself later referred to this as her "false self." But she felt the erotic masculine sensations that she also felt in her real life, with her female lover, as she pictured strapping on a dildo and penetrating me. In this fantasy, Amy had my husband being the one on the outside, in the position of exclusion and jealousy.

When Amy did feel conscious jealousy, she would feel like exploding with rage, and she would speak of her fantasy wish: "Throw you against the wall and fuck you!" She remembered a scene of accidentally going into her parents' bedroom when they failed to close their door during sex. Afterwards, everyone in the family was mortified with embarrassment and shame, staring down at their plates at the dinner table, and not being able to look at each other. Nobody could speak about these sexual things in her family, even though there was so much sexualized enactment going on in her family all the time. With all this enactment, someone was always excluded. One of Amy's most anguished early memories was of being three years old and being caught in a terrifying trap, in between the conflict between her parents, when her father returned home after an extramarital affair. Her father's sexual affairs were frequent, and Amy's mother was the most aggrandized of victims of her husband's exclusion. In this three year old's memory, Amy ran downstairs to open the door for her father, who was banging persistently on a door that had been locked with a new lock that he couldn't open. Her mother screamed at Amy from upstairs, "If you open that door, I will kill you!" Her father screamed, over and over, "Open the door!"

Three-year-old little Amy was paralyzed, and she ran towards the door, and then ran away from it, as her mother screamed again: "If you open that door, I will kill you!"

Amy's mother's jealousy, and Amy's mother's betrayals pervaded the household as Amy grew up. Naturally, Amy got some relief from the traumatizing effect of these scenes by eroticizing them. She would create triadic sexual scenarios in fantasy, and then in transference fantasy, where she could be in control by creating the fantasy. By making herself the audience in a scene of passionate lovemaking between myself and my husband, she managed to include herself, and avoid her own jealousy. By being my lover, in her mind, and having my husband banging on the door from the outside, the way her father had banged on the door that night when she was three, Amy became the one in control. In her fantasy, Amy had my husband in the helpless position of jealous rage and frustrated sexual desire—implying also frustrated cravings for maternal nurturance from the preoedipal level. In this way, Amy could avoid conscious jealousy and all the threats of overwhelming feeling that came with it. Later in treatment, Amy would have to feel this emotional need behind sexual desire more consciously. She had a dream where she associated to my needs being overwhelming, as she threw one eel after another over the side of a boat. However, when I interpreted that these eels also represented her own needs being felt as overwhelming to her, she had to admit to the conscious state of need, having been defensive in response to my interpretation. Once she consciously began to own her needs, she had a chance for the child part of her—which she felt through loss and mourning of injuries and losses—to grow up. She then had her full feminine side organically emerge, as well as a natural (not "false self") masculine side that wanted to develop. Amy began to own and integrate all the parts of herself that had been partially repressed and projected, as well as having been often dissociated.

Jealousy could be owned and tolerated in symbolic fantasy, when mourning of childhood losses (Kavaler-Adler, 1992, 1993, 1996, 2003b, 2007), such as emotional abandonment by her mother, could be felt with the support of the analyst and the analytic "holding environment" (Winnicott, 1965). This helped Amy to be able to commit to her long-term lesbian lover. This occurred even though Amy became conscious of desires for male penetration and male love in the later stages of her analysis, when oedipal desire, conflict, and jealousies became felt, and her feminine self emerged in full desire to surrender to male love and male phallic penetration. In her own words, Amy no longer felt like "a hamster on a wheel," who was always drawn away from her lover to want emotional and erotic affairs with others. She became more present with her lover, as all parts of herself could be accepted both by her and by her lover and long-term partner. In fact, throughout her analysis, Amy had feared that she was betraying her lover by having fantasies of making love to me, and by actually calling flower shops to send me long-stemmed roses, until she could put these gifts of love into words at a symbolic level.

In the middle of enjoying fantasies of lovemaking with me in her mind, Amy would stop and express anger about being lulled into such desires by analysis. She would fear that she was betraying her lover, and feared her lover would become highly enraged and jealous if she knew. One day, she confessed to her lover that she had actually sent me long-stemmed red roses, which was what she used to send her lover. She was extremely relieved when her lover understood that these kinds of things could take place in analysis. Amy had feared the wrath of her monumentally jealous and retaliatory mother. But she was met with a very different response. The Greek tragedy in her mind did not play itself out in a triad of jealous competition between her external world lover and her transference mother/lover (her female analyst). Seeing this, Amy could begin to relax.

Gradually Amy began to enjoy the feminine side of her development. She stood up to her lover, when her lover questioned why she wanted to dress differently. Her lover was shocked when Amy was considering wearing a dress. Ultimately, Amy decided to wear elegant pants suits, with a touch of jewelry. As Amy's fears of jealousy within herself and within others lessened, she was able to articulate her needs and desires in words. Then her need for powerful erotic fantasies in analysis lessened. Very significantly, her sex life with her lover/partner improved.

Clinical vignette: 5
Simon: the man who was haunted by jealous thoughts

Simon said his relationship with Rachel was different than any relationship with women in his past. He felt more exposed to being truly known by Rachel, unlike with former girlfriends. He felt challenged with Rachel because of the intense periods of sustained intimacy with heights of sexual passion. Yet, somehow Simon continued to experience Rachel as a mystery, despite how many facts she shared about her life. Also, with Rachel, Simon was haunted by fears that had never plagued him before. In fact, in the past he had been the one to cheat in a relationship, and he never thought of it as a betrayal at the time. He was shocked when his former girlfriend's jealousy resulted in a breakup of a relationship of several years.

Now, with Rachel, Simon could not stop imagining that Rachel was with another man. He tried to deny to himself how deeply threatened he felt by such fears. In fact, it took much time for him to admit to himself that he actually felt haunted on a continuing basis by the fear that Rachel was with another man. Symptomatically, when Simon called Rachel on his cell phone, and she wasn't immediately available, he would begin to "freak out." If Rachel did not answer the call and say "Simon?" instantly he would start to imagine that she was out on a date with another man, or that she was in bed with another man. In his therapy sessions, Simon assured me that he never had such suspicious thoughts before about another woman. He said that it was something about Rachel that unnerved him. He wondered whether it was a combination of her deep emotional and sexual availability that made him feel ongoing terror about losing her. However, Simon's terror of losing Rachel was often overwhelmed by his sense of enraged, and very self-righteous, aggression towards her. In fact, Simon explained this by interpreting her possible betrayal of their monogamous contract as a deliberate attempt to traumatize him, taking advantage of his revealing his sensitive nature to Rachel.

Where Simon's suspicions originated was only partially apparent to Simon. He referred to Rachel having kept one secret from him at the beginning of their relationship. But could such a small transgression really arouse his constant state of haunted terror and of exquisitely sensitive vulnerability? Simon asked this to himself. How could he be almost feeling like he was losing his mind, simply over suspicious thoughts about Rachel's commitment to him? He could not believe it himself how haunted he was by suspicions that Rachel was with another man. He brought this one shred of rational reason for suspicion into the consulting room, and shared his thoughts while lying on the couch in his psychoanalytic therapy session. He would repeat this shred of rational reasoned suspicion over and over again, as he obsessed about why he could not trust Rachel, and why this led to him being distant from the woman who he said he was most passionately "in love" with.

So we talked about Rachel's resistance to his interrogation of her about things in the beginning of their relationship. They had already decided to commit themselves to each other, and he assumed that she was being honest in saying she had not dated anyone else since that time. But then Rachel casually mentioned that she had gone on a date with a medical doctor on a certain day, which Simon quickly calculated was after he and Rachel had met and decided to get serious (meaning to each of them exclusively dating each other). Simon went into a tailspin. He kept checking the date over and over again in his mind, and then he asked Rachel if she was sure she hadn't seen anyone but him after a certain date, prior to that when they had a serious conversation about commitment. Rachel stuck to her story of absolute exclusivity with him. Simon reacted by feeling like he was losing his mind.

Eventually Rachel admitted that she had gone on one single date then because the guy looked so handsome in the picture she saw of him through an online dating service. She admitted that his lucrative income had also attracted her. Rachel defended herself by saying that she had been feeling very insecure about managing her life on the income she had. She said she just couldn't resist going on one date with this guy to check him out, even though she immediately decided to stay fully committed to Simon, as soon as she actually spent an evening with this other guy. But this did not appease Simon's fears about Rachel's loyalty to him at all! In fact his fear increased. After all, he tortured himself with obsessional thoughts because he had caught Rachel in a lie, even after he had committed himself to her, and even after she had proclaimed her commitment to him. Simon couldn't forget this one incident, even though it was right at the beginning of their relationship, when they had just begun talking about seriously being together, way before they had even considered moving in together. Simon could not stop having the disturbing and perseverating thought: "If she lied once she could lie again," and the accompanying thought: "Is she with another man now? Is she looking for a better catch, someone cuter, smarter, or richer?" He thought he was being rational, since he had caught her in a lie about being with another man. Yet the intense haunting nature of his jealousy obsession suggested— even to him—that he might be "a little nuts," because ever since that early time, Rachel had shown herself to be totally commit- ted to the exclusive monogamy of their agreed-upon relationship. Not knowing about how he might be unconsciously projecting his own wandering ways nor appreciating how Rachel might serve as a transference representative of a figure from his past, left Simon in the dark, continually crying out in therapy, "Why can't I forget this thing? It's killing me!" He found himself being more distant from Rachel than ever. He feared he would destroy the whole rela- tionship, especially the most intimate sexual and emotional shar- ing that he and Rachel had enjoyed.

In analysis, Simon was to learn that Rachel indeed represented a transference figure, in fact the ultimate transference figure: his mother. Disturbing memories began coming back to him. One particular traumatic memory reared its head. When he was in his latency years, his mother—who was a fairly well-known actress before her marriage to his father—had run away from the family. She had left him and his younger sister all alone with a father who was emotionally detached, and who was very rarely at home. In fact, when he and his sister weren't in school, they were often in the care of young teenage babysitters, with whom they felt quite inse- cure. Years later, one of the former babysitters, whom he met when away at a university, told him that his father had been seduced by his runaway mother into living half the time with her and also serving as her agent so she could try to get back into show business. That was disturbing enough to hear, but then the former babysitter told him that his father would talk about how his wife resented ever having left show business to become a mother. Simon was devastated when he heard this, even though he was then of college age, and no longer at home longing for a mother who left him.

As his psychoanalyst, I said to Simon that it made sense that with such a traumatic experience of abandonment by his mother, he might have trouble trusting women. I also said that the fact that his mother's feelings had been building up to the point of run- ning away to New York City to a hotel and leaving the family, also would make a case in his mind for suspicions about the underlying motives of women. After all, Simon learned that women who might on the surface be "playing their role" well—the role of devotion to caring for another, or others—might secretly be harboring desires to depart and to get rid of those who they supposedly care about, or those that they are caring for. Simon said that "Yes," he could see that that all made sense. However, Simon didn't really "get it" on an emotional level. After all, to his conscious mind Rachel seemed nothing like his mother, and to his conscious mind he was "over all that," about his mother leaving him and his sister behind to go back into show business in New York. To his conscious mind, all that was irrelevant to his current state since it was years ago.

Then something came alive in the transference with me that made Simon think again. He began to fail to show up for sessions. He actually began to forget a lot of his sessions, and hadn't even thought of setting a reminder alert on his phone so that he wouldn't forget. He was vague and distant in his sessions. When I tried to explore his unconscious "forgetting," he got defensive. He said that he forgot a lot of things, not just his therapy sessions. He had been forgetting things for years. I suggested that forgetting things was a way of forgetting things that are too painful to remember, like the inconstancy of women, which he generally interpreted as betrayal and abandonment. Suddenly, Simon turned his accusing tone and accusing looks (not seen fully while on the couch) on me. He said that he thought I had ulterior motives in charging for the sessions that he forgot and didn't show up for. He never had a problem with the understood commitment that he would pay for his session times before, even if he couldn't attend, especially when he didn't ask for rescheduling for his missed sessions ahead of time.

Now—and it did seem sudden to me—Simon began to wonder if I really took pleasure in his not showing up, so that I could earn money for sessions I did not have to work in. He even went on to say that: "No woman could be trusted!" He suddenly launched into suspicion of me even though he intellectually knew that I had been the one trying to reach him by phone and email when he wouldn't be showing for his session times. In contrast to me enjoying his absences so I could get paid for no work, I had spent the sessions wondering how to reach him, and wondering what was going on for him.

Intellectually, Simon knew this, but emotionally, he needed an opportunity to see me as the betraying woman. Unconsciously, he may have needed to distrust me, so he could work out his trouble trusting women. He was becoming very afraid of being alone for the rest of his life. He was afraid he would not be able to sustain love for any woman, due to his deep distrust of women, despite his intellectual excuses for his mother and for Rachel. We are still in the process of understanding Simon's distrust of me, and therefore understanding his fear of trusting women. The hurt and pain that Simon suffered as a child, when he was rejected by his mother—at least rejected in terms of being cared for daily by her—is beginning to surface.

Some of Simon's pain is related to how disturbing to him it is to have so much anger at his mother, as well as having so much anger towards me and Rachel. He is remembering an agony that he had repressed for a lifetime. When his mother left the family home, and left him, he was forced to close off his internal subjective experience, in order to psychologically survive. Simon had no choice but to repress his anger and rage. He had to cooperate with the program his mother and father had set up because he was totally dependent on them for his survival. And for psychic survival, he had to repress the intensity of his feeling. He had to go along with the program then, and now he felt like he was being forced to go along with the program of attending sessions regularly in analysis. So we looked at how trapped he felt and how angry that made him towards me. Outside of the transference, he knows it's his choice to attend therapy sessions or not. Yet, he is reliving the time of his mother's rejection of the care for him and his sister. It is inevitable that he should feel like rebelling against my program of setting time frames. But under the rage about being forced to go wherever his parents wanted him to go is Simon's deep hurt about being rejected by his one and only mother. He feels too hurt to just feel anger and self-righteous rage. He carries a deep wound of narcissistic injury, which is part of what sets him up to be so overtaken by jealousy. Unconsciously—for a lifetime—he has always doubted that he could be truly wanted! Just like Othello, he may doubt he is OK, underneath his surface functioning in the world.

Conclusion

In this contribution, I have shared case examples of those who have triadic oedipal stage jealousy at a symbolized level, in contrast to those with enactments of primal envy. Jealousy can be worked with analytically, that is, by means of interpretation of the unconscious. Those stuck in enactments of primal (oral) envy, are primarily stuck in the paranoid-schizoid position, where differentiated whole object jealousy is not yet on the horizon, and where symbolization of such affect states of envy and jealousy is not developed. I have also shared the dilemma of a patient who has suffered unresolved oedipal stage jealousy, with possible underlying preoedipal merger wishes as well, in the mind of a psychoanalyst.

Although the focus of this chapter was on jealousy, and not on the mourning process necessary to resolve the neurotic self-sabotage involved when jealousy remains unconscious, the clinical necessity for mourning as a developmental process has been indicated in each case. My longer clinical cases on the "developmental mourning" (Kavaler-Adler, 1992, 1993, 1995, 1996, 2003b, 2004, 2006, 2007, 2013a, 2013b) process itself can be read in my books and articles. Particularly relevant, and particularly relevant in relation to mourning of guilt and loss, as in Melanie Klein's "depressive position," are two clinical books: *Mourning, Spirituality, and Psychic Change: A New Object Relations View of Psychoanalysis* (Kavaler-Adler, 2003a, Gradiva Award from NAAP 2004), and *The Anatomy of Regret: From Death Instinct to Reparation and Symbolization through Vivid Case Studies* (Kavaler-Adler, 2013a).

Martin Bergmann (1987), in his book, *The Anatomy of Loving*, speaks of the ubiquitous human fantasy that true love will somehow rid someone of their feelings of both envy and jealousy. Obviously, when people do not enter analysis, both their feelings of envy and jealousy and their belief that love could rid them of such feelings would remain predominantly unconscious. However, in psychoanalysis we have the opportunity to bring these shame-ridden and guilt-laden feelings—as well as the never conceptualized unconscious beliefs attached to them—to consciousness. In this way, we not only help our psychoanalytic patients, we also grow to understand the predicaments of the human condition in greater depth.

In the same book, Bergmann refers to the danger of failed analyses, in which envy and jealousy are not addressed as human phenomenology, and where the normal human mourning for the loss of the oedipal love object is not undertaken by the patient. He references Freud (1916d) speaking about patients who consider themselves to be the grandiose exceptions, who would presume to not have to face the mental prohibitions against incest, nor to have to face being jealous of rivals. These are those "oedipal victors" who can only see themselves as the objects of jealousy but not as those with jealousy within themselves.

I agree with both Freud and Martin Bergmann that nobody can sustain healthy development and healthy and sustained intimate relationships without facing the limitations of the human condition. The human condition requires that we mourn, with true grief affect, and with conscious awareness of what must be relinquished, to move on to adult human relations. To mourn, one must symbolize the original primal love objects, and the old infantile or oedipal mode of relationship. The old mode of attachment needs to be "let go" of, while one relinquishes possessive wishes towards those objects, including "omnipotent" attempts to control those onto whom those primal "jealous" objects are projected.

We may retain our old symbiotic and oedipal relationship constellations in fantasy, but in analysis, we need to make unconscious fantasies conscious so that we don't persist in acting them out, rather than just enjoying the former experiences as symbolic level fantasies. In the end, we do have to move on to different forms of relatedness, in which separation-individuation loss is felt, and in which oedipal loss of the incest object is tolerated through mourning as well. Only then can we move on to seeing who we are truly with within the present, in the external world, outside the internal world scenarios that press unconsciously for repetition. The journey of grief, mourning, and loss is a difficult one, particularly for those with failures in primal preoedipal mothering, if only in the later periods of separation-individuation (Mahler, Pine, & Bergman, 1975). With those who have had more adequate mothering, and mother image internalization in the preoedipal years, the oedipal stage relinquishment of an incestuous love object, and the relinquishment of the regressive oedipal rival object, which foments intense feelings of jealousy, are somewhat less difficult. This is true, since what I call normal "developmental mourning" (Kavaler-Adler, 1992, 1993, 1995, 1996, 2003b, 2004, 2005a, 2006, 2007, 2013a, 2013b), in these developmentally higher level cases, is not compounded by the patient needing to navigate the traumatic void, rage, and unsymbolized grief of the "abandonment depression" (Masterson 1976, 1981) that is consequent to primal developmental arrest. The "abandonment depression" is, after all, primal object-loss due to the disruption of "good enough mothering" and of the self-cohesion of "going-on-being" (Winnicott, 1965, 1971).

Nevertheless, we all need to mourn and relinquish the old relationship constellations. We need to mourn both those with bad object attachments (Fairbairn, 1952), and those with overstimulating, but yet adequate oedipal stage attachments. The technique of interpretation in psychoanalysis remains our main tool to help people understand what they are carrying with them from the past, which needs to be understood (forgiven) and somewhat relinquished, to move on.

CHAPTER TWELVE

Jealousy in countertransference

Dhwani Shah

To experience jealousy is to experience mental torture. Jealousy feels visceral and urgent, pressing for action or relief. One literally feels torn up inside, imprisoned in a cage of longing and exclusion. Searing hot-blooded psychic pain combined with unrelenting desire feels unbearable and excruciating. Jealousy does not have the advantage of being an experience that feels noble or moral. In fact, it is quite the reverse—it feels shameful and filled with hatred. Roland Barthes (1977) describes it well:

> As a jealous person, I suffer fourfold: because I am jealous, because I reproach myself for my jealousy, because I fear that my jealousy is hurting the other, because I allow myself to be enslaved by banality: I suffer from being excluded, from being aggressive, from being crazy, and from being common. (p. 146)

The dreaded consequences of jealousy surround us: Old and new stories of jealous lovers murdering and committing unspeakable acts of cruelty are commonplace from reality television shows on television to the ancient myths of Greece. Jealousy haunts all of us—as Freud (1922b) wrote: "Jealousy is one of those affective states ... that may be described as normal. If anyone appears to be without it, the inference is justified that it has undergone severe repression and consequently plays all the greater part in his unconscious mental life" (p. 223). Despite this ubiquity, our experiences of jealousy as psychoanalysts and psychotherapists are not readily discussed with a few notable exceptions including Searles (1986), Lewin (2011), and Wurmser and Jarass (2008b). This is especially curious considering the centrality of the experience of jealousy in psychoanalytic theorizing, foremost in the oedipal struggles of childhood and the intense rivalries and passions between parents and children that need to be confronted and mourned. As the Freud quote above states, jealousy is a fundamental experience in every person's life and childhood. For it to be missing indicates it has "gone underground," banished from consciousness.

Over the past several decades, there has been a growing interest in exploring the analyst's emotional reactions to the patient in an honest manner. In contemporary analytic theory, there is general agreement that countertransference is an unavoidable and indispensable tool the analyst can use in the service of furthering the analytic process. Such consensus has only gradually evolved, though. Over the course of psychoanalytic theorizing, three perspectives on countertransference have been noticeable: (i) in traditional usage, countertransference was viewed as an obstacle to the analytic process, based on one's own personal history and biases, that interferes with free floating attention and unconscious communication between the patient and the analyst (Freud, 1910d); (ii) then, countertransference came to be regarded as a consequence of projective identification of the patient's self or internalized objects (Heimann, 1950; Racker, 1957) and therefore a helpful source for understanding the patient's internal world, and, finally (iii) countertransference was posited to be a reverie-based method of emotional containment for the patient's unbearable affects and fantasies (Bion, 1963; Oelsner, 2013). Numerous authors have addressed the analyst's experience of painful negative emotional states, including experiences of greed (Akhtar, 2013c), boredom (Hirsh, 2008), hopelessness

(Shah, 2015), sadism (Gabbard, 1996), perversity (Ogden, 1996), and envy (Steiner, 2011). Why has jealousy been largely ignored in this discussion? One could argue that perhaps it has to do with the emotional discomfort over the experience of jealousy, but this does not feel sufficient—greed, envy, and sadism are obviously very disruptive and difficult emotions to tolerate in the analytic setting but have been discussed openly and in detail.

The central argument of this chapter is to make the case that jealousy is indeed an emotional experience that is especially difficult for an analyst to come to terms with because of its unique qualities that differentiate it from other negative emotional experiences. Specifically, jealousy always involves a third object—real or imagined (or both). Psychoanalysis and psychoanalytic psychotherapy is at its core a two-person experience: In a private setting, apart from the rest of the world, we are with our patients in a passionate yet controlled relationship. The experience of jealousy disrupts this primordial peaceful Eden for both the patient and the therapist, reminding them both of their triadic shock at learning that whoever they love and imagine they possess has others in life: mothers, fathers, real and imagined lovers—an internal "secret garden" that none of us can ever fully be a part of (Britton, 1998). We are all excluded from paradise.

To avoid this shock, it is tempting to "coast" in a two-person experience without dealing with the complexity of this triadic experience (Hirsch, 2008). The analyst can feel she is in a privileged role of being the exclusive caretaker to someone in need, an experience from early in childhood prior to the discovery and shock of the third represented in the primal scene. This avoids the narcissistic blow to omnipotence that occurs when we discover that those we love most have others in their lives they love, possibly (terribly) more.

The importance of the analytic setting being a holding environment and a place of safety in order for the process to unfold may unwittingly be what also conveniently allows us not to experience jealousy with our patients consciously. The analyst's careful listening to unconscious themes in the manifest material and allowing himself to be affected and tuned in to his patient's free associations and subtle or unstated emotional experiences deepens the dyadic experience for both parties. The more powerful the experience, the greater the risk of jealousy for both the patient and the analyst when the inevitable truth of triadic reality occurs. The analyst, however, is at risk in a particular way because of his need to be both intimately involved with the patient as well as respectful of the patient's boundaries. Unconscious jealousy on the part of the analyst can lead to possessiveness, seductiveness, and a rupture of boundaries or a stalemate in treatment. If the analyst is able to bear the onslaught of jealousy in the treatment and use this experience to understand the patient's experience, however, a movement towards triadic reality can occur within the analytic space, and the patient can begin to learn the difficult task of balancing exclusivity and sharing, loving without total possession (Wurmser, 2008).

Defining jealousy

Prior to exploring the analyst's experiences of jealousy, it would be worthwhile to first explore the experience of jealousy in greater depth. Psychoanalysts have viewed jealousy as a primary emotional experience that can be conscious or unconscious (Wurmser, 2008). Others have highlighted jealousy as a defense against other affective states, including envy (Riviere, 1932), guilt (Wurmser, 2008), and emptiness (Blevis, 2009), or as a defense against intimacy (Coen, 1987). Freud originally described jealousy as an affective state with three layers: competitive, or "normal" jealousy, projected jealousy, and delusional jealousy. Interestingly, Freud (1922b) was quick to bypass "normal jealousy":

> There is not much to be said from the analytic point of view about normal jealousy. It is easy to see that essentially it is compounded of grief, the pain caused by the thought of losing the loved object, and the narcissistic wound, in so far as this is distinguishable from the other wound; further, of feelings of enmity against the successful rival, and of a greater or lesser amount of self-criticism which tries to hold the person himself accountable for his loss. Although we may call it normal, this jealousy is by no means completely rational, that is, derived from the actual situation, proportionate to the real circumstances and under the complete control of the conscious ego; for it is rooted deep in the unconscious, it is a continuation of the earliest stirrings of the child's affective life and it originates in the Oedipus or family complex of the first sexual period. (p. 221)

What Freud stated as "easy to see" is, even in Freud's in-depth description, emotionally complex from an experiential point of view. This chapter will focus on this "normal" jealousy, consciously and unconsciously experienced by the analyst. Why was Freud so quick to bypass "normal jealousy"? It is known that Freud considered himself a jealous person and his theorizing of the jealous rivalry in the Oedipus complex was motivated by his own self analysis (Baumgart, 1990). Psychoanalytic historians have also noted Freud's intense jealous rivalries with others in his inner circle (Makari, 2008). Perhaps Freud himself was uncomfortable with this especially torturous emotional experience.

Regardless of the reasons for doing so, Freud may have unwittingly minimized the complex and unique qualities of the experience of "normal" jealousy for the analyst. Unlike other affective states, jealousy involves emotions between three people, not two: the lover, the beloved, and the rival. Jealousy is a complex brew. Towards the rival, one feels varying degrees of hatred, envy, admiration, and competitiveness. Jealousy induces complex feelings towards the beloved as well including unbearable longing, intense grief, and psychic pain over the loss of love, rage over being replaced, and guilt over this hatred. Narcissistic injury, helplessness, and the shame of exclusion accompanied by self-criticism are acutely felt as well (Akhtar, 2009; Auchincloss & Samberg, 2012). Importantly, the jealous individual is tortured by being simultaneously included and excluded: It is essentially an "inside out" experience symbolized by the primal scene. Because of his desire, he is on the "inside" longing painfully for his beloved, while simultaneously being "outside," excluded by a rival she prefers: "… ravaged, yet burned with desire, he errs endlessly in jealousy's labyrinth, incapable of finding an exit" (Blevis, 2006, p. 3). There are no gray areas in the experience of jealousy; emotionally it is a zero sum game: "You love him, not me; I am nothing to you." As Wurmser (2008) notes, jealousy:

> … involves a regression to strictly Oedipal states of mind such that the object of desire and the rival are felt to be more intact, powerful, and sexually flourishing than is the jealous self, which is experienced as weak, inadequate, and desperately dependent on the love of the desired object and often of the rival as well. (p. 32)

Jealousy and the triadic experience

Underlying the experience of jealousy is a secret hope of exclusivity and possessiveness:

> ... at its core, there is a sheltered ... the fantasy of an all powerful twosome unity from which everybody else, even the entire world, should be banished ... the essence of jealousy lies in this absoluteness and exclusivity of the demanded relationship. (Wurmser, 2008, p. 5)

Attachment research has demonstrated jealous responses as early as four months old (Hart, Carrington, Tronick, & Carroll, 2004). Hart et al. argue that the loss of exclusiveness represents momentary disrupted attachment and the infant's expression of jealousy through emotions such as sadness functions to solicit caregiving: "... jealousy protest signifies the meaningfulness of the attachment relationship" (p. 72). Interestingly, the level of intensity of attachment to the mother predicted the jealous response, a finding that will be discussed later in this chapter on the analyst's emerging awareness of her jealousy as the relationship with the patient deepens.

The fantasy of a return to a "twosome unity" of an exclusive relationship to avoid triadic reality is discussed in every psychoanalytic tradition. The idealization of a merger with a powerful and loving caregiver, a "completeness that closes in on itself" (Lacan, 1973, p. 116) is an extremely powerful one, warding off the horror of separateness and loss. The shock of a child's learning that his beloved mother, his everything, is involved with others (often represented and symbolized as father) is a crushing experience for the child. This defeat forces him to realize one can no longer retain a claim of omnipotence to the desire of the other: "The discovery of the oedipal triangle is felt to be the death of the couple ... in this phantasy the arrival of the notion of the third always murders the dyadic relationship" (Britton, 1998, p. 37). It is here where jealousy finds its origins: in the moment of realization of a third, a moment of exclusion from the comfort and safety of the loving dyadic union:

> In jealousy I feel: "I am the one who has been excluded from love. I am standing outside of an intimate relationship that is particularly precious to me." Behind jealousy, there is always a sense of loss, and with that, acute pain and sadness, but also a feeling of humiliation and shame ... I am the excluded third and want to be the excluding first ... I am excluded from belonging ... and my pain and shame are so strong that I want to hurl myself against this exclusion, but feel helpless to do anything about it. (Wurmser, 1998, p. xi)

These experiences are of course recreated and reenacted on the analytic stage between analyst and analysand, both participating in a fantasied dyadic relationship. The "arrival of the notion of the third" is always looming, threatening to disrupt the happy couple at any time: When we claim to be one of the "happy pair", we rid ourselves by projection of that aspect of ourselves which is forever "unfilled with the pain of longing" and with it we project our potential for envy and jealousy … clinically, this is familiar and frequent in analysis in various intensities. (Britton, 1998, p. 124)

The emergence of acute conscious jealousy in the analyst

There is an absence of a detailed discussion on the topic of the analyst's experience of jealousy in psychoanalytic literature, with one notable exception: Harold Searles. In a series of intriguing and boldly honest papers (Searles, 1986), he describes the experience of jealousy in the analyst and its therapeutic possibilities in depth, which I will quote in more detail below. Searles viewed the experience of jealousy as inevitable for both analyst and patient alike and described his own struggles with jealousy in a manner that would be difficult even for the contemporary analyst well versed in the importance of putting words to countertransference experiences. He also noted that his conscious experiences of being jealous of patients grew as the treatment deepened and felt the experience of jealousy in the analyst heralded the opportunity to understand the patient's jealousy in an in-depth manner. The experience of jealousy in the countertransference emotionally communicates to the analyst the experience of the patient's struggles which he is not yet conscious of, as this case illustrates.

Clinical vignette: 1

> Deven was a twenty-seven-year-old adopted Sri Lankan postdoctoral student in political science with a history of depression and difficulty in maintaining long-lasting relationships with women. He began analysis because of a personal academic interest in psychoanalytic theory and was eager to start on couch four times a week. As the analysis progressed past a year, it became clear that Deven loved to use obsessional and intellectualized language that intrigued me yet kept me at arm's length. Conceptual insight came

readily to both of us and Deven seemed pleased with our relationship and his newfound understanding of himself. Despite these "insights," nothing really appeared to be changing in his life—his mood remained low, he struggled completing his work, and his interest in pursuing any romantic involvement waned even further. In the sessions, although his enthusiasm appeared to continue, it seemed the analysis was an analysis in name only—all of the motions and procedures were in place but there was a lack of depth and relatedness despite our fondness for one another. It was as if there was a barrier we could not cross together. I could not feel his presence with me in any sustained meaningful way—it was as if he did not leave any impact on me, despite the fact that I thought about him often and struggled to feel closer to him. Any discussions about these experiences between us led to further theorizing and conceptual understandings but no meaningful change.

Towards the beginning of his second year of analysis, Deven took me by surprise with the announcement that he had decided to cut back his analytic sessions, perhaps even terminate temporarily. He had discovered a psychotherapist, Rose, who practiced mindfulness meditation and yoga. She had been encouraging him to end his analysis and start a two-month intensive mind body workshop with her. Deven spoke about her in a surprisingly tender and passionate fashion and said that he felt "truly and fully" understood by her—I could feel for the first time a true longing in Deven for some type of contact that went beyond theories and ideas. I felt my heart racing and my face flushed—an acute sense of loss gripped my abdomen, and although it took me some time to consciously face it, I was jealous. In response, I offered some rambling thoughts about the benefits of mindfulness and therapy, which I now see as a way of me desperately trying to include myself in his newfound interest which felt too painful to be excluded from. This also continued the typical intellectualized intimacy we both found safe. Deven reassured me that the analysis was indeed helpful but he didn't feel it was reaching him at the level Rose did. He found her presence warm and inviting: "She brings out something in me I can't put into words—it's as if she intuitively knows me and understands how to draw me out." The discomfort over my jealousy increased hearing these words—I realized that I wished I had the powers Rose did to bring him to life.

Although it took some time, over the course of the analysis after this point, the jealousy I felt over being excluded from Deven and Rose had important roots in Deven's childhood experience. My jealousy resonated with a deep feeling of exclusion and shame Deven felt growing up in his household. Adopted at the age of two by a wealthy Irish Catholic family, with no siblings, Deven grew up feeling profoundly different from his adopted family, whom he felt were "more guardians than parents." He especially felt a profound mismatch with his mother. Coming from a strict and abusive household, Deven's mother had difficulty with being playful or genuinely affectionate with him. He did feel a great deal of love for his father, who encouraged his intellectual passions and abilities, but felt their relationship ended there. One aspect of Deven's experience that was not fully conscious but which emerged in the analysis after my experience of jealousy was powerful feelings of exclusion and jealousy from both of his parents as a couple. Deven's parents had been teenage lovers and spent all of their time together running a business. They were both in their forties when they adopted Deven, and he often felt excluded from their "inner circle." Reflecting on the first year of the analysis, I realized that the lack of spontaneity and relatedness in our relationship together (to which we both contributed) mirrored his situation growing up with his distant mother and cerebral father. The acute jealousy I experienced upended my role as an emotionally distant parent to a more primal experience from Deven as a young boy excluded from a couple that shared a special bond together. Using this experience as a guide allowed Deven and I to begin to explore his need to protect himself from intimacy to avoid the possible experience of shame and exclusion that he experienced as a child.

My feelings of acute jealousy that broke through my defenses around keeping Deven emotionally distant from me involved a rival, a "third" that interrupted a fantasized dyadic union between us. My experiences of jealousy towards Rose allowed for a deepening of my understanding of Deven's own experience of the exclusion and jealousy he felt throughout his life. While Rose was an actual person in Deven's life that heralded these experiences in our treatment, strangely enough, jealousy can also occur intrapsychically between parts of oneself and the analysand, as discussed below.

The analyst's jealousy of patient's internal objects

Although Searles was one the first to acknowledge the presence of acute conscious jealous feelings in the analyst and their usefulness in understanding the patient's often unconscious emotional experience, he went several steps further in his understanding of jealousy in the analyst which are surprising but clinically useful. His major contribution is the concept of jealousy occurring intrapsychically between a person's internal objects—an internal jealousy of a part of one's own self. Searles (1986) felt this type of jealousy "is a major factor in maintaining the disharmony of the [patient's] internal object world and in preventing him from experiencing a single, whole and continuous identity" (p. 100). Simplified, the dilemma is as follows: Growing up, the patient experienced the parent narcissistically and passionately involved with one aspect of the patient's existence, such as her body, her intellect, or her ideal (from the past or in the future). This creates dissociation in the patient's experience of this aspect of herself which she then feels jealous of—it is as if the parent and this aspect of the patient have a love affair that the patient is excluded from:

> The patient comes to realize that he is not after all at the center of the life of a mother or father who had appeared selflessly devoted to him … he now realizes the parent's interest was essentially narcissistic and that, to the extent that he has been a truly separate person at all to the parent—the parents loves an image of the child that the child is jealous of. (p. 116)

The analyst's role is to allow himself to become actively engaged with the patient to the point where he begins to experience consciously feelings of jealousy that the patient has been previously unconscious of via projective identification. By doing so, the analyst can then begin to help the patient become aware of and integrate this aspect of herself. This intrapsychic jealousy that occurs in the analyst can take many forms in the analyst's countertransference. Searles describes being excluded and jealous of his patient's preoccupations with his hallucinations, jealous of an idealized image of Searles that the patient seems to be enamored with; even jealous of a man's lavish preoccupation with his penis:

> The analyst finds to his astonishment that he is feeling jealous as regards to the patient's intimate and fascinated relationship with

the latter's own penis. The analyst, that is, first comes to feel as his own the jealousy which the patient himself has dissociated for so many years, jealousy referable to his mother's relationship with his penis. (p. 105)

This strange type of intrapsychic jealousy is best illustrated by Searles's descriptions of patients' jealousy of their own bodies or body parts. Searles describes to his surprise feeling jealous of his patient's constant focus (positive or critical) on a particular body part, for example as stated above a man's penis or a woman's legs, and realizing that the jealousy he is feeling mirrors an internal jealousy on the part of the patient:

> It is inherent in the successful analyzing of this "intrapsychic" jealousy that the analyst become able to experience it vis a vis the relationship between the patient and the body parts in question, before the patient can be expected to become aware of, and integrate, the strangely jealousy-ridden relationship between herself and one or another introject represented by the body parts in question. (p. 105)

The analyst first comes to feel as his own the jealousy which the patient herself has dissociated from childhood, a jealousy of a caregiver's focus on that aspect of the patient's body.

Clinically, this is often seen in patients with eating disorders and body image distortions—a parent's exclusive focus on a child's body image or a particular aspect of a child's body becomes idealized. The child then feels a dissociated separateness from her body, as if her body existed in the third person. Such children often measure their bodies, abuse them, or speak about them as an almost separate entity as if they do not inhabit them (Schwartz & Ceaser, 2005). As a patient once noted about her mother: "She loved my body but not my soul." This aspect of the patient could never feel fully lived in and owned—the body cannot then be a source of pleasure or sexuality. Unconsciously the body belongs to the parent. The analyst's experience of jealousy about being excluded from this body image that the patient is focused on allows him insight into the patient's intrapsychic internal rivalry between the imagined parent, body and self.

In a similar fashion, Searles also discusses feeling excluded and jealous of his patient's idealized images of him—one patient imagines his tanned and sculpted body at the beach; another constantly admires his writing but appears to devalue Searles's actual presence: "I experienced uncomfortable stirrings of jealousy of the relatively admired author Searles whose works this scornful man was sure I could not have possibly written" (p. 108). Searles was able to trace these jealous experiences to his patient's early experiences of having a caregiver love an idealized image of the patient either in the future or the past, preferring this image over the actual patient as a person. The jealousy the analyst feels towards the patient's possession of his idealized image reflects a similar jealousy the patient feels towards her own internalized ideal that she imagines she is excluded from: "That experience with her left me well able to believe that similar jealousy was mobilized within her on occasions when she sensed that I was visualizing her as being a capable person" (p. 116). This unconscious internal jealous struggle leads the patient to feel excluded and not integrated with her ideal which can lead to a negative therapeutic reaction.

The analyst's jealousy of patient's inanimate objects

Another interesting and surprising insight Searles discusses is the patient's and the therapist's jealous reaction to inanimate objects. Searles (1986) gives vivid descriptions of his patient's feeling jealous over "things" the analyst possesses, including the analyst's chair, desk, and even the office plant. Conversely, the analyst also may experience jealousy of objects patients are enamored with that the analyst feels excluded from. Clinically, the analyst can experience this unusual type of jealous reaction to patients who use drugs, as this case illustrates:

Clinical vignette: 2

John, a twenty-eight-year-old chemical engineer, began treatment for depression and chronic marijuana use. At the urging of his increasingly frustrated wife, John attempted a variety of treatments for his marijuana use and low mood that he described as failures, in part because he felt disengaged with "the annoying self-help mantras" of the therapists he worked with. Despite his struggles with depression and chronic marijuana use, John functioned highly at work and was dedicated to his job. But despite his numerous successes at work, John struggled with his feelings of low self-worth and a constant feeling of being undervalued and disrespected. He felt isolated from his wife, whom he described as constantly irritable and demanding of his attention and time. John did not feel close with anyone in his life; he found himself uncomfortable in most social situations and preferred to be alone in his own thoughts. In his initial sessions with me, John often appeared bored and disengaged, focusing on his disappointments with his colleagues at work and his wife who he complained was demanding and constantly "nagging" him. After several sessions like these, I found myself struggling to find some area where John felt alive. I noticed that he never spoke about his marijuana use in detail, only discussing it as a "thing that my wife wants out of my life and I need to stop." I commented on his lack of interest in speaking to me about what it was like for him to smoke marijuana and he replied flatly, "Do you really want to know, or are you asking me so you can figure out how to get me to stop?" I replied that it seemed there was a part of him that wanted me to really know what it was like for him but he assumed I would play the part of others in his life that wanted him to stop. Over the course of the next several months, John slowly began to describe his passion for cultivating and growing marijuana in the basement of the old family home where his parents still lived after retirement. He would carefully study the art of horticulture online and plant a variety of different species, picking the right soil, carefully paying attention to the pH and the quality of the nutrients in the plants. He would then harvest and "cure" the buds, preparing them for his use. He grew animated discussing this process and I found myself at first fascinated and taken in by the process. As time went on, and our relationship deepened, however, I began to find myself annoyed when he brought up the plants again. It seemed any time we made progress in him being able to speak truthfully about his experience to me, the next session would turn to his "secret garden." In these moments, I imagined what his plants looked like and how tenderly he probably cared for them. I began to interrupt his reveries about horticulture with questions about the effects of this hobby on his daily life and his relationship with others, including myself and his wife. His affect shifted and he began to show up late to sessions, which increased my feelings of frustration at his lack of interest in our work together—something he would never do to those precious plants of his I imagined with annoyance! This thought surprised me and allowed me to realize that I was jealous of John's relationship with his plants, a feeling that I was certain John's wife felt as well. An insight occurred to me about John's past that felt relevant but only emerged as emotionally meaningful later in treatment: John's mother suffered from anorexia nervosa and spent hours when John was a child weighing herself in her bathroom with the door locked. Feeling shut out of being able to be with his mother and his jealousy of her constant preoccupation with her body and not him was enacted in my jealous feelings of him being with his marijuana plants when our relationship began to deepen.

John's preoccupation with his marijuana plants is a reminder of our continuous involvement with "things" in our lives that are deeply meaningful to us and the constructive, sustaining, and symbolic significance of the inanimate world (Akhtar, 2003). In addictions, inanimate objects like the plants of John's fascination can take on especially powerful meanings. These include the symbolized lack of felt human connection, the need for control, and the need to use physical objects to ward off mental pain and anguish: "Addictions make psychic pain bearable. Beautiful objects make the addiction bearable" (ibid., p. 17). Allowing myself to examine my own jealous reactions to John's absorption with his marijuana plants led us to be able to speak to his unbearable jealousy towards his mother's preoccupation with her body and his feeling of exclusion from her. While the conscious experience of jealousy for the analyst is obviously disrupting and uncomfortable, if reflected on and mentalized it can serve as a potential guide to understanding. There are also significant dangers of not attending to his powerful emotion as discussed below.

Chronic and unconscious jealous countertransference dilemmas

While emerging acute conscious jealous feelings in the analyst can lead to a deepening of the analytic experience, chronic unconscious jealousy on the part of the analyst can lead to either impasses or seductive acting out behaviors. As stated above, based on the frame and nature of his work with patients, the analyst is placed in a position that makes him especially prone to jealousy. Despite being actively involved and hearing the patient's most intimate details and fantasies the analyst is also excluded from fully participating in the unfolding intimacy—his responsiveness and engagement is in the service of the understanding and helping of the patient, not for pure gratification. The analyst is actively engaged and simultaneously excluded from fully participating in this passionate encounter; he is both "inside and out." This can lead to a peculiar type of isolation and loneliness. Being lonely in the company of others is fertile ground for unbearable jealousy. Searles (1986), in his honest and endearing way, states this clearly:

> It should be seen that the loneliness, in reality, of the analyst's work is such as to make him highly prey to feeling reality based jealousy in the analytic setting. The lonely nature of one's work as an analyst is an immensely powerful reality factor which tends to require one to repress the feelings of jealousy to which the work renders one so vulnerable—including feelings of jealousy of that partially split off aspect of oneself which enjoys, transitorily at least, relatively close communion with the patient ... the analyst is rendered lonely by his necessarily predominant attunement to aspects of the patient which are unconscious and which may not emerge into relatively full awareness for years ... also transference can feel lonely that the patient is relating to an image of the analyst that has little basis at times in the analyst's own identity. (p. 135)

Countertransference jealousy and the observing transference

There is a particular transference reaction that is especially prone to cause loneliness and jealousy in the analyst—the patient placing the analyst in the position of the excluded observer. This often occurs in the context of a patient being preoccupied with someone (or something) outside of the analytic setting that has no direct relationship with what is happening explicitly in the analytic process. In these situations, the analyst often feels excluded and left to helplessly observe the details of the patient's life with no real involvement—the transference is essentially one of the analyst being an observer to the patient's life (Steiner, 2011). This can lead to unconscious jealous reactions in the analyst which can enact the need to include himself in order to avoid the pain of exclusion and the discomfort of jealousy. Steiner (ibid.) discusses this observing transference and the difficulty it poses to the analyst:

> The observing transference is also difficult for the analyst to toler-ate, and I have found that it is particularly conducive to enactments. This is especially the case when material is brought involving pas-sionate feelings with no direct transference link—often, for exam-ple, when contentious incidents, say with a parent, a spouse or rival are reported. In these situations the analyst may try to force himself back into the primary role. (p. 87)

On an unconscious level, the analyst is reacting to losing the position of the patient's "primary object" and left to be an observer excluded from the action. This place of the excluded jealous observer is often unconscious and can lead to the analyst needing to force himself back into being on the inside by collapsing triadic reality. As Steiner notes, one enactment that can occur is an overt attempt to include oneself by over-interpreting transference themes in the content of the patient's associations. Although it is always important to understand the transference implications of all of the patient's associations, the jealous analyst may fall prey to actively imagining that all the patient's associations have some transference theme when in fact the important transference-countertransference theme is the cocreation of a feeling of exclusion and jealousy on the part of the analyst from the patient's inner world.

Clinical vignette: 3

> Molly began treatment with me after her analyst of twenty years passed away. She was a fifty-seven-year-old magazine editor and a mother of two boys, aged eighteen and sixteen. Despite a twenty-year treatment, Molly was significantly impaired in her ability to function due to severe anxiety and somatic symptoms including intermittent pains in her throat and neck, with no clear medical cause. She spoke in a rapid and loud fashion staring straight ahead with only intermittent eye contact, with a flurry of complex ideas and verbiage that often caused me to feel confused and worried that I could not understand her. I began to also feel ashamed that I could not keep up with her complex ideas and thoughts that seemed to relentlessly take up the entire session.

Most of her associations involved angry struggles with her ex-husband and her two sons, both of whom had developmental delays and behavioral issues. I found myself struggling to gain a foothold into her ideas and thoughts and wondered how often and when I could interrupt her to get a word in. Molly seemed to not want me to speak but she also was desperate to convey the urgency and severity of her situation and her symptoms to me. Although at the time I did not realize it, my senses of wanting to talk and interrupt her came from a feeling of jealousy over being excluded from her associations—they contained no meaningful bridge to our relationship or her present emotional state. I began to attempt to bring Molly into the "here and now" in our relationship together by commenting on how she might be feeling overwhelmed and frustrated in here with me as she did with her ex-husband. She agreed with this assessment but went on to talk about her situation in the same manner as before, effectively ignoring the comment. I began to feel left out and ignored, forced into the role of simply observing her associations without making any impact at all. This was the role that Molly occupied in her family—being the fourth in a family of eight, born prematurely with a neurological disorder that affected her ability to walk, Molly grew up watching her brothers and sisters play together without her. Her mother was diagnosed with lupus and was often bedridden. When her mother was awake, she preferred the company of her eldest sons, leaving Molly alone with her books. Over time, allowing myself to be more comfortable in the role of the observer and understanding its meaning to Molly let me be less jealous of her associations and allowed me to be more responsive and attuned to her suffering.

Molly's crushing jealous experiences growing up forced her to use what Lewin (2011) describes as a defense of parallel identification, a manic defense that creates a non-penetrating state of relatedness in the transference that effectively blocks any ability for the analyst to reach the patient:

> The patient, anaesthetized to the conscious pain of jealousy, becomes emotionally frozen. This blocks the back-and-forth energy-flow of projective/introjective processes between patient and therapist, in

turn distancing the therapist from the efficacy of internally articu-
lating her countertransference. (p. 552)

Painfully bearing the position of the excluded observer can allow a
place of empathy and respect for the patient's struggles which can lead
to reduction in this defensive identification.

Jealousy and seduction

Another method of the analyst avoiding conscious chronic jealousy is
an enactment of various forms of seduction with the patient. Seduction
can of course take on many forms in the analytic setting, ranging from
verbal enactments to sexual acting out on the part of the analyst. This is
a very obvious yet overlooked defense against the awareness of jealous
feelings—a seduction collapses the triadic space and the pain of exclusion by creating a magical atmosphere of there being only two with no
rivals or observers. Several authors have discussed the seductive nature
of the analytic setting in its exclusive focus on the relationship between
the analyst and the analysand and how this is a necessary condition for
the emergence of transference and a deepening of the analytic process
(Maroda, 1998). In these conditions, the analyst and patient are both
vulnerable to jealous reactions when a third is introduced: "The discovery of the oedipal triangle is felt to be the death of the couple ... in
this phantasy the arrival of the notion of the third always murders the
dyadic relationship" (Britton, 1998, p. 37).

One form a seduction can take is to avoid triadic themes of jealousy,
competitiveness, and sexuality by focusing on preoedipal conflicts
involving separation and attachment to a maternal figure. In their discussion of a girl's developmental move from an exclusive relationship
with the mother to a triadic sexual competitive relationship involving the father, Kulish and Holtzman (2008) describe how the analyst
can impede a woman's progress towards a triadic experience with the
father because of jealousy. When jealous and competitive feelings begin
to emerge in the transference between female analysts and their female
patients, a female analyst may resist being seen as the rival mother;
instead, the analyst can move the analysis back to mother/daughter
issues and focus on conflicts surrounding safety and attachment, ignoring the competitive strivings of the patient:

Some female analysts respond defensively to the competition and envy of their female patients and often resist being seen as the rival triadic mother. Instead, they tend to get involved—or lost—in earlier "pre-Oedipal" mother/daughter issues, or to become identified with their patients. They may become "too maternal" and overprotective. (p. 166)

This maternal "overprotectiveness" shields the analyst from her own jealous reactions to her patient's competitive wishes to take on the father as the love object and seductively eliminates the rival in the oedipal triangle. In a similar manner, male analysts, in an effort to avoid their own possessive and jealous feelings, may infantilize their female patients by taking on an overly paternal transference to avoid themes involving jealousy and sexuality, unconsciously seducing their patients into a magical union between the two with no rivals (ibid.). In these cases, one finds an emphasis on a split between the idealized all loving "good mother" and the devalued cruel "bad mother." The analyst inhabits the role of the good parent, loving and caring for the patient who has been damaged and hurt. This seductively protects the couple from any intrusions from the "bad parent," who is split off and displaced on a person outside the therapeutic situation—usually a spouse or an actual parental figure (ibid.). In effect, the analyst communicates to the patient, "Your parents were cruel and hurt you. I will be the loving parent you never had and not hurt or abandon you—no one will come between us." As Maroda (1998) notes:

> If I, the analyst, am not the bad object, and the patient needs to experience "someone" in that role, who else is left? ... That is why the safest possible situation for both patient and therapist is simply to stay outside the transference-countertransference interplay and let the real parents, spouse, boss, colleagues, etc. be the bad objects. (p. 23)

This phenomenon is common in case discussions where colleagues often vent their frustrations about the patient's parents and the harm they did. Although it is often the case that parents do significant harm to their children, the moral outrage and aggression towards the patient's parental figures may be ways of coping with unconscious jealous possessiveness towards their patients and the need to be the good object to preserve a dyadic union.

Jealousy and the lovesick analyst

These themes of seduction and possessiveness of the patient are overtly seen in boundary violations between analyst and patient. Sexual boundary violations often begin with a lonely, "lovesick" analyst feeling the need to have the exclusive love of a patient he views as special (Gabbard & Lester, 1995). The lovesick analyst harbors an unconscious or conscious fantasy that love is healing, and that a psychic cure will occur if she loves her patients more completely than their parents did—a common fantasy of patients entering analysis as well. This "love cure" is threatened by the emergence of conscious feelings of jealousy which interrupt the fantasy of the union between the two lovers. The analyst, lonely and jealous, needs to possess the patient fully in order to eliminate any jealous feelings; he must know that the patient is fully his without any rival. A magical seductive space is created to harbor this illusion and perpetuate the fantasy of magical union.

Conclusion

This chapter has focused on the analyst's experience of jealousy in the analytic setting. Jealousy was understood as a complex triadic emotional experience that creates an unbearable "inside out" experience that can be conscious or unconscious. The analyst is especially prone to jealousy because of his struggle of being intimately involved with the patient as well as being deprived of receiving the same nurturance in return. Acute emerging conscious experiences of jealousy in the analyst as the treatment deepens can lead to a deeper understanding of the patient's own struggles with jealousy and exclusion. Acute jealous reactions can take the form of jealousy over actual persons in the patient's life or jealousy of a patient's internal objects. Chronic, often unconscious jealous reactions in the analyst can lead to a stalemate in treatment or seductive acting out. Various forms of countertransference jealousy were discussed as well as the analyst's methods of defending against jealousy, including possessiveness, regression to preoedipal conflicts, splitting, and seduction.

EPILOGUE

CHAPTER THIRTEEN

The anguish of triangulation: a concluding commentary

Mary Kay O'Neil

> YOU CAN ONLY BE JEALOUS OF SOMEONE WHO
> HAS SOMETHING YOU THINK YOU OUGHT TO HAVE
> YOURSELF
>
> Margaret Atwood, The Handmaiden's Tale (p. 183)

Jealousy is a ubiquitous human feeling.[1] Jealousy, as experienced in life, is conveyed in literature, in film, in art, in music as well as in psychoanalytic theory and practice. Milan Kundera (1984), in *The Unbearable Lightness of Being*, describes the human triangle of jealousy.

> Back at home, after some prodding from Tereza, he admitted that he had been jealous watching her dance with a colleague of his. "You mean you were really jealous?" she asked him ten times or more, incredulously, as though someone had just informed her she had

> been awarded a Nobel Peace prize. Then she put her arm around
> his waist and began dancing across the room. The step she used
> was not the one she had shown off in the bar. It was more like a
> village polka, a wild romp that sent her legs flying in the air and her
> torso bounding all over the room, with Tomas in tow. Before long,
> unfortunately, she began to be jealous herself, and Tomas saw her
> jealously not as a Nobel Prize, but as a burden, a burden he would
> be saddled with until not long before his death. (p. 56)

Tomas's jealousy was evoked by Tereza's dancing partner; hers, by her
thoughts of the other women in Tomas's life—especially his mistress
Sabrina. Tereza's "prodding" was also self-serving—she wanted to confirm that she was attractive enough to Tomas that he could be jealous of
a dancing partner. Tomas's "burden" arose from her neediness and his
shame/guilt that he could not be faithful to her. This scene involving
three people is also vividly portrayed in the film of Kundera's book.

Oscar Wilde (1891), in *The Picture of Dorian Gray*, conveys jealousy
and the feared loss of youthful beauty evoked by art.

> I am jealous of everything whose beauty does not die. I am jealous
> of the portrait you have painted of me. Why should it keep what I
> must lose? Every moment that passes takes something from me and
> gives something to it. Oh, if it were only the other way! If the pic-
> ture could change, and I could be always what I am now! Why did
> you paint it? It will mock me some day—mock me horribly! (p. 31)

Can more be learned about jealousy from this volume? In this concluding
chapter, I try to find the words to say what I learned about *jealousy* from
the contributors. First, it is clearly documented that much more has been
written (in psychoanalytic theory and clinical vignettes) about envy than
jealousy. Second, despite the division of the chapters into three realms—
developmental, cultural, and clinical—to a greater and lesser extent,
each of the authors addresses all three areas. Indeed, to grapple with
understanding jealousy, every contributor, beginning with Akhtar, goes
beyond psychoanalytic writing and calls on poetry, novels, plays, film,
art, popular song, classical music to provide penetrating interpretations
of this enigmatic emotion. These cultural portrayals of jealousy seem
necessary to fully understand jealousy and its clinical manifestations.

The nature of jealousy

Despite the paucity of psychoanalytic writing about jealousy, especially when compared with the proliferation of written discourse on envy, there is general agreement that jealousy involves three elements and envy involves two. Jealousy always occurs with three (real or imaginary) as in the three-sided triangle. All three sides are necessary; the sides touch but do not interact; each side is self-contained yet interdependent. Jealousy can be "normal," harmless, even motivating. But jealousy, like envy, can be painful, malignant, and destructive. There is also agreement on a difference between the two, at least in theory: envy develops preoedipally beginning with mother and baby while the capacity to experience jealousy requires a higher level of ego integration and develops later at the oedipal stage. Yet, both emotions can be experienced throughout life. In his introductory overview in Chapter 1, Akhtar provides a comprehensive definition of jealousy, a history of psychoanalytic understanding of this emotion, including the three types—competitive, projected, and delusional—and confirms its portrayal in our culture. However, psychoanalysts, including this volume's contributors, struggle with understanding the differences between jealousy and envy. Frequently, the two emotions, as well as their developmental correlates, are confused. Anderson, in Chapter 2, offers a reason for this confusion; she asserts that the lack of distinction and of attention to jealousy may be because "jealousy and envy are intertwined." Envy is the desire to have for yourself what someone else has, and jealousy, which includes envy, also wants the other person not to have it. In envy, both people can have what is good if there is enough to go around; envy becomes malignant when there is not enough and the good is depleted, in reality, or in imagination. In contrast, jealousy's destructive aim is to take the good and to deprive the other—to bring about loss. Jealousy occurs when one person (the subject) wants to take a third (person or quality) away from the second person (object).

To clarify further, when is envy not intertwined with jealousy? When is it simply envy and when is it harmful or not to the other? Envy is envy when a person wants what the other person has but does not want to take it away from the object of envy. For example, a person wants to be loved just as another person appears to be loved. Nonmalignant envy is not destructive to the other person, it is a wish, a want—"I wish I had a wife like yours, or your power or your money." It can even motivate a person to strive to fulfil a wish or achieve what is wanted. Envy becomes malignant when the envier fears that his need could drain the other person and when the need is so great that there is little regard for the other.

Certainly, envy and jealousy, both normal and pathological, occur in all pairs. These pairs can be lovers, couples, parents, children, grandparents, siblings, friends, therapists, patients, both genders, and all sexual orientations. Subject and object are interchangeable, that is, either or both can experience the emotion at one time or at the same time. There is anguish in both envy and jealousy but the anguish is different. Envy is painful when one is not able (in imagination, or in reality, or due to lack of opportunity or not enough to go around) to get for oneself what is felt to be needed and what another person has. Jealousy is painful for both the jealous person (the subject) and the one who has what another person wants (the object) and even painful at times for the third person (the wanted). Jealousy is painful due to its destructiveness (only one person, not two can have the third), for example, I want to take your husband/wife from you. It is also painful due to the underlying feelings of shame and guilt at wanting to take someone/something from the other person, while either a sense of omnipotence or of powerlessness can drive the jealousy or intensify the suffering. Suffice it to say that the difference between jealousy and envy is complicated and that psychoanalytic attempts to differentiate these emotions, their nature, and development (from Freud and Klein to the present day) continue in this volume and will continue within psychoanalysis.

Jealousy as a developmental experience

When and how does the capacity to feel jealousy develop? In classical psychoanalytic theory, the oedipal phase of development stimulates a child's capacity to be jealous. Three people are involved—mother, father, and child. Theoretically, the child wants to be the sole possessor of the parent of the opposite sex and competes for love with the parent of the same sex. All analysts know this theory. Usually, when the child's feelings are absorbed as non threatening and boundaries are maintained, the child grows up with the ability to use jealousy competitively and nondestructively. In theory, the wanted person is the parent of the opposite sex but in reality jealousy can be experienced between any two people who want the third. Certainly, the capacity to experience jealousy develops further over time in various life experiences.

Anderson tells of a mother's jealousy of her as the child's therapist. In fact, the mother became so jealous of the attachment the child had with the therapist that she removed her child from treatment. It was painful for this mother to see her child attached to another therapeutically mothering person; she feared loss of her child's attachment and love. Anderson recognized her unconscious wish to have a special relationship with the child and struggled with this countertransference wish, long after wondering if she should have been more attentive to the mother's needs rather than simply pleased with the good work she and the child were doing. The therapist and the child[2] also experience loss—an aspect of the painfulness of triangulation.

Kobrick (personal communication), cringed when a child coming out of a session called her "mommy" in front of the waiting mother, supporting Anderson's experience. Kobrick, in Chapter 10, also recalled through drawings and a ballad a childhood experience understood in her analysis of thirty years previously. Her mother's fear of the ill will of her own relatives' envy and jealousy toward Kobrick's family of origin left a residue. Kobrick became aware of the danger of jealousy and felt a need to protect herself: "I too became adept at navigating and avoiding the anticipated attacks of envy and jealousy, whilst experiencing a sense of loss and at times a sense of humiliation. I kept valued belongings, accomplishments and relationships hidden and out of sight from the intruders." Kobrick as well as monitoring the development of jealousy within herself also tracks, like Anderson, the connection and distinction between envy and jealousy within psychoanalysis, from Freud (1922b) to Lewin (2011).

Parents are not the only ones who kindle jealousy; siblings, as Robertson, in Chapter 3, asserts, are also major contributors—they are rivalrous with each other and for the parents' attention. A child, while loving a new sibling, may secretly wish and even threaten to harm a brother or sister. A six-year-old boy blurted out feelings about his month-old sister, "Ever since that baby came, nobody reads to me, nobody talks to me, nobody plays with me!" An older sibling went around asking neighbors if anyone wanted to buy the baby, and a third ignored her. Yet, all three were delighted to have a sister. Sensitive parents absorb the older child's painful loss of position by offering substitutes and special age-appropriate attention. Expressions of anger, aggression, and denial may be evident. It is also possible that siblings are more able to love a brother or sister of the opposite sex with less jealousy. The three boys in the examples above became protective of their sister while they frequently fought with each other. Robertson demonstrates that "Sibling relationships have been marked by jealousy since the dawn of our species" (e.g., from the Bible, Cain and Abel, Joseph and his brothers). He draws attention to the psychoanalytic focus on the developmental effects of the parent-child relationship at the expense of the impact of sibling relationships. After noting the sparse literature dealing with the "horizontal axis" of sibling relations, he addresses sibling ambivalence with a quote:

> ... the ecstasy of loving one who is like oneself is experienced at the same time as the trauma of being annihilated by one who stands in one's place. There are various forms of the sibling complex and its accompanying fantasies; the intruder, the rival, the imaginary twin, bisexual fantasies, the narcissistic double; sibling incestuous fantasies ...

Robertson's clinical example of malignant jealousy—a brother for a sister—demonstrates the painful effect of jealousy on the object. His vignette of a brother harmfully jealous of a sister calls into question the notion that jealousy is less intense with gender opposites. Perhaps gender differences lead only to less intense nonmalignant jealousy, and malignant jealousy can occur in any sibling gender combination because parental sensitivity, personality, and circumstances can also be determining factors. Robertson does more: he affirms a central premise: "How sibling jealousy is dealt with by an individual will long affect such crucial matters as future object choices, the nature of friendships through the life cycle, and the ability to live as a productive member of human groups."

Besides parents and siblings, friendships contribute to the development of jealousy. Zadie Smith (2016) in her recent novel, *Swing Time*, portrays jealousy between two brown (mixed racial) girls who became friends in childhood. Each imagined that the other had what she wanted whether it was talent, looks, parental attention, or maternal qualities. Mothers were involved and in fact provoked jealousy in their daughters by being destructively critical of the other's parents and their lifestyle. The girls' eventual differentiation allows them to develop a separate sense of self but not without painful longing for each other. Kieffer, in Chapter 4, to illustrate further aspects of development, discusses jealousy in adolescent girls. She draws on Elena Ferrante's quartet

of books, *The Neapolitan Novels*, about a friendship within a patriarchal culture (the Messogiorno of southern Naples). Whether rebelling
against or accepting their birth culture, the girls' friendship, perme-
ated periodically by mean acts of jealousy, persists throughout their
lifespan. The support of their friendship sustains them and contributes
to development, despite what Akhtar referred to as competitive
jealousy. Although Kieffer contributes three sensitive case vignettes to
illustrate especially the common patient fantasy that "Your life is better
than mine," as well as the development of adolescent jealousy, she uses
Ferrante's writing to illustrate more fully her understanding of jealousy
in adolescent girls. With her conclusion, Kieffer confirms that literature
can underline and contribute to psychoanalytic theory: "It is the task of
the adolescent to negotiate an adult identity separate from their family
of origin, and to create new bonds in which they will come to recognize
self in relation to other. The work of Elena Ferrante has illustrated some
of the struggles that girls face, particularly in adolescence, on the road
to womanhood."

What if the capacity for jealousy does not develop; what if a person
never feels jealous? The saying, "She doesn't have a jealous (mean)[3]
bone in her body" is often heard. Dimitrijevic, in Chapter 5, asserts that
jealousy may be absent from some people's behavior and conscious
awareness. Jealously, frequently the cause of intense mental pain (e.g.,
longing, hopelessness, helplessness) may be defended against with
avoidance ("no love, no loss"), denial ("I am not a jealous person"),
idealization ("One day there will be a perfect world in which we will all
be equal"). These defenses may be due to trauma or deprivation—it is
just too painful to admit that others have more, better or good fortune
and supportive circumstances. In Winnicottian terms, such defenses
(however pathological) against a painful experience may be a person's
only way of maintaining a sense of self. It is also asserted that there
is a healthy absence of jealousy which is especially evident in friend
relationships. The social support received from friends is so valued that
jealousy is not experienced. In fact, a person cannot be friends with a
person who evokes jealousy. Freud wrote very little about friendship
and it is well known that his anxiety about being the subject or object of
jealousy kept him from friendship or relations with valued colleagues
unless he was in charge. Using Schiller's *Ode to Joy* which was set to
music by Beethoven in his Ninth Symphony, Dimitrijevic describes
how devastating it was for Beethoven not to have close relationships:
"I haven't a single friend; I must live alone" (cited in Kerst, 1905, p. 41).

He could find only within himself the ideal, and wrote his jubilant music at a time of personal misery.

Following on the Oxfordian studies of *Othello* by Feldman (1952, 1954), "the first psychoanalyst to take up Freud's call to question the authorship of Shakespeare's works," Waugaman, in Chapter 6, questions the authorship of Shakespeare's *Othello*. His thesis, like that of psychoanalysts before him, is that one needs life experience to write so perceptively about psychological issues, in this case, pathological jealousy. He supports his thesis and suggests that Edward de Vere, the 17th Earl of Oxford, rather than William Shakespeare, is the true author of *Othello*. This suggestion is substantiated by evidence from De Vere's life that jealousy was intensely experienced and lived out in various situations and relationships. Additionally, evidence of De Vere's particular involvement in the social situation of the time, including his knowledge of Queen Elizabeth's reaction to the play, is also offered as support for De Vere's authorship. Dimitrijevic provides further insight into Freud's inability to write about and perhaps even be aware of his own experience of jealousy. Was he jealous that the writer of *Othello* could have deep insight into the psychological causes and effects of this human emotion before he did? To put a fly in the ointment, Freud's (1968a) statement that "It is quite inconceivable to me that Shakespeare should have got everything second-hand—Hamlet's neurosis, Lear's madness, Othello's jealousy etc." (p. 140) could also be construed as jealousy on Freud's part. Freud, the great psychologist and prized author must have wondered how one man before him could have written so insightfully about human psychology. Even Des Rosiers, in Chapter 7, questioned why Freud mentioned jealousy in *Othello* so infrequently and apparently denied similarities between *Othello* and his own oedipal situation. At the end, Waugaman proposes that consideration of multiple authorships of Shakespeare's works could lead to deeper understanding of connections between life and literature. The question of whether or not an author needs to have life experience to write insightfully about deep emotion and psychological experiences has been long debated by many. Leaving authorship aside, the to date unanswered question can still be asked: Does one have to experience jealousy to write deeply about such emotion[4] or for that matter to be helpful to others suffering from jealousy through analysis or psychotherapy?[5]

Jealousy as a cultural experience

The quintessential portrayal of jealousy—the "green eyed monster"—in Shakespeare's *Othello* highlights the destructiveness of malignant jealousy. Various contributors utilized *Othello* in their own way to give their view of this intensely destructive emotion. Des Rosiers reads deeply, considering in minute detail the underlying theme of racial identity intertwined with jealousy. For him, jealousy in *Othello* is not just about sex and power. It is also about race, about an internalized self-image, about introjected and projected cultural images, aspirations, and expectations. He focuses on cultural attitudes and their effect on the man of color "out of Africa," the father of the horde—the color divisions and hierarchies in our society. Color—black—denotes subjugation, demeaned self-image, while lack of color—white—denotes primacy and enhanced self-image through entitlement. The interaction of the two main characters, Iago and Othello, tells much about the destructiveness of the jealous person, the propensity to experience jealousy in its most lethal form due to an internalized sense of self as lower and as well the role of the desired innocent white/pure/virginal woman as the essential third in the triangle. The oedipal rebellion of Desdemona marks her to become the evoker of male jealousy. Des Rosiers also touches on the possibility of unconscious homosexual desires as a motivator of jealous activity. After recalling the terrible murderous effects of Iago's "Satanic" jealousy on Desdemona and Othello, he asserts the Othello complex which involves themes of race, sex, power, and leads to evoked and/or projected jealousy. Insightful analytically, "The *Othello complex* refers to a whole range of amorous and hostile desires that a black man feels for a white woman, the love of his life but of whose sincerity he is never sure. Positively, the black man arranges his personality into a false self in order to *survive* (author's italics) in a white society at the price of a hysterical conversion—"'I am not what I am.'" Des Rosiers's thesis is supported by calling on the life experience of well-known authors (Dumas and Pushkin), both of mixed racial background, and their portrayal of jealousy in the characters who populate their novels. In summary, he concludes that "The Othello complex plays a fundamental role in our understanding of the worldwide phenomenon of racism against blacks, negatively cathected as the receptacles of primitive aggression and repudiated aspects of the ego."

Zeichner, in Chapter 8, clarifies and harkens back to earlier developmental chapters before discussing jealousy in cinema. He notes that both jealousy and envy are rooted in unresolved childhood trauma, that jealousy is something every child suffers when a third person (father or sibling) intrudes between the self and the mother and that adult pathological jealousy is related to unresolved early attachments. He utilizes several films to demonstrate how jealousy in women and in men is differentially expressed. He contrasts normal and pathological jealousy in the two women protagonists of the movie, *Play Misty for Me* (1971). Certainly, jealousy occurs due to a triangle in which Dave and two women provide the three sides. Zeichner's analysis of the film illustrates vividly the relationship between degrees of jealousy and the level of ego development. Tobi has a well-developed ego and is aware of her normal jealousy and manages her feelings constructively and self-protectively. In contrast, the more seriously disturbed Evelyn, whose jealousy seems due to relational hunger and fear of abandonment, lacks self-awareness, cannot tolerate her feeling, and resorts to murderous acts. Zeichner's second film, *Disclosure* (1994), which also portrays triangulation, deals with career, love, and gender jealousy and here two men and a woman are equally jealous. The third film, *Possession* (1981), has two men as protagonists who attempt to possess the same woman who does not want to be possessed but seeks sexual fulfillment. The men seek to fulfill and be fulfilled by vying with each other and imaginary potency. It is both a drama and supernatural horror film which is bizarre and confusing. However, when viewed as a film of jealousy, as Zeichner does, I could see clearly the obsessive preoccupation, anger/rage, shame, and destructiveness of jealousy. The fourth example, *The Room* (2003), is the familiar story of jealousy in a love triangle. Suffice it to say that although "one of the worst films ever made" this has become a cult film because it so resonates with the audience and their own experiences, however imaginary. Not only does the reader learn about various types of jealousy as portrayed in the different films but also that different cinematography conveys these variations. Zeichner concludes his chapter with salient points: jealousy is an irresistible force which, whether overcome or not, when present causes suffering, controls and destroys lives; though normal and experienced by everyone at one time or another, it can tragically be one of the most destructive of human emotions.

Jealousy in the treatment experience

Since so little is written by Freud and in subsequent psychoanalytic literature about jealousy, I wondered how well we work with jealous patients.
Undoubtedly, as the four contributors to the clinical realm underline, we
learn from patients and from experience. In Chapter 11, Kavaler-Adler
asks: "What role can we play as psychoanalytic clinicians in transforming
potential destructive aggression, in the form of the green-eyed monster
of jealousy (murderous as in *Othello*), into the more benign experience
of symbolized hostile fantasy where self-reflection can be employed to
tame the monster?" When pathological, the envious person experiences
little differentiation between self and other; envy is self-sabotaging and
must be resolved before a person can experience the love/hate of oedipal level jealousy. The first clinical vignette, Vivian, illustrates clearly the
primitive confusion between envy and projected jealousy. Therapeutically the analyst must bear the projection and it is this difficult tolerance
that provides the curative component (creation of transitional space)
with such a patient. Helen, in the second case, experiences the painfulness and deleterious effect on self-esteem of being the imagined object
of jealousy. The effect on self-esteem is due to the shame, guilt, and fear
of punishment—the self-hate that jealousy evokes. Even though Helen's
obsessive jealous anxiety probably developed at the oedipal phase with
a seductive mother and punitive father, her jealousy fears were evoked
by a competitive sister. Three other cases of both men and women teach
that if jealousy is to be analyzed productively, the analyst must recognize the patient's level of ego development to distinguish between more
primitive envy and the capacity to experience higher level jealousy.
Whether envious or jealous, there is a need to mourn loss, either the
loss of envy—a person cannot have what is felt to be needed—or the
powerlessness of jealousy—a person cannot have what the other person
has and the guilt involved wanting it from another to have for oneself.
Kavaler-Adler brought me full circle to the distinction between envy
and jealousy as she emphasized the necessity of sound psychoanalytic
assessment of the underlying ego structure to treat jealous patients.

Jealousy can persist over time and become a character trait. In
Chapter 9, Jack and Kerry Novick's patients called attention to "retroactive jealousy" and its obsessive-compulsive quality. "Prospective
jealousy" with its compulsive fantasy of sexual behavior of another person in the future rather than the past is also described. The men they

treated came for help because they could not stop thinking about past loves, previous or subsequent sexual involvement, or a current love's future sexuality. This sort of jealousy occurs in women as well but more often between mothers and children, where there is a denial of separateness and jealousy of anyone who might come between them, including the analyst. The terms "retroactive or prospective jealousy" have otherwise not been used in the psychoanalytic literature although Freud (1922b) described "projective jealousy" as the attribution of the desire to betray one's lover to him/her and then feeling suspicious of an imagined rival. Despite differences in description, time, phase of development, and gender, the Novicks shed light on jealousy's underlying dynamics of omnipotence, denial of separateness to defend against powerlessness, and helpless anxiety due to traumatic experiences. Understanding of jealousy is increased by the Novicks' dynamic insight and their therapeutic technique based on their two-system (e.g., open and closed) responses to helplessness. The aim was to help the difficult-to-treat jealous men to own their hostility. An additional goal was to help them recognize (overcome) their limitations to find pleasure in their own powers and their present reality, and to help the mothers and children accept the inevitability of separateness due to growth over time. The song, utilized by the Novicks, "I Wonder Who's Kissing Her Now," makes abundantly clear not only the defensive painful preoccupation of this kind of jealousy but also the reality of separateness. Written in 1909 not long before WWI and sung in its entirety with its verse about the reality of separateness, the song's message was later diluted. After WWII only its nostalgic chorus without the verse was sung, thereby supporting the cultural ethos of the ideal 1950s postwar family. A book (made into a 2014 film), *Testament of Youth: An Autobiographical Study of the Years 1900–1925*, written by Vera Brittain in 1933 portrays jealousy stimulated by war from different perspectives—men's jealousy of other men going to war, women's jealousy of soldiers and of other women whose loves survived, soldiers' jealousy of men back home and of each other's women at home—demonstrates the relationship of trauma, helplessness, anxiety, separation, and loss as well as current cultural reality to the ubiquitous feeling of jealousy. Again I was brought to the necessity of distinguishing between "normal vs. pathological" jealousy.

Analysts accept normal jealousy and treat pathological jealousy. It is in clinical encounters with jealous patients that the analyst's own experience of jealousy intrudes. Kobrick's awareness of how her fear of others' jealousy had developed allowed her to understand jealousy in her work with patients. She recognizes in contrast to envy which arises in a more conscious realm, that jealousy is hidden and protected from others. Shame, fear of malevolent and destructive forces, low self-esteem, insecurity, all contribute to the pain of jealousy. Describing her work with three patients, Ophelia, Horatio, and Hawk, Kobrick demonstrated analysts' excruciating experience of their own jealousy and their patients' jealousy aroused by their fantasies or observations of their analysts' lives. Along with the idealization, "Oh! To live in my patient's fantasies of me," comes the analyst's trepidation of inevitable future devaluation, "I could not resist wondering ... who was she talking about and how hard the impact would be when I fell from the pedestal she created." An analyst can best bear the affective storms of jealousy if he/she is open to their own and their patients' experiences. Even with openness, an analyst can be provoked to expression of personal feeling. For example, Kobrick, in Chapter 10, admitted anger when a patient brushes too close to the depths of jealousy in the analyst. Her final paragraph, "Jealousy betwixt envy had made an unbidden entrance onto the stage of my personal landscape and paradoxically I needed to open the door to differentiate self and other, and sameness and difference within relatedness. The ghosts of jealousy needed to be met in the darkest corners to find light and understanding" corroborates the interweaving of envy and jealousy, jealousy's destructive potential, the reality of separateness, and need for openness.

Shah, in Chapter 12, deepens our understanding of the analyst's experience of jealousy. For anyone, intense jealousy can be mental torture, involving longing, exclusion, shame, and hatred. This is equally true for the analyst/therapist despite a paucity of discussion within the psychoanalytic literature on jealous countertransference. Are we as analysts ashamed of the intensity of our jealous feelings which deepen as the therapeutic relationship deepens? Can we experience various forms of jealousy for people and inanimate objects in our patients' lives? Is jealousy especially difficult for the analyst to admit because a third person or object is introduced into the dyad of the close therapeutic relationship? Do we fear the interference of jealous affect when we encourage patients' expressions of feelings? While we do not have the privilege of expressing our own inner reactions we must be aware and use these reactions constructively. Are we jealous of the care our patients receive through our efforts—the only reciprocation being the opportunity to work and receive remuneration in our chosen method? Can unconscious jealous reactions lead to therapeutic impasses or destructive acting out? Can the degree of satisfaction in an analyst's life affect the intensity of jealous reactions? Yes!, is the answer to all of these questions as Shah substantiates in his thoughtful contribution with his case examples, his summary of the literature, and a confirmation in his concluding paragraph.

Jealousy as a learning experience

Jealousy is a complex and difficult emotion, experienced by all in various intensities and at different times. It is commonly confused with envy. Despite the editors' request that each contributor write about a different aspect of jealousy, and each personalized the assigned topic, all struggled to differentiate envy and jealousy. All noted the paucity of literature on jealousy per se in contrast to the proliferation of psychoanalytic writing on envy. Moreover, for me, jealousy was clarified in the following ways. I learned that envy is a part of jealousy but without the third person or the same kind of destructiveness. Jealousy is a common human experience and like envy can be constructive in evoking ambition and productive competition. It can also be pathological and destructive to greater or lesser degrees. Although jealousy develops later than envy, the parental or oedipal situation is not the only contributor; siblings, friends, colleagues, even strangers also provoke and contribute to its development. Since it is such a ubiquitous human experience, jealousy permeates all forms of our culture—poetry, (auto) biographies, mysteries, novels, song, classical music, films, art, attitudes, and prejudices. In fact, it seems jealousy appears more in the popular culture than in the psychoanalytic literature. Opera, the most passionate and complex of art forms in which jealousy constitutes a major theme[6] curiously does not seem to enter the thoughts of the contributors. However, psychoanalytic understanding has been increased by the authors' thoughtful contributions to this volume. The triangulation of jealousy is painful to all three participants as other difficult-to-bear feelings underlie the experience. Jealousy can be long lived, it is no respecter of gender, age, or life circumstances; it evokes shame, guilt, anger, hatred, cruelty, fears of exclusion, separation, and loss. The absence of jealousy makes us less human, less relational, and in analytic terms usually it is a defense against pain. Bearing the jealousy of patients and being aware of the derivatives and nature of our own jealousy contributes to becoming good enough analysts/therapists.

NOTES

Chapter One

1. The current nosological system of psychiatry (DSM-V, 2013) mentions jealousy in two contexts: delusional disorder—jealous type—and obsessive jealousy. The former refers to an encapsulated delusion of infidelity without auditory hallucinations and other grossly disorganizing features of psychosis. The latter refers to a "non-delusional preoccupation with a partner's perceived infidelity" (p. 139). The assignment of the latter category to the broad group of obsessive compulsive disorder is questionable in my mind. The non-psychotic jealous person does not experience his suspicions as ego-dystonic. In fact, he is inclined to regard such doubts as plausible. He draws considerable masochistic gratification from them. Moreover, while the true obsessional who obtains temporary relief upon being told that what he fears shall not come true, the

241

jealous person bristles at such reassurance and begins to pile up more evidence to prove himself right.

2. In bestowing such importance upon the role of sibling relationship in personality development, Klein was noticeably ahead of her times.

3. Elsewhere, I have elucidated the role of lightheartedness in the capacity for being playful (Akhtar, 2011, pp. 65–84).

4. The intimacy and precision of Wisdom's (1976) description makes one wonder if the boy in question was actually his own child. If true, this will not be the first instance of such a sort in psychoanalytic literature. Many analysts, beginning with Freud (1920g), have used observations regarding their children or grandchildren to make a theoretical point.

5. For a detailed explication of the role inanimate objects play in human mental life, see Akhtar (2003, 2005).

6. This list is restricted to high-quality films and does not refer to the mediocre (and simply bad) movies that are the daily staple of TV channels like Lifetime Movies.

7. While a systems-based approach to jealousy, especially in the setting of marital therapy, might be useful in certain situations, I do not have experience in couples work and suggest that the interested reader look up pertinent literature from this sub-specialty (especially S. Friedman, 1989; Guerin, Fay, Burden, & Kautto, 1987; Pam & Pearson, 1994).

8. Klein (1928), however, believed that "Jealousy plays a greater part in women's lives than in men's, because it is reinforced by deflected envy of the mate on account of the penis" (p. 195). She also held that women possess a greater capacity for disregarding their own wishes and for sacrifice. Putting these two observations together, Klein concluded that women are capable of emotions that range from "the most petty jealousy to the most self-forgetful loving-kindness" (p. 195).

Chapter Four

1. The reader might wonder what had been my husband's motives in sending flowers at a time when I was likely to be busy with patients: I had recently returned to work on an essentially full-time basis after our son turned three, and my husband (as well as our son) had been having some conflicted feelings about seeming to be suddenly second-place to my work life. Thus, the feelings of jealousy had been mutual, to some degree.

2. Much of the book is written in a Neapolitan dialect and the transition back and forth between dialect and classical Italian provides a glimpse into some of the oscillating identifications with which Elena, the narrator, struggles.

3. A series of 1960s Italian films satirized this double standard, for example, *Divorce Italian Style* (1961), *Seduced and Abandoned* (1964), and filmmaker, poet, and philosopher, Pier Paolo Pasolini (1965) conducted interviews in a satirical documentary that explored the mores of the Mezzogiorno.

4. Nevertheless, as was reported in the February 21, 2016 Travel section of *The New York Times*, the popularity of Ferrante's books have sparked an interest in Neapolitan tourism; the city had formerly had a negative reputation for crime and the crumbling of architectural structures and other amenities that had kept tourists away. It is ironic that Ferrante's critique of her loved and hated neighborhood may lead to its revival.

5. Of course, this is not a fixed state: Mutual recognition is always in danger of breaking down and must be restored.

Chapter Five

1. This is a very literal translation of "Eifersucht ist eine Leidenschaft,/Die mit Eifer sucht, was Leiden schafft." Grillparzer masterfully uses the frequent situation that two (or more) German words can be combined to produce a new one whose meaning is completely unrelated to its sources.

2. See Paquette and Dumont (2013) in this regard.

3. For psychoanalytic discussions of these notions see Benjamin (1988); S. A. Mitchell (2000).

Chapter Six

1. "Oxfordians" agree with Sigmund Freud that Edward de Vere, Earl of Oxford (1550–1604) probably wrote under the pen name "William Shakespeare."

2. Only in the 1954 article does Feldman connect the play with de Vere's life.

3. See my chapter "The Theme of Betrayal in the Works of 'William Shakespeare,'" in Akhtar (2013a).

4. In his classic study, Irving Janis (1972), using a term coined in 1952 by William H. Whyte, observed that defenders of a contested theory often fail to consider alternative theories, overrate their expertise, and gain group cohesiveness through deep hostility toward those who critique their theory or offer conflicting evidence.

5. Naturally, they then seize on mistaken connections, such as the alleged connection between the name of Shakspere's son, Hamnet, and Shakespeare's play *Hamlet*. Further, they mistakenly claim that Shakespeare "was not all that learned" (Stanley Wells, in the 2012 film *Last Will and Testament*); that words of the sixteenth-century dialect of the Stratford region appear in Shakespeare's works; that Shakespeare made errors about Italy that prove he never visited that country; that he also made errors in the use of legal terminology that prove he did not attend law school; etc.

6. The hyphenated form of the name was never used by the businessman from Stratford, while it often appeared on the literary works. Hyphenated last names were uncommon in the Elizabethan era, though Ben Jonson and other writers used them for obviously assumed names. In his 1616 *Collected Works*, Jonson, that recognized master of literary ambiguity, even spelled the pen name "Shake-Speare," along with several other assumed names in that capitalized-hyphen-capitalized format. In all of Jonson's lists of actors' names in that book, he did not use that format for any other real names.

7. For example, the Shakespeare scholar Stanley Wells (2003) has said he is 100 percent certain that "Shakspere" of Stratford wrote the works of Shakespeare. He added that he is unwilling to read any contrary evidence until it is 100 percent proven that Edward de Vere wrote Shakespeare. Wells seems proud of how closed-minded he is.

8. It was a servant. De Vere's motives are unknown. His guardian, the future Lord Burghley, secured de Vere's acquittal (saving him from a death sentence) with the preposterous conclusion that the servant committed suicide on de Vere's fencing foil, and on the grounds that de Vere acted in self-defense ("se defendo," self-deprecatingly mocked in *Hamlet* when the gravedigger says Ophelia's death from possible suicide must have been "se offendendo").

9. James Schiffer (2002) is surprised that so few critics have linked *Othello* with some of the sonnets (e.g., 35, 105, 138, 144)—"Central to each work is the experience of triangulation, jealousy, and radical uncertainty ... The protagonists' experience of jealousy in both works is greatly

exacerbated ... by uncertainty" (p. 326). "The Sonnets poet is divided in complex ways, not only between two loves, but also between rival versions of the young friend and dark lady, as well as of himself. In relation to the young friend, the poet vacillates between hyperbolic praise ... and recrimination of the friend's 'sensual fault[s]'" (p. 327). Schiffer speculates that *Othello* and some of the sonnets were written around the same time. Other Shakespeare scholars may hesitate to acknowledge the connections Schiffer highlights because of their unwillingness to link these literary works with their author's life experiences. Lyric poetry such as sonnets are usually highly personal and autobiographical.

10. Cf. Sonnets 86–90.

11. An anonymous 1578 poem featuring a betrayed female speaker seems to be de Vere's effort to show that he could in fact understand his wife's point of view. This poem is a fascinating prototype of some of Shakespeare's most memorable female characters. See chapter three in Waugaman (2014).

12. On the other hand, a March 1575 letter from the queen's physician, Richard Masters, alleges that Anne sought an abortion from him a week after de Vere departed for the Continent. We can only speculate as to her reasons.

13. One of the best references on Shakespeare's intimate knowledge of Italy is Roe (2011). Anderson (2005) writes of the profound impact de Vere's year in Italy had on his subsequent writing. He adds, "For such an autobiographical artist as the Earl of Oxford, extreme agony and disturbance in life ultimately provided profound inspiration" (p. 118).

14. See chapters six and seven in Waugaman (2014).

15. Whigham and Rebhorn (2007) gloss "formal" as meaning "sane," inadvertently supporting my attribution of the *Arte* to de Vere, since the OED's sole example of this meaning of "formal" (4.c) is in Shakespeare's (1623) *The Comedy of Errors*.

16. Freud's (1912e) admonition that the psychoanalyst mirror back the patient's transference was probably influenced by Hamlet's famous advice to the actors that "the purpose of playing [acting] ... is, to hold, as t'were, the *mirror* up to nature" [III, ii, 21–23; emphasis added].

17. Cf. *The Tempest* (1623), when Prospero conjures up a masque to entertain Miranda and Fernando; Fernando says, "This is a most majestic *vision*, and/Harmoniously charming."

18. If we instead emphasize "under their own *names*," we might think of de Vere using his initials rather than his name ("E. O." for "Edward

Oxenford") for several of his poems published in the many editions of the popular Elizabethan book of song lyrics, *Paradise of Dainty Devises*.

19. The first play to bear this pen name was the 1598 edition of *Love's Labors Lost*. This is the only play that used the "Shakespere" spelling, which is closer to the spelling of the Stratford businessman's name. The next three plays used the "Shake-speare" spelling. Starting in 1599, only the familiar unhyphenated "Shakespeare" spelling was used, as though the hyphen was undermining the official effort to suggest that the Stratford man was the author. But, after Queen Elizabeth was replaced by King James in 1603, the hyphen was once again frequently used, including in the 1640 "second edition" of the *Sonnets*.

20. It is likely that Christopher Marlowe was the "rival poet" of the *Sonnets*, and it is even possible that de Vere had him killed. De Vere attempted to fight a duel with Sir Philip Sidney (Queen Elizabeth stopped the duel); he later boasted he could have Sidney killed and not be caught.

21. Janet Adelman (1992) does draw attention to King Lear's demented suspicion that his daughters are illegitimate.

22. These are the dates given by Ogburn and Ogburn (1952) in *This Star of England*.

23. This pen name seems similar to "anonymous," but in Greek, it means "lawless; impious; unconventional; or unmusical." These poems are reprinted in Davison's (1602) anthology, *A Poetical Rhapsody*. To my knowledge, Eric Miller (2012) was the first to attribute the "Anomos" poems to de Vere.

Chapter Seven

1. Act IV, Scene III, 50–52, p. 359.
   I called my love false love; but what said he then?
   Sing willow, willow, willow
   If I court more women, you'll couch with more men.

2. I'll tear her all to pieces [...] Arise, black vengeance (Act III, Scene III, 447, p. 310) I will chop her into messes ... (Act IV, Scene I, 193, p. 336). These images of fragmentation compress the traumas suffered by black bodies and projected onto Desdemona.

3. My mother had a maid call'd Barbary (Act IV, Scene III, 25).

Chapter Eight

1. This camera technique would be utilized later in American "slasher" films like *Halloween* (1978) but predates them by several years.
2. "Spaghetti Westerns" are a subgenre of Western movies that became popular in the mid-1960s.

Chapter Nine

1. In this chapter we have chosen to use "I" when referring to the analyst in actual clinical interactions, and the collective "we/our/us" when describing our joint, general theoretical, technical, and clinical formulations. The "I" is an attempt to capture some of the immediacy of the work and it also adds another layer of confidentiality to the reported clinical material.
2. Allen Creek Preschool in Ann Arbor, Michigan is a psychoanalytic preschool founded in 1996 by a group of psychoanalytic colleagues and community leaders. Information can be found on the website at allencreek.org and descriptions of programs and conceptual foundations in our book, *Emotional Muscle: Strong Parents, Strong Children* (2010).

Chapter Eleven

1. See Kavaler-Adler (1993) for a view of jealousy in Charlotte Brontë's (1853) novel, *Villette*, versus primal envy in Emily Brontë's (1847) *Wuthering Heights*.
2. See Masterson (1981) on "Transference Acting Out."
3. See Winnicott (1971) on "The Capacity for Play" in this regard.

Chapter Thirteen

1. This is not to say that animals cannot be jealous but here only people are being discussed.
2. In a parting dream, the child clearly expressed the value of their work together and a wish to maintain an attachment to be revisited in later years.
3. "Mean" is commonly substituted for "jealous."
4. I think not. For example, both Emily (*Wuthering Heights*, 1847) and Charlotte (*Jane Eyre*, 1847) Brontë wrote passionately and with deep

understanding of the human experience of love, despite the fact that they lived very secluded, passionless (in the usual sense of passion/love) lives. They had a marvelous ability to put their internal passions and life losses through circumstances into written words.

5. Many analysts are gifted in understanding (empathizing with) the emotions of others whether they have felt or experienced the same as their patients. They use their empathy to be helpful to others.

6. For example, in *La Traviata* (Verdi, 1853), when Violetta refused Alfredo and falsely declared her love for another to protect his family's reputation, Alfredo in a fit of jealous rage evoked by painful rejection denounced his former love, shaming her in front of other guests.

REFERENCES

Adams, F., Hough, W., Howard, J., & Orlob, H. (1909). "I wonder who's kissing her now." Written for the play, *The Prince of Tonight*. www.internationallyricsplayground, accessed March 3, 2017.

Adelman, J. (1992). *Suffocating Mothers: Fantasies of Maternal Origins in Shakespeare's Plays, Hamlet to The Tempest*. New York: Routledge.

Adler, A. (1928). *Understanding Human Nature*. London: Allen & Unwin.

Affair to Remember, An (1957). Directed by L. McCarey. Twentieth Century Fox production.

Agamben, G. (2009). The friend. In: *What Is an Apparatus? And Other Essays* (pp. 25–37). Stanford, CA: Stanford University Press.

Akhtar, S. (2000). Mental pain and the cultural ointment of poetry. *International Journal of Psychoanalysis, 81*: 229–243.

Akhtar, S. (2003). Things: developmental, psychopathological, and technical aspects of inanimate objects. *Canadian Journal of Psychoanalysis, 11*: 1–44.

Akhtar, S. (2005a). *Objects of Our Desire*. New York: Random House.

Akhtar, S. (2005b). Early relationships and their internalization. In: E. S. Person, A. M. Cooper, & G. O. Gabbard (Eds.), *Textbook of Psychoanalysis* (pp. 39–56). Washington, DC: American Psychiatric Publishing.

Akhtar, S. (2009). *Comprehensive Dictionary of Psychoanalysis*. London: Karnac.

Akhtar, S. (2011). *Matters of Life and Death: Psychoanalytic Reflections*. London: Karnac.

Akhtar, S. (Ed.) (2013a). *Betrayal: Developmental, Literary, and Clinical Realms*. London: Karnac.

Akhtar, S. (2013b). *Psychoanalytic Listening: Methods, Limits and Innovations*. London: Karnac.

Akhtar, S. (2013c). Meanings, manifestations, and management of greed. In: S. Akhtar (Ed.), *Greed: Developmental, Cultural, and Clinical Realms* (pp. 131–158). London: Karnac.

Anderson, M. (2005). *Shakespeare by Another Name: The Life of Edward de Vere, The Man Who Was Shakespeare*. New York: Gotham.

Anonymous (1589). *Art of English Poesy*. Kent, OH: Kent State University Press, 1970.

Anzieu, D. (1989). *The Skin Ego*. C. Turner (Trans.). New Haven, CT: Yale University Press.

Appignanesi, L. (2011). *All about Love. Anatomy of an Unruly Emotion*. London: Virago.

Aristotle (circa 4th century BC). *Rhetoric*. J. Freese (Trans.). Cambridge, MA: Loeb Classical Library, 1924.

Aron, L. (2006). Analytic impasse and the third: Clinical implications for intersubjectivity theory. *International Journal of Psychoanalysis, 87*: 349–368.

Atwood, M. (2014). *The Handmaid's Tale*. Toronto: EMBLEM McClelland & Stewart.

Auchincloss, E., & Samberg, E. (2012). *Psychoanalytic Terms and Concepts*. New Haven, CT: Yale University Press.

Balint, M. (1968). *The Basic Fault: Therapeutic Acts of Regression*. London: Tavistock.

Barag, G. (1949). A case of pathological jealousy. *Psychoanalytic Quarterly, 18*: 1–18.

Bartels, A., & Zeki, S. (2000). The neural basis of romantic love. *Neuroreport, 11*: 3829–3834.

Bartels, A., & Zeki, S. (2004). The neural correlates of maternal and romantic love. *Neuroimage, 21*: 1155–1166.

Barthes, R. (1977). *A Lover's Discourse: Fragments*. New York: Hill & Wang.

Basic Instinct (1992). Directed by Paul Verhoeven, produced by Carolco Pictures.

Baumgart, H. (1990). *Jealousy: Experiences and Solutions*. Chicago, IL: University of Chicago Press.

Beebe, B., Cohen, P., & Lachmann, F. (2016). *The Mother-Infant Interaction Picture Book. Origins of Attachment*. New York: W. W. Norton.

Beethoven, L. V. (1824). *Symphony #9 in D minor*, Op. 125.

Beguiled, The (1971). Directed by D. Siegel. Maplaso Company production.

Benjamin, J. (1988). *The Bonds of Love: Psychoanalysis, Feminism, and the Problem of Domination*. New York: Pantheon.

Benjamin, J. (1995). *Like Subjects, Love Objects: Essays on Recognition and Sexual Difference*. New Haven, CT: Yale University Press.

Benjamin, J. (1998). *The Shadow of the Other: Intersubjectivity and Gender in Psychoanalysis*. New York: Routledge.

Benjamin, J. (2002). The rhythm of recognition: comments on the work of Louis Sander. *Psychoanalytic Dialogues, 12*: 43–54.

Benjamin, J. (2004). Beyond doer and done to: an intersubjective view of thirdness. *Psychoanalytic Quarterly, 73*: 5–46.

Bergmann, M. (1987). *The Anatomy of Loving*. New York: Columbia University Press.

Bible, Revised Standard Edition (1973). Oxford: Oxford University Press.

Bion, W. R. (1959). Attacks on linking. *International Journal of Psychoanalysis, 40*: 308–315.

Bion, W. R. (1962). A theory of thinking. *International Journal of Psychoanalysis, 43*: 306–310.

Bion, W. R. (1963). *Elements of Psycho-Analysis*. London: Heinemann.

Bishop, B. (2004). "Othello": faith and doubt in the good object. *British Journal of Psychotherapy, 21*: 300–310.

Blevis, M. (2009). *Jealousy: True Stories of Love's Favorite Decoy*. New York: Other Press.

Blos, P. (1967). The second individuation process of adolescence. *Psychoanalytic Study of the Child, 22*: 162–186.

Blos, P. (1968). Character formation in adolescence. *Psychoanalytic Study of the Child, 23*: 245–263.

Bohm, E. (1967). Jealousy. In: A. Ellis & A. Abarbanel (Eds.), *Encyclopedia of Sexual Behavior* (pp. 567–594). New York: Hawthorne.

Bollas, C. (2015). Psychoanalysis in the age of bewilderment: on the return of the oppressed. *International Journal of Psychoanalysis, 96*: 535–551.

Bond, R. W. (Ed.) (1902). *The Complete Works of John Lyly*. Oxford: Clarendon.

Bonomi, C. (2015). *The Cut and the Building of Psychoanalysis, Volume I: Sigmund Freud and Emma Eckstein*. London: Routledge.

Bowlby, J. (1980). *Loss: Sadness and Depression*. New York: Basic Books.

Brenman, E. (1985). Cruelty and narrow-mindedness. *International Journal of Psychoanalysis, 66*: 273–281.

Brittain, V. (1933). *Testament of Youth: An Autobiographical Study of the Years 1900–1925*. London: Penguin Classics, 1989.

Britton, R. (1998). *Belief and Imagination: Explorations in Psychoanalysis*. New York: Routledge.

Britton, R., Cohen, D., & Mitchell, J. (2009). Siblings in development. In: V. Lewin & B. Sharp (Eds.), *Siblings in Development: A Psychoanalytic View* (pp. 112–145). London: Karnac.

Brontë, C. (1847). *Jane Eyre*. London: Penguin Classics, 2006.

Brontë, C. (1853). *Villette*. New York: Modern Library, 2001.

Brontë, E. (1847). *Wuthering Heights*. New York: Random House, 2009.

Brooke, R. (1908). Jealousy. In: *Collected Poems of R. Brooke* (p. 45). New York: Astounding Stories, 2015.

Brunswick, R. (1929). The analysis of a case of delusional jealousy. *Journal of Nervous and Mental Disease, 70*: 1–22.

Brusset, B. (2011). La projection pour le meilleur et pour le pire. *Revue française de psychanalyse, 75*: 681–695.

Buss, D. (2000). *The Dangerous Passion: Why Jealousy Is as Necessary as Love and Sex*. New York: Free Press.

Burton, R. (1632). *Anatomy of Melancholy*. New York: The New York Review of Books Press, 2001.

Butler, J. (2002). Melancholy gender: refused identification. In: M. Dimen & V. Goldner (Eds.), *Gender in Psychoanalytic Space* (pp. 3–20). New York: Other Press.

Buunk, B. P., & Hupka, R. B. (1987). Cross-cultural differences in the elicitation of sexual jealousy. *Journal of Sex Research, 23*: 12–22.

Cardanus, G. (1573). *Comforte Complete*. T. Bedingfield (Trans.). London: Thomas Marsh, 1998.

Carnochan, P. (2011). Jealousy and the capacity to imagine: commentary on paper by Stephanie Lewin. *Psychoanalytic Dialogues, 21*: 580–588.

Castiglione, B. (1528). *The Art of the Courtier*. New York: Charles Scribner's Sons, 1903.

Chatterji, N. (1948). Paranoid jealousy. *Samiksa, 11*: 14–24.

Chimbos, P. D. (1978). *Marital Violence: A Study of Interspouse Homicide*. San Francisco, CA: R & E Research Associates.

Cinthio, G. (1565). Hecatommithi. *Encyclopædia Britannica, 11th ed.* (p. 44). Cambridge: Cambridge University Press, 1911.

Clanton, G., & Smith, L. G. (1998). *Jealousy*. New York: University Press of America.

Coen, S. (1987). Pathological jealousy. *International Journal of Psychoanalysis, 68*: 99–108.

Coleridge, S. (1987). *Collected Works of Samuel Taylor Coleridge: Lectures 1808–1819*. London: Routledge & Kegan Paul.

Coles, P. (2003). *The Importance of Sibling Relationships in Psychoanalysis.* London: Karnac.

Coles, P. (2014). The transgenerational pattern of trauma transmission. In: K. Skrzypek, B. Maciejewska-Sobczak, & Z. Stadnicka-Dmitriew (Eds.), *Siblings: Envy and Rivalry, Coexistence and Concern* (pp. 113–122). London: Karnac.

Crichton, M. (1994). *Disclosure.* New York: Alfred A. Knopf.

Davids, M. F. (2011). *Internal Racism. A Psychoanalytic Approach to Race and Difference.* New York: Palgrave Macmillan.

Davies, J. M. (2004). Whose bad objects are we anyway? Repetition and our elusive love affair with evil. *Psychoanalytic Dialogues, 14*: 711–732.

Davison, F. (1602). *A Poetical Rhapsody.* H. E. Rollins (Ed.). Cambridge, MA: Harvard University Press, 1931.

De Paola, T. (1973). *Nana Upstairs & Nana Downstairs.* New York: G. P. Putnam's Sons.

De Steno, D. A., & Salovey, P. (1996). Genes, jealousy, and the replication of misspecified models. *Psychological Science, 7*: 376–377.

De Vere, E. (1593). *Venus and Adonis.* Attributed to William Shakespeare. New York: W. W. Norton, 1996.

Diagnostic and Statistical Manual of Mental Disorders-V (2013). Washington, DC: American Psychiatric Publishing.

Dimen, M. (2003). *Sexuality, Intimacy, Power.* Hillsdale, NJ: Analytic Press.

Dimitrijevic, A. (2015). Being mad in early modern England. *Frontiers in Psychology, 6*: 1740.

Dimitrijevic, A. (in press, a). Is integration possible for psychoanalysis? In: A. Borgos & F. Eros (Eds.), *Psychopolitics.* Budapest: Central European University.

Dimitrijevic, A. (in press, b). A mixed-model for psychoanalytic education. *International Forum of Psychoanalysis.*

Diner (1982). Directed by B. Levinson, produced by Metro Goldwyn Mayer Studios.

Dirty Harry (1971). Directed by D. Siegel, produced by Warner Brothers Studios.

Disclosure (1994). Directed by B. Levinson, produced by Warner Brothers Studios.

Divorce Italian Style (1961). Directed by P. Germi, produced by Luxe Films.

Dostoyevsky, F. (1881). *The Brothers Karamazov* (p. 381). R. Pevear & L. Volokhonsky (Trans.). Introduction by Malcolm Jones. New York: Alfred A. Knopf, 1992.

Dowling, S., Lament, C., Novick, K. K., & Novick, J. (2013). Dialogue with the Novicks. *Psychoanalytic Study of the Child, 67*: 137–145.

Dumas, A. (1844). *The Three Musketeers.* New York: Oxford Classics, 1991.

Dumas, A. (1846). *The Count of Monte Cristo*. New York: Bantam Classics, 1984.

East of Eden (1955). Directed by E. Kazan. Warner Brothers production.

Edward, J. (2011). *The Sibling Relationship: A Force for Growth and Conflict*. Lanham, MD: Rowman & Littlefield.

Evans, W. N. (1975). The eye of jealousy and envy. *Psychoanalytic Review, 62*: 481–492.

Eyes Wide Shut (1999). Directed by S. Kubrick. Warner Brothers production.

Fairbairn, W. R. D. (1944). Endopsychic structure considered in terms of object-relationships. *International Journal of Psychoanalysis, 25*: 70–92.

Fairbairn, W. R. D. (1952). *Psychoanalytic Studies of the Personality*. London: Routledge & Kegan Paul.

Falzeder, E., & Brabant, E. (Eds.) (1993). *The Correspondence of Sigmund Freud and Sándor Ferenczi*. Cambridge, MA: Belknap Press, 2000.

Fast, I. (1984). *Gender Identity: A Differentiation Model*. Hillsdale, NJ: Analytic Press.

Fatal Attraction (1987). Directed by A. Lyne. Paramount Pictures production.

Feldman, A. B. (1952). Othello's obsessions. *American Imago, 9*: 147–164.

Feldman, A. B. (1954). Othello in reality. *American Imago, 11*: 147–179.

Fenichel, O. (1935). A contribution to the psychology of jealousy. In: *The Collected Papers, First Series* (pp. 349–362). New York: W. W. Norton, 1953.

Ferenczi, S. (1909). Introjection and transference. In: E. Mosbacher (Trans.), *First Contributions to Psychoanalysis* (pp. 35–93). London: Karnac, 1980.

Ferenczi, S. (1912). On the part played by homosexuality in the pathogenesis of paranoia. In: E. Mosbacher (Trans.), *First Contributions to Psychoanalysis* (pp. 154–186). London: Karnac, 1980.

Ferrante, E. (2012). *My Brilliant Friend*. New York: Europa Editions.

Ferrante, E. (2013). *The Story of a New Name*. New York: Europa Editions.

Ferrante, E. (2014a). *Those Who Go and Those Who Stay*. New York: Europa Editions.

Ferrante, E. (2014b). *The Neapolitan Novels of Elena Ferrante*. New York: Europa Editions.

Ferrante, E. (2015). *The Story of the Lost Child*. New York: Europa Editions.

Freud, S. (1897). Letter 75 to Wilhelm Fliess. *S. E., 1*: 268–271. London: Hogarth.

Freud, S. (1900a). *The Interpretation of Dreams*. *S. E., 4–5*: 1–626. London: Hogarth.

Freud, S. (1909d). Notes upon a case of obsessional neurosis. *S. E., 10*: 153–320. London: Hogarth.

Freud, S. (1910d). The future prospects of psych-analytic therapy. *S. E., 11*: 139–152. London: Hogarth.

Freud, S. (1911c). Psycho-analytic notes on an autobiographical account of a case of paranoia. *S. E., 12*: 9–88. London: Hogarth.

Freud, S. (1912e). Recommendations to physicians practising psycho-analysis. *S. E., 12*: 109–120. London: Hogarth.

Freud, S. (1912–13). *Totem and Taboo. S. E., 13*: 1–162. London: Hogarth.

Freud, S. (1916d). Some character-types met with in psycho-analytic work. *S. E., 14*: 310–333. London: Hogarth.

Freud, S. (1919h). The uncanny. *S. E., 17*: 217–252. London: Hogarth.

Freud, S. (1920g). *Beyond the Pleasure Principle. S. E., 18*: 7–64. London: Hogarth.

Freud, S. (1922b). Some neurotic mechanisms in jealousy, paranoia and homosexuality. *S. E., 18*: 221–233. London: Hogarth.

Freud, S. (1924d). The dissolution of the Oedipus complex. *S. E., 19*: 171–188. London: Hogarth.

Freud, S. (1926d). *Inhibitions, Symptoms and Anxiety. S. E., 20*: 75–175. London: Hogarth.

Freud, S. (1928b). Dostoevsky and parricide. *S. E., 21*: 177–196. London: Hogarth.

Freud, S. (1930a). *Civilization and Its Discontents. S. E., 21*: 80. London: Hogarth.

Freud, S. (1931b). Female sexuality. *S. E., 21*: 223–243. London: Hogarth.

Freud, S. (1955c). Memorandum on the electrical treatment of war neurotics. *S. E., 17*: 211–216. London: Hogarth.

Freud, S. (1968a). *The Letters of Sigmund Freud and Arnold Zweig*. New York: Harcourt Brace,

Freud, S. (1990). *The Letters of Sigmund Freud and Eduard Silberstein, 1871–1881.* Cambridge, MA: Harvard University Press.

Friday, N. (1985). *Jealousy*. New York: Perigord.

Friedman, S. (1989). Strategic reframing in a case of delusional jealousy. *Journal of Strategic and Systemic Therapies, 8*: 1–4.

Frye, N. (1986). *Northrop Frye on Shakespeare*. New Haven, CT: Yale University Press.

Gabbard, G. O. (1996). *Love and Hate in the Analytic Setting*. Lanham, MD: Jason Aronson.

Gabbard, G. O., & Lester, E. P. (1995). *Boundaries and Boundary Violations in Psychoanalysis*. Washington DC: American Psychiatric Publishing.

Garner, E. (1954). "Misty". From the album, *Contrasts*. Chicago, IL: Universal Recording Studio.

Gay, P. (1988). *The Godless Jew*. New York: W. W. Norton.

Gay, P. (1998). *Freud: A Life for Our Time*. New York: W. W. Norton.

George, C., & West, M. L. (2012). *The Adult Attachment Projective Picture System: Attachment Theory and Assessment in Adults*. New York: Guilford.

Gerhardt, J. (2009a). The roots of envy: the unaesthetic experience of the tantalized/disposed self. *Psychoanalytic Dialogues, 19*: 267–293.

Gerhardt, J. (2016). Libidinal and destructive envy: relationally speaking, "I can be like you, therefore I am". *Psychoanalytic Perspectives, 13*: 1–23.

Gilligan, C. (1983). *In a Different Voice.* Cambridge, MA: Harvard University Press.

Gilmartin, B. G. (1986). Jealousy among the swingers. In: G. Clanton & L. G. Smith (Eds.), *Jealousy* (pp. 152–158). Lanham, MD: University Press of America.

Goleman, D. (1995). *Emotional Intelligence.* New York: Bantam.

Graduate, The (1967). Directed by M. Nichols. Lawrence Turman production.

Green, A. (1980). The dead mother. In: A. Weller (Trans.), *Life Narcissism, Death Narcissism* (pp. 185–221). London: Free Association.

Grillparzer, F. (1830). Epigrams. In: *Franz Grillparzer Collected Works, Volume 1* (p. 389). Munich, Germany: Holzinger Verlag, 1960.

Grossmann, K. E., Grossmann, K., & Waters, E. (Eds.) (2006). *Attachment from Infancy to Adulthood: The Major Longitudinal Studies.* New York: Guilford.

Guardian, The (2009). Howard Jacobson's top 10 novels of sexual jealousy. November 4. Accessed at www.theguardian.com/books/2009/nov/03/howard-jacobson-top-10-sexual-jealousy, on September 6, 2016.

Guerin, P. J., Fay, L. F., Burden, S. L., & Kautto, J. G. (1987). *The Evaluation and Treatment of Marital Conflict: a Four-Stage Approach.* New York: Basic Books.

Halloween (1978). Directed by D. Carpenter, produced by Compass International Pictures.

Hardy, T. (1891). *Tess of the d'Urbervilles.* London: Penguin, 2003.

Hart, S. L., Carrington, H. A., Tronick, E. Z., & Carroll, S. R. (2004). When infants lose exclusive maternal attention: is it jealousy? *Infancy, 6*: 57–78.

Heimann, P. (1950). On counter-transference. *International Journal of Psychoanalysis, 31*: 81–84.

Hirsh, I. (2008). *Coasting in the Countertransference: Conflicts of Self Interest between Analyst and Patient.* New York: Analytic Press.

Hirsch, I. (2011). Narcissism, mania and analysts' envy. *American Journal of Psychoanalysis, 71*: 363–369.

Hirsch, I. (2014). Narcissism, mania, and analysts' envy of patients. *Psychoanalytic Inquiry, 34*: 408–420.

Houzel, D. (2001). The "nest of babies" fantasy. *Journal of Child Psychotherapy, 27*: 125–138.

Janis, I. L. (1972). *Victims of Groupthink: A Psychological Study of Foreign-policy Decisions and Fiascoes.* New York: Houghton Mifflin.

Johnson, S., Steevens, G., & Reed, I. (Eds.) (1813). *The Plays of William Shake-speare in Twenty-One Volumes*. London: J. Nichols & Sons.

Jones, E. (1929). Jealousy. In: *Papers on Psychoanalysis* (pp. 282–295). London: Bailliere, Tindall, and Cox, 1950.

Jonson, B. (1616). *Collected Works*. London: William Stansby.

Kaës, R. (2009). *Le complex fraternal*. Paris: Dunod.

Kaplan, H., & Saddock, B. (1985). *Comprehensive Textbook of Psychiatry/IV*. Baltimore, MD: Williams & Wilkins.

Kaplan, L. (1995). *Adolescence: The Farewell to Childhood*. New York: Touchstone.

Kaplan-Solms, K., & Solms, M. (2000). *Clinical Studies in Neuro-Psychoanalysis: Introduction to a Depth Neuropsychology*. London: Karnac.

Kavaler-Adler, S. (1992). Mourning and erotic transference. *International Journal of Psychoanalysis, 73*: 527–539.

Kavaler-Adler, S. (1993). *The Compulsion to Create: a Psychoanalytic Study of Women Artists*. London: Routledge.

Kavaler-Adler, S. (1995). Opening up blocked mourning in the preoedipal character. *American Journal of Psychoanalysis, 55*: 145–168.

Kavaler-Adler, S. (1996). *The Creative Mystique: From Red Shoes Frenzy to Love and Creativity*. London: Routledge.

Kavaler-Adler, S. (1999). Interview with Frank Summers. *Division Review (The Newsletter of Division 39)*. Washington, DC: The American Psychological Association.

Kavaler-Adler, S. (2003b). Lesbian homoerotic transference in dialectic with developmental mourning: on the way to symbolism from the protosymbolic. *Psychoanalytic Psychology, 20*: 131–152.

Kavaler-Adler, S. (2004). Anatomy of regret: the critical turn towards love and creativity in the transforming schizoid personality. *American Journal of Psychoanalysis, 64*: 39–76.

Kavaler-Adler, S. (2005a). The case of David: nine years on the couch for sixty minutes, once a week. *American Journal of Psychoanalysis, 65*: 103–134.

Kavaler-Adler, S. (2006). My graduation is my mother's funeral: transformation from the paranoid-schizoid to the depressive position in fear of success, and the role of the internal saboteur. *International Forum of Psychoanalysis, 15*: 117–136.

Kavaler-Adler, S. (2007). Pivotal moments of surrender to mourning the parental internal object. *Psychoanalytic Review, 94*: 763–789.

Kavaler-Adler, S. (2013a). *The Anatomy of Regret: From Death Instinct to Reparation and Symbolization through Vivid Case Studies*. London: Karnac.

Kavaler-Adler, S. (2013b). *Klein-Winnicott Dialectic: Transforming Metapsychology and Interactive Clinical Theory*. London: Karnac.

Kernberg, O. F. (1975). *Borderline Conditions and Pathological Narcissism*. New York: Jason Aronson.

Kerst, F. (1905). *Beethoven: The Man and the Artist, as Revealed in His Own Words*. H. E. Krehbiel (Trans.). New York: B. W. Huebsch.

Kerst, F., & Krehbiel, H. E. (Eds.) (1964). *Beethoven: The Man and the Artist, as Revealed in His Own Words*. New York: Dover.

Kieffer, C. C. (2008). On siblings: mutual regulation and mutual recognition. *Annals of Psychoanalysis, 36*: 161–173.

Klein, M. (1927). Criminal tendencies in normal children. In: *Love, Guilt and Reparation and Other Works 1921–1945* (pp. 170–185). New York: Free Press, 1975.

Klein, M. (1928). Early stages of the Oedipus conflict. In: *Love, Guilt and Reparation and Other Works 1921–1945* (pp. 186–198). New York: Free Press, 1975.

Klein, M. (1946). Notes on some schizoid mechanisms. *International Journal of Psychoanalysis, 27*: 99–110.

Klein, M. (1952). Some theoretical conclusions regarding the emotional life of the infant. In: *Envy and Gratitude and Other Works 1946–1963* (pp. 61–93). New York: Free Press, 1975.

Klein, M. (1957). Envy and gratitude. In: *Envy and Gratitude and Other Works 1946–1963* (pp. 176–235). New York: Free Press, 1975.

Klein, M. (1975). *Envy and Gratitude and Other Works 1946–1963*. London: Hogarth Press and the Institute of Psychoanalysis.

Klein, M., & Riviere, J. (1964). *Love, Hate and Reparation*. New York: W. W. Norton.

Kohut, H. (1971). *The Analysis of Self: A Systematic Approach to the Psychoanalytic Treatment of Narcissistic Personality Disorders*. New York: International Universities Press.

Kohut, H. (1977). *The Restoration of Self*. New York: International Universities Press.

Kohut, H. (1979). The two analyses of Mr. Z. *International Journal of Psychoanalysis, 60*: 3–27.

Kohut, H. (1982). Introspection, empathy and the semi-circle of mental health. *International Journal of Psychoanalysis, 63*: 395–407.

Kris, E. (1956). On some vicissitudes of insight in psychoanalysis. *International Journal of Psychoanalysis, 37*: 445–455.

Kristeva, J. (1982). *Powers of Horror: An Essay on Abjection*. New York: Columbia University Press.

Kulish, N., & Holtzman, D. (2008). *A Story of Her Own: The Female Oedipus Complex Reexamined and Renamed*. Lanham, MD: Jason Aronson.

Kundera, M. (1984). *The Unbearable Lightness of Being*. New York: Harper Collins.

Lacan, J. (1973). *The Four Fundamental Concepts of Psychoanalysis: Book XI*. New York: W. W. Norton.

Lansky, M. R. (2005). Hidden shame. *Journal of the American Psychoanalytic Association, 53*: 865–890.

Laplanche, J., & Pontalis, J.-B. (1967). *Vocabulaire de la psychanalyse*. Paris: PUF, 1973.

Lasch, C. (1991). *The Culture of Narcissism: American Life in an Age of Diminishing Expectations*. New York: W. W. Norton.

Last Will and Testament (2012). Directed by L. Wilson and L. Wilson, produced by Centropolis Entertainment.

Laura (1944). Directed by O. Preminger. Twentieth Century Fox production.

Layton, L. (1998). *Who's That Girl, Who's That Boy? Clinical Practice Meets Postmodern Gender Theory*. Hillsdale, NJ: Psychoanalytic Press.

Layton, L. (2005). Beyond narcissism: towards a negotiation model of gender identity. In: E. Toronto, G. Ainslie, M. Donovan, M. Kelly, C. C. Kieffer, & N. McWilliams (Eds.), *Psychoanalytic Reflections on a Gender-Free Case: Into the Void* (pp. 227–242). New York: Routledge.

Lewin, S. (2011). Parallel identification: a shield against the assault of traumatic jealousy. *Psychoanalytic Dialogues, 21*: 551–570.

Lewontin, R. (1968). Honest Jim Watson's "big think" DNA. *Chicago Sunday Times, Book Week, 25*: 1–2.

Lockwood, L. (2003). *The Music and Life of Beethoven*. New York: W. W. Norton.

Luzzi, J. (2013). It started in Naples: Elena Ferrante's "Story of a New Name". *New York Times Book Review*, September 9.

MacLachlan, B., & Fletcher, J. (2007). *Virginity Revisited: Configurations of the Unpossessed Body*. Toronto, Canada: University of Toronto Press.

Mahler, M. S., Pine, F., & Bergman, A. (1975). *The Psychological Birth of the Human Infant: Symbiosis and Individuation*. New York: Basic Books.

Makari, G. (2008). *Revolution in Mind: The Creation of Psychoanalysis*. New York: Harper Collins.

Mancia, M. (1981). On the beginning of mental life in the foetus. *International Journal of Psychoanalysis, 62*: 351–357.

Maroda, K. (1998). *Seduction, Surrender and Transformation: Emotional Engagement in the Analytic Process*. New York: Analytic Press.

Masson, J. M. (Ed.) (1985). *The Complete Letters of Sigmund Freud to Wilhelm Fliess, 1887–1904*. Cambridge, MA: Belknap.

Masterson, J. F. (1976). *Psychotherapy of the Borderline Adult: A Developmental Approach*. New York: Brunner/Mazel.

Masterson, J. F. (1981). *The Narcissistic and Borderline Disorders: An Integrated Developmental Approach*. New York: Brunner/Mazel.

Mead, M. (1931). Jealousy: primitive and civilized. In: S. D. Schmalhausen & V. F. Calverton (Eds.), *Women's Coming of Age* (pp. 35–48). New York: Horace Liveright.

Menninger, K. (1938). *Man Against Himself*. New York: Harcourt, Brace.

Mildred Pierce (1945). Directed by T. Garnett. Warner Brothers production.

Miller, E. (2012). *Analytical Notes and Commentary on a Poetical Rhapsody*. www.ericmillerworks.com. Accessed May 4, 2017.

Miller, R. S. (2014). *Intimate Relationships, 7th Edition*. New York: McGraw Hill.

Mish, F. C. (Ed.) (1993). *Merriam-Webster's Collegiate Dictionary (9th Edition)*. Springfield, MA: Merriam-Webster Press.

Mitchell, J. (2003). *Siblings: Sex and Violence*. Oxford: Polity.

Mitchell, J. (2013a). The law of the mother: sibling trauma and the brotherhood of war. *Canadian Journal of Psychoanalysis, 21*: 145–159.

Mitchell, J. (2013b). Siblings: thinking theory. *Psychoanalytic Study of the Child, 67*: 14–34.

Mitchell, S. A. (2000). *Relationality: From Attachment to Intersubjectivity*. New York: Psychology Press.

Mollon, P. (2002). *Shame and Jealousy: The Hidden Turmoils*. London: Karnac.

Morrison, A. (1989). *Shame: The Underside of Narcissism*. New York: Routledge.

Mullen, P. E. (1990). A phenomenology of jealousy. *New Zealand Journal of Psychiatry, 24*: 17–28.

Mullen, P. E. (1996). Editorial: jealousy and the emergence of violence and intimidating behaviors. *Criminal Behavior and Mental Health, 6*: 199–205.

Mullen, P. E., & Martin, J. (1994). Jealousy: a community study. *British Journal of Psychiatry, 164*: 35–43.

Neilson, W. A., & Hill, O. J. (Eds.) (1942). *The Complete Plays and Poems of William Shakespeare: The New Cambridge Edition*. Cambridge, MA: Houghton Mifflin.

Neubauer, P. (1982). Rivalry, envy, and jealousy. *Psychoanalytic Study of the Child, 37*: 121–142.

Neubauer, P. (1983). The importance of the sibling experience. *Psychoanalytic Study of the Child, 38*: 325–336.

New York Times, The (2016). Travel Section, February 21.

Niagara (1953). Directed by H. Hathaway. Twentieth Century Fox production.

Nietzsche, F. (1905). *Thus Spake Zarathustra*. New York: Modern Library Series, 1955.

Novick, J., (1980). Negative therapeutic motivation and negative therapeutic alliance. *Psychoanalytic Study of the Child, 5*: 299–320.

Novick, J., & Novick, K. K. (1996). *Fearful Symmetry: The Development and Treatment of Sadomasochism*. Northvale, NJ: Jason Aronson, 2007.

Novick, J., & Novick, K. K. (2000). Love in the therapeutic alliance. *Journal of the American Psychoanalytic Association, 48*: 189–218.

Novick, J., & Novick, K. K. (2002). Two systems of self-regulation. *Journal of Psychoanalytic Social Work, 8*: 95–122.

Novick, J., & Novick, K. K. (2003). Two systems of self-regulation and the differential application of psychoanalytic technique. *American Journal of Psychoanalysis, 63*: 1–19.

Novick, J., & Novick, K. K. (2004). The superego and the two-systems model. *Psychoanalytic Inquiry, 24*: 232–256.

Novick, J., & Novick, K. K. (2006). *Good Goodbyes: Knowing How to End in Psychotherapy and Psychoanalysis.* Lanham, MD: Rowman & Littlefield.

Novick, J., & Novick, K. K. (2013a). A new model of techniques for concurrent psychodynamic work with parents of child and adolescent patients. In: R. Ritvo & S. Henderson (Eds.), *Psychodynamic Treatment Approaches to Psychopathology: Child and Adolescent Psychiatric Clinics of North America, 22*(2): 331–349.

Novick, J., & Novick, K. K. (2013b). Discussion of the case of Diane. In: H. Basseches, P. Ellman, & N. Goodman (Eds.), *Battling the Life and Death Forces of Sadomasochism: Clinical Perspectives* (pp. 63–78). London: Karnac.

Novick, J., & Novick, K. K. (2013c). Two systems and defenses. *Psychoanalytic Review, 100*: 185–200.

Novick, J., & Novick, K. K. (2015). Working with "out-of-control" children—a two-systems approach. *Psychoanalytic Study of the Child, 69*: 153–188.

Novick, K. K., & Novick, J. (2005). *Working with Parents Makes Therapy Work.* Lanham, MD: Jason Aronson.

Novick, K. K., & Novick, J. (2010). *Emotional Muscle: Strong Parents, Strong Children.* Bloomington, IN: XLibris.

Novick, K. K., & Novick, J. (2012). Some suggestions for engaging with the clinical problem of masochism. In: D. Holtzman & N. Kulish (Eds.), *The Clinical Problem of Masochism* (pp. 51–75). Lanham, MD: Jason Aronson.

Novick, K. K., & Novick, J. (2013a). Concurrent work with parents of adolescent patients. *Psychoanalytic Study of the Child, 67*: 103–136.

Oelsner, R. (2013). Introduction. In: R. Oelsner (Ed.), *Transference and Countertransference Today* (pp. 1–17). New York: Routledge.

Ogburn, C., & Ogburn, D. (1952). *This Star of England.* New York: Coward-McCann.

Ogden, T. H. (1996). The perverse subject of analysis. *Journal of the American Psychoanalytic Association, 44*: 1121–1146.

Ortega, M. J. (1959). Delusions of jealousy. *Psychoanalytic Review, 46D*: 102–103.

Oxford Dictionary of English, 2nd Edition (2003). Oxford: Oxford University Press.

Pam, A., & Pearson, J. (1994). The geometry of the eternal triangle. *Family Process, 33*: 175–190.

Panksepp, J., & Bevin, L. (2012). *The Archeology of Mind.* New York: W. W. Norton.

Pao, P.-N. (1969). Pathological jealousy. *Psychoanalytic Quarterly, 38:* 616–638.

Paquette, D., & Dumont, C. (2013). Is father–child rough-and-tumble play associated with attachment or activation relationships? *Early Child Development and Care, 183:* 760–773.

Paul, L., & Galloway, J. (1994). Sexual jealousy: gender differences in response to partner and rival. *Aggressive Behavior, 20:* 203–211.

Pechter, E. (1999). *Othello and Interpretative Traditions.* Iowa City, IA: University of Iowa Press.

Peck, D. (1985). *Leicester's Commonwealth: The Copy of a Letter Written by a Master of Art of Cambridge (1584).* Athens, OH: Ohio University Press.

Phillips, A. (1994). *On Flirtation.* Boston, MA: Harvard University Press.

Pierloot, R. A. (1988). Impersonal objects in morbid jealousy. *International Review of Psycho-Analysis, 15:* 293–305.

Pines, A. M. (1983). Sexual jealousy as a cause of violence. Paper presented at the annual convention of the American Psychological Association, Anaheim, CA.

Pines, A. M. (1998). *Romantic Jealousy: Causes, Symptoms, Cures.* New York: Routledge.

Pinta, E. (1979). Pathological tolerance. *American Journal of Psychiatry, 135:* 698–701.

Play Misty for Me (1971). Directed by C. Eastwood, produced by Universal Pictures.

Possession (1981). Directed by A. Zulawski, produced by Gaumont Productions.

Pushkin, A. *Polnoe sobranie sochinenii.* (*Table-Talk* the title originally in English). PSS 12:157, Moscow and Leningrad, 1937–1959.

Pushkin, A. (1916). *The Prose Tales of Alexander Poushkin.* T. Keane (Trans.). London: G. Bell and Sons.

Racker, H. (1957). The meanings and uses of countertransference. *Psychoanalytic Quarterly, 26:* 303–357.

Rain Man (1988). Directed by B. Levinson, produced by United Artists.

Rear Window (1954). Directed by A. Hitchcock, produced by Paramount Pictures.

Ricoeur, P. (2008). *Freud and Philosophy: An Essay on Interpretation.* Delhi, India: Motilal Banarsidass.

Riviere, J. (1932). Jealousy as a mechanism of defence. *International Journal of Psychoanalysis, 13:* 414–424.

Robbe-Grillet, A. (1957). *La Jealousie.* Paris: Editions de Minuit, 1980.

Roe, R. P. (2011). *The Shakespeare Guide to Italy: Retracing the Bard's Unknown Travels.* New York: Harper Perennial.

Room, The (2003). Directed by T. Wiseau, produced by Wiseau Productions.

Rouse, W. H. D. (Ed.) (1904). *Shakespeare's "Ovid" Being Arthur Golding's Translation of the Metamorphoses*. London: de La Mare.

Rudnytsky, P. L. (1992). *Freud and Oedipus*. New York: Columbia University Press.

Rustin, M. (2007). Taking account of siblings—a view from child psychotherapy. *Journal of Child Psychotherapy, 33*: 21–35.

Rymer, T. (1693). *A Short View of Tragedy: Its Original, Excellency, and Corruption. With Some Reflections on Shakespear, and Other Practitioners for the Stage*. Menston, UK: Scolar, 1970.

Sachs, H. (2010). *The Ninth. Beethoven and the World in 1824*. New York: Random House.

Sadker, M., & Sadker, D. (1994). *Failing at Fairness: How America's Schools Cheat Girls*. New York: Charles Scribner's Sons.

Sandler, J., & Freud, A. (1983). Discussions with Anna Freud on "The Ego and the Mechanisms of Defense": the ego and the id at puberty. *International Journal of Psychoanalysis, 64*: 401–406.

Schiffer, J. (2002). Othello among the sonnets. In: P. C. Kolin (Ed.), *Othello: New Critical Essays* (pp. 325–345). London: Routledge.

Schiller, F. (1785). Ode to Joy. In: *Complete Poetical Works and Plays*. Hastings, UK: Delphi Classics, 2013.

Schmidberg, M. (1953). Some aspects of jealousy and of feeling hurt. *Psychoanalytic Review, 40*: 1–16.

Schore, A. N. (1991). Early superego development: the emergence of shame and narcissistic affect regulation in the practicing period. *Psychoanalytic Contemporary Thought, 14*: 187–250.

Schwartz, H., & Ceaser, M. (2005). The patient with bulimia. In: H. Schwartz (Ed.), *Psychodynamic Concepts in General Psychiatry* (pp. 335–357). Washington, DC: American Psychiatric Press.

Searles, H. (1979). The analyst's experience with jealousy. In: L. Epstein & A. H. Feiner (Eds.), *Countertransference* (pp. 305–327). New York: Jason Aronson.

Searles, H. (1986). *My Work with Borderline Patients*. Lanham, MD: Jason Aronson.

Seduced and Abandoned (1964). Directed by P. Germi, produced by Luxe Films.

Segal, H. (1974). *Introduction to the Work of Melanie Klein*. New York: Basic Books.

Shackelford, T. K., Buss, D. M., & Bennett, K. (2002). Forgiveness or breakup: Sex differences in responses to a partner's infidelity. *Cognition and Emotion, 16*: 299–307.

Shaffer, P. (1979). *Amadeus*. London: National Theatre, November 2.

Shah, D. (2015). Hopelessness in the countertransference. In: S. Akhtar & M. K. O'Neil (Eds.), *Hopelessness: Developmental, Cultural, and Clinical Realms* (pp. 181–200). London: Karnac.

Shakespeare, W. (1598). *Love's Labor's Lost*. In: G. B. Evans, J. M. Tobin, H. Baker, A. Barton, F. Kermode, H. Levin, H. Smith, & E. Edel (Eds.), *The Riverside Shakespeare* (pp. 208–250). Boston, MA: Houghton Mifflin 1997.

Shakespeare, W. (1600). *The Merchant of Venice*. In: G. B. Evans, J. M. Tobin, H. Baker, A. Barton, F. Kermode, H. Levin, H. Smith, & E. Edel (Eds.), *The Riverside Shakespeare* (pp. 284–318). Boston, MA: Houghton Mifflin, 1997.

Shakespeare, W. (1600). *Much Ado About Nothing*. In: G. B. Evans, J. M. Tobin, H. Baker, A. Barton, F. Kermode, H. Levin, H. Smith, & E. Edel (Eds.), *The Riverside Shakespeare* (pp. 361–398). Boston, MA: Houghton Mifflin, 1997.

Shakespeare, W. (1603). *Hamlet*. In: G. B. Evans, J. M. Tobin, H. Baker, A. Barton, F. Kermode, H. Levin, H. Smith, & E. Edel (Eds.), *The Riverside Shakespeare* (pp. 1183–1245). Boston, MA: Houghton Mifflin, 1997.

Shakespeare, W. (1603). *Othello, The Moor of Venice*. M. Neill (Ed.). Oxford: Oxford University Press, 2006.

Shakespeare, W. (1623). *The Comedy of Errors*. In: G. B. Evans, J. M. Tobin, H. Baker, A. Barton, F. Kermode, H. Levin, H. Smith, & E. Edel (Eds.), *The Riverside Shakespeare* (pp. 111–137). Boston, MA: Houghton Mifflin, 1997.

Shakespeare, W. (1623). *Cymbeline*. In: G. B. Evans, J. M. Tobin, H. Baker, A. Barton, F. Kermode, H. Levin, H. Smith, & E. Edel (Eds.), *The Riverside Shakespeare* (pp. 1565–1611). Boston, MA: Houghton Mifflin, 1997.

Shakespeare, W. (1623). *The Winter's Tale*. In: G. B. Evans, J. M. Tobin, H. Baker, A. Barton, F. Kermode, H. Levin, H. Smith, & E. Edel (Eds.), *The Riverside Shakespeare* (pp. 1612–1655). Boston, MA: Houghton Mifflin, 1997.

Shakespeare, W. (1623). *The Tempest*. In: G. B. Evans, J. M. Tobin, H. Baker, A. Barton, F. Kermode, H. Levin, H. Smith, & E. Edel (Eds.), *The Riverside Shakespeare* (pp. 1656–1688). Boston, MA: Houghton Mifflin, 1997.

Shakespeare, W. (1623). *First Folio: Mr. William Shakespeare's Comedies, Histories, & Tragedies*. London: Edward Blount, and William & Isaac Jaggard.

Shakespeare, W. (1640). *Poems by Mr William Shakespeare: The Sonnets, Second Edition*. London: The Cotes.

Shapiro, J. (2010). *Contested Will: Who Wrote Shakespeare?* New York: Simon & Schuster.

Sherwin-White, S. (2007). Freud on brothers and sisters: a neglected topic. *Journal of Child Psychotherapy, 33*: 4–20.

Siedenberg, R. (1952a). Fidelity and jealousy: socio-cultural considerations. *Psychoanalytic Review, 54D*: 27–52.

Siedenberg, R. (1952b). Jealousy: the wish. *Psychoanalytic Review, 39*: 345–353.

Smith, Z. (2016). *Swing Time*. Toronto, Canada: Hamish Hamilton.

Solms, M. (2013). The conscious id. *Neuropsychoanalysis, 15*: 5–19.

Solms, M., & Turnbull, O. (2002). *The Brain and the Inner World: an Introduction to the Neuroscience of Subjective Experience*. New York: Other Press.

Solomon, M. (2003). *Late Beethoven. Music, Thought, Imagination*. Berkeley, CA: University of California Press.

Sophocles (429 BC). *Oedipus Rex*. New York: Dover Thrift Editions, 1991.

Spenser, E. (1579). *The Shepheardes Calendar*. London: Hugh Singleton.

Spielman, P. M. (1971). Envy and jealousy: an attempt at clarification. *Psychoanalytic Quarterly, 40*: 59–82.

Spillius, E. B. (1993). Varieties of envious experience. *International Journal of Psychoanalysis, 74*: 1199–1212.

Steiner, J. (2011). *Seeing and Being Seen: Emerging from a Psychic Retreat*. New York: Routledge.

Strode, W. (1620). On jealousy. In: T. Frazer (Ed.), *Selected Poems of William Strode*. Exeter, UK: Shearsman, 2001.

Strozier, C. B. (2001). *Heinz Kohut: The Making of a Psychoanalyst*. New York: Macmillan.

Suddenly Last Summer (1959). Directed by J. Mankiewicz. Columbia Pictures production.

Sullivan, H. S. (1953). *The Interpersonal Theory of Psychiatry*. New York: W. W. Norton.

Summers, F. (1999). *Transcendence of the Self: An Object Relations Model of Psychoanalytic Therapy*. Hillsdale, NJ: Analytic Press.

Summers, F. (2013). *The Psychoanalytic Vision*. London: Routledge.

Testament of Youth (2014). Directed by J. Kent, produced by BBC Films.

Tolstoy, L. (1889). The Kreutzer Sonata. In: *The Kreutzer Sonata and Other Short Stories* (pp. 64–152). Mineola, NY: Dover Editions, 1993.

Toohey, P. (2014). *Jealousy*. New Haven, CT: Yale University Press.

Trevarthen, C. (1996). Lateral asymmetries in infancy: implications for the development of the hemispheres. *Neuroscience and Biobehavioral Reviews, 20*: 571–586.

Verdi, G. (1853). *La Traviata*. Opera, first performed March 6, 1853, Teatro la Fenice, Venice.

Verdi, G. (1887). *Otello*. Opera, first performed February 5, 1887, Teatro alla Scala, Milan.

Vivona, J. M. (2007). Sibling differentiation, identity development, and the lateral dimension of psychic life. *Journal of the American Psychoanalytic Association, 55*: 1191–1215.

Vivona, J. M. (2010). Siblings, transference, and the lateral dimension of psychic life. *Psychoanalytic Psychology, 27*: 8–26.

Waelder, R. (1936). The principle of multiple function: observations on multiple determination. *Psychoanalytic Quarterly, 41*: 283–290.

Wagenknecht, E. (1972). *The Personality of Shakespeare*. Norman, OK: University of Oklahoma Press.

Waugaman, R. M. (2014). *Newly Discovered Works by "William Shake-Speare," a.k.a. Edward de Vere, Earl of Oxford*. Oxfreudian Press (ebook).

Weiss, E. (1934). Bodily pain and mental pain. *International Journal of Psychoanalysis, 15*: 1–13.

Wells, S. (2003). *Shakespeare: For All Time*. Oxford: Oxford University Press.

Whigham, F., & Rebhorn, W. A. (Eds.) (2007). *The Art of English Poesy*. London: Cornell University Press.

White, G. L., & Devine, K. (1991). Romantic jealousy: therapists' perception of causes, consequences and treatment. In: G. L. White & P. E. Mullen (Eds.), *Jealousy: Theory, Research, and Clinical Strategies* (pp. 244–264). New York: Guilford.

White, G. L., & Mullen, P. E. (Eds.) (1989). *Jealousy: Theory, Research, and Clinical Strategies*. New York: Guilford.

Whyte, W. (1952). Groupthink. *Fortune*, March 1952: 114–117, 142, 146.

Wilde, O. (1891). *The Picture of Dorian Gray*. Dover Thrift Editions, 1993.

Winnicott, D. W. (1931). A note on normality and anxiety. In: *Through Paediatrics to Psycho-Analysis*. London: Hogarth.

Winnicott, D. W. (1960). Ego distortion in terms of true and false self. In: *Maturational Processes and the Facilitating Environment* (pp. 140–152). New York: International Universities Press, 1965.

Winnicott, D. W. (1965). *The Maturational Processes and the Facilitating Environment: Studies in the Theory of Emotional Development*. New York: International Universities Press.

Winnicott, D. W. (1971). *Playing and Reality*. London: Tavistock.

Winnicott, D. W. (1975). *Through Paediatrics to Psycho-Analysis*. London: Hogarth and the Institute of Psychoanalysis.

Wisdom, J. O. (1976). Jealousy in a twelve-month-old boy. *International Review of Psychoanalysis, 3*: 365–368.

Wurmser, L. (1996). Trauma, inner conflict, and the vicious cycles of repetition. *Scandinavian Psychoanalytic Review, 19*: 17–45.

Wurmser, L. (2007). *Torment Me, but Don't Abandon Me: Psychanalysis of the Severe Neuroses in a New Key*. Lanham, MD: Rowman & Littlefield.

Wurmser, L., & Jarass, H. (Eds.) (2008a). *Jealousy and Envy: New Views About Two Powerful Emotions*. New York: Analytic Press.

Wurmser, L., & Jarass, H. (2008b). Pathological jealousy: the perversion of love. In: L. Wurmser & H. Jarass (Eds.), *Jealousy and Envy: New Views about Two Powerful Emotions* (pp. 1–24). New York: Analytic Press.

INDEX

For Product Safety Concerns and Information please contact our EU
representative GPSR@taylorandfrancis.com
Taylor & Francis Verlag GmbH, Kaufingerstraße 24, 80331 München, Germany

www.ingramcontent.com/pod-product-compliance
Lightning Source LLC
Chambersburg PA
CBHW050703280326
41926CB00088B/2442

9 781782 206446